ORAL INTERPRETATION
OF
FORMS OF LITERATURE

ORAL INTERPRETATION
OF
FORMS OF LITERATURE

BY

MARGARET PRENDERGAST McLEAN

NEW YORK UNIVERSITY

AUTHOR OF "GOOD AMERICAN SPEECH"

E. P. DUTTON AND COMPANY, INC.

PUBLISHERS   NEW YORK

Campbell and Hall
3.38

1-29-57 Jlm
2-20-57 cdm

ACKNOWLEDGMENTS

My first deep debt of gratitude is to the two greatest teachers I have known, who were also the most lovable of men:

First, to the late Leland Powers of the Leland Powers School, Boston—one of the finest, most skillful, and most inspiring dramatic artists of all time—who gave me the basic and fundamental principles underlying the art of the oral interpretation of literature, and who taught me how to apply those principles to given selections.

Second, to the late William Tilly of Columbia University—whose scholarly influence in the field of speech education has left its impress throughout the world, and whose wide vision kept his work on the most exalted plane, while it remained intensely practical—who gave me an insight into the science of speech and its application to the art of pronunciation both in daily life and in the art of the professional speaker.

I am also deeply indebted to another rare teacher, Mr. Albert H. Johnstone, of Kansas City, Missouri, whose scholarly and systematic manner of presenting his subjects to his students gave me my first acquaintance with the basic principles within different forms of literature which determine the general manner of oral interpretation of those forms.

I wish to express my most sincere appreciation of the extreme kindness and courtesy extended to me by the authors and publishers with whom I have come in contact in the preparation of this book. Almost without exception they have gone out of their way to do me favors and to extend their help, and to give me the benefit of their extensive knowledge and wide experience.

For their gracious permissions to use lines, extracts, and complete selections from copyrighted material I wish to acknowledge my great debt to the following authors, publishers and copyright owners, and to express my deep and sincere appreciation:

To Dr. Frederick Herbert Adler, Professor of English, Western Reserve University, for the sonnet "A Bit of Mull," from his book, *Leaven for Loaves*, published by Harold Vinal, New York, 1927; and for the poem, "Christmas in Bethlehem," by Elizabeth S. Noble, which he kindly sent to me privately.

To The American Book Company, for lines from *Forms of English Poetry*, by C. F. Johnson, and from *History of English Literature*, by R. P. Halleck, both of which books are copyrighted.

For the extracts from the epic poem, *The Kalevala*, translated by John Martin Crawford; for the extract from the essay, "The Spirit of Theodore Roosevelt," in *The Most Interesting American*, by Julian Street; and for the poems, "The Message of the Rose," by Bessie Chandler, "In Arcadia," by R. F. W. Duke, Jr., "Always When There is Music," by David Morton, from *The Century Magazine;* all of which are used by permission of D. Appleton-Century Company, Inc., Publishers, and owners of the copyrights.

To Walter H. Baker Company, Publishers, for lines from the one-act play "Will o' The Wisp," by Doris Holman.

For lines from *Everyday Problems in Teaching*, by M. V. O'Shea, Copyright 1912, used by special permission of the Publishers, The Bobbs-Merrill Company.

To Brandt & Brandt, for "Nos Immortales," by Stephen Vincent Benét, from *Ballads and Poems*, published by Farrar & Rinehart, Inc. Copyright, 1918, 1920, 1923, 1925, 1929, 1930, 1931, by Stephen Vincent Benét.

To Dr. Nicholas Murray Butler, President of Columbia University' for an extract from his address, "The Will of Peace."

To Chapman & Grimes, Publishers, for the poem, "The Coyote," by Badger Clark, from the book *Grass Grown Trails*.

To Catherine Cate Coblentz, for the sonnet "Stone Walls of New England," published first in *St. Nicholas*, and later in Braithewaite's 1926 *Anthology of Magazine Verse*.

To F. S. Crofts & Co., Publishers, for lines from *Oral Interpretation of Literature*, by Professor Algernon Tassin of Columbia University.

To E. P. Dutton and Company, Publishers, for lines from *The Speaking of English Verse*, by Elsie Fogerty, and from *Lyric Poetry*, by Ernest Rhys; for lines and charts from the 1935 revised edition of *Good American Speech*, by Margaret Prendergast McLean; for the poem, "Ah! Sun-Flower," by William Blake, from *Poems and Prophecies;* and for the poems, "Ad Ministram," by Thackeray, "A Dirge," by W. Johnson-Cory, "Encouragements to a Lover," by Sir John Suckling, "In Memoriam," by R. M. (Milnes), Lord Houghton, "Mary," by C. Tennyson-Turner, and "Wail of the Cornish Mother," by R. S. Hawker, from the Everyman edition of *Palgrave's Golden Treasury*.

To John Day Company, Inc., Publishers, for lines from *South of the Sun*, by Russell Owen.

For lines from *Life and Literature*, by Lafcadio Hearn, and from "A Horse Thief," by William Rose Benét; for an extract from "The American Ideal," from *Sidelights*, by G. K. Chesterton; for the poems "The Skater of Ghost Lake," and "The Woodcutter's Wife," from *Golden Fleece*, by William Rose Benét; for the poems, "Desertion" and "The Soldier," from *The Collected Poems of Rupert Brooke;* for the sonnet, "To My Father," from *Poems of Iris Tree;* and for the poem, "This Out of All," from *The Slender Singing Tree*, by Adelaide Love, which are used by permission of the Publishers, Dodd Mead and Company, Inc.

For lines from "Mr. Lobel's Apoplexy," from *Sundry Accounts*, by Irvin S. Cobb, Copyright 1922 by Doubleday, Doran & Company, Inc.

For lines from Act Three of *The Vortex*, by Noel Coward, copyright 1924, reprinted with permission from Doubleday, Doran and Company, Inc.

For the sonnet "They Brought Me Tidings," from "Sonnets of a Portrait-Painter," from *Selected Poems* of Arthur Davison Ficke, copyright 1926 by Doubleday, Doran and Company, Inc.

To Ethelean Tyson Gaw, for the privilege of including in my book her poem, "The Voice of Francis Drake," which is reprinted by permission of *The Lyric West*, where it first appeared. I am indebted to Braithewaite's 1926 *Anthology of Magazine Verse* for my first acquaintance with this poem.

To Ginn and Company: Publishers, for lines from *Handbook of Poetics*, by Francis B. Gummere.

To Alice Rogers Hager for the privilege of reprinting her poem, "Saga of the Silver Bird." I am indebted to Braithewaite's 1928 *Anthology of Magazine Verse*, for my first acquaintance with this poem.

To Harcourt, Brace and Company, Inc., for lines from *Main Street*, by Sinclair Lewis; and for lines from the stories, "How They Broke Away to Go to the Rootabaga Country," "What the Six Girls with Balloons Told the Gray Man on Horseback," and "The White Horse Girl and the Blue Wind Boy," from *Rootabaga Stories*, by Carl Sandburg.

To Mr. Robert Cortez Holliday for lines from his essay "On Wearing a Hat," from his book *Walking Stick Papers*.

To Henry Holt and Company, Publishers, for the poem "Silver," from *Peacock Pie*, by Walter de la Mare.

To Houghton Mifflin Company, for lines from *A Hand Book of Oral Reading*, by Emerson Lee Bassett; from "A Soldier Fallen in the

Philippines" by William Vaughn Moody; from *A Study of Poetry*, by Bliss Perry; from "Patterns," by Amy Lowell; from *The Popular Ballad*, by Francis B. Gummere; from "The Symbolic Value of English Sounds," in *Views About Hamlet and Other Essays*, by Albert Harris Tolman; from *The Teaching of Poetry in the High School*, by Arthur H. Fairchild; from "Words," in *Essays in Idleness*, by Agnes Repplier; for the poems "To a Friend," by Amy Lowell, and "In An Atalier," in *The Poems of Thomas Bailey Aldrich*.

To P. J. Kenedy and Sons, Publishers and Booksellers, for the poem "The Conquered Banner," from *Poems: Patriotic, Religious, Miscellaneous*, by Abram J. Ryan.

To the Library Company of Philadelphia for lines from *The Philosophy of the Human Voice*, by Dr. James Rush.

To Mr. Robert Littell and to the Press Publishing Company, for lines from Mr. Littell's article "East River," which appeared in *The World* (New York City), Aug. 27, 1930.

To Little, Brown & Company, Publishers, for four lines from one of *The Poems of Emily Dickinson*, and for lines from the play, *Craig's Wife*, by George Kelly.

To Lothrop, Lee and Shepard Company, for lines from the poem, "Aspect of the Pines," by Paul Hamilton Hayne.

To John W. Luce & Company, for lines from "The Loot of Loma," from *The Last Book of Wonder*, by Lord Dunsany.

For lines from *A History of English Literature*, by Neilson and Thorndyke, and from *The Beginnings of Poetry*, by Francis B. Gummere; for lines from the poems, "Tristram," by E. A. Robinson, from "Spanish Waters" and "A Wanderer's Song," in *Poems and Plays of John Masefield;* "A Woman is a Branchy Tree," in *Collected Verse*, by James Stephens; "On First Seeing the Ocean," in *Collected Poems*, by John G. Neihardt; "An Old Woman of the Roads," in *Poems*, by Padraic Colum; for the long extract from "The Oldest English Epic," Beowulf, translated in the original metres by Francis B. Gummere; for the poems, "O World Be Nobler," from *Collected Poems* Vol. I, by Lawrence Binyon, "I Never See the Red Rose Crown the Year," from *Poems and Plays of John Masefield;* "The Return of Morgan and Fingal," from *Collected Poems*, and "Why He Was There," from *Sonnets*, by E. A. Robinson; "The Lover Tells of the Rose in His Heart" from *Collected Poems*, by William Butler Yeats; all of which are used by permission of the Macmillan Company, Publishers.

ACKNOWLEDGMENTS xi

To Mr. John S. Montgomery of New York for the poem "Ulysses Returns," from *Ulysses Returns and Other Poems*, by Roselle Mercier Montgomery.

To David Morton of Amherst College for his sonnets, "Fields at Evening," "Guest," and "Visitor," from his book of poems *Harvest*, and for the sonnet "The Revealer," from his book of poems *Earth's Processional*.

To Mr. Gilbert Grosvenor, editor of *The National Geographic Magazine*, for lines from the article "The Perhahera Procession of Ceylon," by G. H. G. Burroughs, which appeared in the July, 1932 issue of *The National Geographic Magazine*.

To the New York Times for lines from the *Book Review* section, Oct. 26, 1930; from the *Magazine* section, Feb. 1st, 1931, Oct. 4, 1931, Jan. 22, 1933; from the issue of May 9, 1932; and from "Letters to the Editor," March 12, 1934.

To the *New Outlook*, and to Mr. Frank A. Tichenor, Publisher, for the poem "Mother," by Willard Wattles, which was first published in the *New Outlook*. I am indebted to Braithwaite's 1926 *Anthology of Magazine Verse*, for my first acquaintance with this poem.

To Parker Garrett of London, Solicitors for the estate of Oscar Wilde, for lines from Wilde's play, "The Importance of Being Earnest."

To Charles A. Scribner's Sons, Publishers, for lines from *The Development of the Drama*, by Brander Matthews; from *The Forms of Prose Literature*, by J. H. Gardiner; from *The Interpretation of Poetry and Religion*, by George Santayana; and from *Types of the Essay*, by B. A. Heydrick; for lines from the poems "The Song of the Chattahoochie," by Sidney Lanier, and from "This Quiet Dust," by John Hall Wheelock; and for an extract from the address, "The Will of Peace," by Dr. Nicholas Murray Butler.

To Frederick A. Stokes Company, Publishers, for lines from the poems, "The Highwayman" and "Drake", in *Collected Poems*, by Alfred Noyes. Copyright 1906.

I am especially and particularly indebted to the following individuals and firms for their timely and more than generous assistance in my hour of need, and I extend to each of them my grateful appreciation:

To Mr. George Morley Acklom, of E. P. Dutton and Company, to the office of Miss Anita Brown of New York, to Miss Betty Margot Cassie, of White River Junction, Vermont, to Mrs. Catherine Cate

Coblentz, of Washington, D. C., to the Book Editorial Department of P. F. Collier and Son Corporation, to the editors of "Education," and to the Palmer Company, Publishers, to Miss Helen R. Gilbert, of Ginn and Company, and to Mr. Harold Vinal, of Vinal Haven, Maine, for their assistance in finding the *addresses* of the *owners of copyrights*.

To Miss C. E. Sauer, of G. P. Putnam's Sons, to Mr. N. L. Somers, Treasurer of D. Appleton-Century Company, to Miss Dorothy Fisk of Harper & Brothers, and to Miss Barbette Thompson of the permissions department of The Macmillan Company, I am greatly indebted for their patient, continued and invaluable assistance in discovering who were the *owners* of copyrights.

I WISH TO EXPRESS MY APPRECIATION:

To Dr. Frederick Herbert Adler, to Walter H. Baker Company, to Catherine Cate Coblentz, to Ethelean Tyson Gaw, to Alice Rogers Hager, to Mr. Robert Cortez Holliday, to Mr. Robert Littell, to Mr. R. S. Watson, of Charles Scribner's Sons, to Miss C. E. Sauer of G. P. Putnam's Sons, and to Miss Barbette Thompson of The Macmillan Company, for their especial courtesy, encouragement and good wishes.

To Mr. John Macrae, President, and to Mr. Elliott Macrae, Treasurer, of E. P. Dutton and Company, for their patient, constructive and continuous help.

To Mr. R. W. Sailor, of the Cayuga Press, of Ithaca, N. Y., for his splendid co-operation and valuable suggestions and advice.

To Dr. Dorothy I. Mulgrave, Assistant Professor of Education, New York University, to Dr. Letitia Raubicheck, Director of Speech Improvement of the Board of Education of the City of New York, and to Edith Warman Skinner, of the Cornish School of Seattle, Washington, for their constant encouragement and unfailing confidence.

To my sister, Mrs. C. S. Atherly, for her most valuable help with the proofs and for additional favors and courtesies far too extensive and too personal to enumerate.

And last and most of all, to my husband, for his encouragement, his co-operation, his confidence, his vision, and his incomparable assistance, from the day the book was begun until it was completed, including the laborious and exacting task of correcting proofs.

CONTENTS

PART ONE

CONTENTS

English Vowels—Descriptive Chart of English Vowels
with Specimen Words—Sentences Containing the
Vowels—Phonetic Letters for English Diphthongs
with Specimen Words—Length or Duration of English
Sounds—Vowels—Consonants—Diphthongs—Practice
Work.

VI. Dramatic Values of Different Sounds.   45

VII. Groups of Sounds in Connected Speech and Their
     Significance in the Oral Interpretation of
     Literature.   53
     A Syllable—Formation of Syllables in Speech—Com-
     binations of Syllables—Stressed Syllables—A Word—
     Examples of Word Separation and of Word Blending—
     A Stress Group—The Thought Value of Stress Groups
     —The Rhythmic Value of Stress Groups—The Breath
     Group—Length of Breath Groups—Breath Groups and
     Pauses—A Stressed Syllable an Essential Part of
     Separate Words, Stress Groups and Breath Groups—
     Stress and Meaning—What Syllables Should be
     Stressed?—Stress a Sufficient Number of Syllables—
     Avoid Stressing the Wrong Syllable—Do not Stress too
     Many Syllables—Use Different Degrees of Stress—
     Very Strong Stress—Strong Stress—Secondary Stress
     —Mark the Stressed Syllables when Studying a Selec-
     tion—Accepted Weak Forms Result From Very Weak
     Stress—Words Which Have Strong and Weak Forms—
     Sentences for Practice of Weak Forms.

VIII. General Pauses in Oral Reading.   67
      Why Should One Pause in Reading?—Mark Places
      where Pauses Should be made—Frequency of Pauses in
      Reading—Pauses Should be Timed—Pauses Must be
      Filled with Meaning—Tense Pauses—Empty Pauses—
      Sentences, Punctuation Marks and Pauses—Extracts
      for Observation—Exercises for Practice.

IX. Rhythm and Metre.   79
    Rhythm—Rhythm and Spoken Language—The Natu-
    ral Rhythm of English Speech—The Rhythm of En-
    glish Prose—Examples of Rhythmic Prose from News-
    papers and Magazines—Examples of Formal Rhythmic
    Prose—Rhythm and Prosody—The Rhythm of English

PART TWO

PREFACE

Modern thinkers in the educational field are realizing more and more the high educational value of dramatic presentation of subject-matter. The radio and the motion pictures have had great influence in this awakening and have made valuable contributions to the practical application of the idea.

Science, history, geography, literature, and other subjects, all come to life and reality when presented in dramatic or pictorial form. The radio play, *The Invention of the Printing Press*, or the talking picture, *The Life of Louis Pasteur*, makes a deeper and more lasting impression on the minds of both young and old than would be gained, in most cases, from the reading of many books or of learning many lessons in the old way. There is great truth in the old sayings, "it is not what you say that counts but the way you say it," and, "actions speak louder than words."

A recognition of the value of drama in the presentation of ideas is not new, it is only an old understanding being put into use anew. The ancients knew full well that ideas could be presented to the masses most effectively when clothed in dramatic guise. Native and savage tribes in all times and in all lands have appreciated this same fundamental law.

Our educational problem of today resolves itself into that of awakening the interest of the masses in the things that will help them to help themselves and each other to a higher and finer and happier life. A wide and thorough acquaintance with literature broadens the understanding, deepens the sympathies, and helps to give a perspective of the ideals of life that can be gained in no other way.

Much of our literature is fundamentally dramatic and must have the living voice and speech and proper bodily reaction to bring out its richest essence and its deepest truths. The charm and the beauty of poetic literature which lie so largely in the magic of its rhythm and the music of the patterns of its sounds, can be brought into living reality only by means of speech and voice.

The day is close at hand, if indeed it is not already here, when students of all ages will first have their interest in literature awakened by having it presented to them, or by being permitted to present it themselves, in appropriate dramatic form—a form they will understand and appreciate. When their vital interest in a piece of literature has been aroused they will be ready to study its details, its mechanism, its history, and its place in the world of letters.

Before an oral reader is ready to attempt the dramatic presentation of a given selection of literature he must first have a clear understanding of the purpose of the writer of that piece of literature, and an understanding of the general demands made by the particular form of literature through which the writer expresses his purpose; and his voice and speech and body must be adequately trained.

It is hoped that this text may be of practical assistance to students and teachers in giving them some acquaintance with the forms of literature that best lend themselves to oral interpretation, and in giving them some suggestions as to the general manner of presenting those forms with dramatic significance, sincerity and truth.

MARGARET PRENDERGAST McLEAN

CHAPTER I.

PURPOSE OF THIS BOOK
AND
SUGGESTIONS FOR THE STUDY OF IT.

PURPOSE

The subject matter of this book is necessarily divided into two parts. It has been very difficult to determine which of the two parts should be considered first. It seems that each should precede the other, but since this is impossible the material necessary for a *general background of the whole subject* and the more technical matter have been considered in Part One.

Part Two is devoted to the consideration of the material for which the background is a necessity and to which the technical matter is to be applied.

The purpose of the book is to give definite and practical suggestions that will enable a serious, earnest student to read aloud—or recite from memory—from the great mass of literature, *any* selection or portion of a selection, *that is suitable for oral presentation*, in a way that will reveal the author's purpose, meaning and moods, truly, interestingly, and sincerely, giving pleasure and profit to his hearers, by acquainting them with the *literature*, while he himself remains inconspicuously in the background.

This accomplishment is possible only when one has learned the *basic principles underlying the oral interpretation of each of the forms of literature* that are *suited* to *oral presentation*, and has practiced *applying* the principles on at least one representative example of each of these forms, until he has *mastered the technique of reading that particular form*. In order to do this he must know, in each case:—

1. *What* is to be done.

1

2. *Why* each particular thing should be done in preference to some other thing.

3. *How* it *can* be done most effectively;

and then he must practice *doing* it until he can do it simply, adequately, and well.

Part One considers, as fully as possible, *what* is to be done, and gives the background and reasons *why* it should be done, as well as the most essential technical details of *how* it *can* be done.

Part Two considers briefly the different forms of literature that are best suited to oral presentation; gives the outstanding characteristics of each form; outlines the demands these characteristics make upon the oral interpreter; and shows—or tries to show—how the *technique* of oral interpretation can be *applied* to each of these representative forms of literature in order that the reader may *meet the demands made by the literature itself.*

This chapter gives suggestions for a practical plan of procedure in studying the text. By following these suggestions as closely as seems advisable, the book may be made to serve its purpose to the greatest possible advantage in the shortest time and with a minimum of effort on the part of the student.

Statements from unimpeachable authorities have been quoted in many instances to give the student confidence that the subject matter of the text is wholly trustworthy.

Suggestions for the Study of the Book

Part One

CHAPTERS II to XI inclusive, deal with some phases of the technique of oral expression. They give some of the *means* by which the oral reader of literature *may attain* the *end* he seeks. Read these chapters thoughtfully several times. Study Chapter V, *The Sounds of Spoken English,* intensively, and as soon as possible, commit all of it to memory. Adequate oral interpretation of literature is impossible without the application of the principles given in this chapter.

Begin at once to make practical application of the principles given in these early chapters, to the actual experience of interpreting literature. Refer to them continually as each form of literature, or each individual selection, is studied, in order that they may be of help at the precise moment that help is needed.

All technical laws and principles are to be used as *servants*. Their only use in the world is to help the interpreter to accomplish his purpose. Call on them on the slightest provocation, make practical and constant use of them for all occasions, but keep them in their proper place which is always *out of sight*. They must be completely concealed, unheard, unseen, but they must always be on duty. There must *seem* to be *no* technique and no consciousness of behavior.

If an audience is aware of a reader's technique it is proof that he has not assimilated it sufficiently; that he has not practiced his reading until his technique has become a part of him as a fixed habit, and he can forget about it. Although the technique must be entirely submerged and out of sight, and the reader must forget it in his finished reading, it must always be in its place, as the framework of a building must always be in its place, performing its indispensable function, *unseen*. If the framework is weak or unsteady the whole structure becomes weak and unsteady and unreliable, and finally but inevitably falls.

Faithful application of the suggestions made in Chapter XI, on general suggestions for preparing a selection for oral interpretation, should be made use of from the beginning.

PART TWO

1. Study Chapters XII, XIII and XIV.

Prepare the extract *The Shipwreck* from *David Copperfield*, or the *Simple Narrative without Dialogue*—or a similar extract of your own choice—according to instructions given.

Remember that you must *seem* to be telling the story in your own words, and you must be sincerely eager to interest and entertain *others* by the telling, so that the selection will be *theirs* after you have read it to them. Strive to keep the dews of freshness and spontaneity upon it. Be sure that you *understand* and *apply* the *general principles* of story telling.

Continue to work on this selection until it is as nearly perfect as possible, then work on some of the short extracts which show the different rhythms of different stories. The manner of *expressing the thought* and the *general spirit of the story must produce the rhythm.* It must be an integral part of the story itself, not something added to it.

When the technique of reading a simple story properly has been fairly well mastered, extracts from more difficult stories and from those containing dialogue, should be undertaken. Use those given in the text or supply others of your own choice.

2. Study Chapter XVII, *Lyrical Poetry*, and Chapter XVIII, *The Ballad*. Prepare—according to instructions, *The Saga of the Silver Bird*, or some other simple modern ballad in which there is no dialogue. Apply the knowledge gained in the study of a *prose story* and in the study of *Lyrical Poetry*, to the ballad. A ballad must be read with a vigorous rhythm which is one of its distinguishing characteristics.

Continue to work on this selection, applying the general principles of oral interpretation of ballads, until it is mastered. Read other ballads given in the text or select other similar ones, mastering the technique of reading each type, *narrative, lyrical* and *dramatic*.

Consider how the interpretation of a ballad *resembles*, and how it *differs* from, the interpretation of a story.

3. Study Chapter XIX, *The Song or True Lyric*. Undertake the oral interpretation of lyrics in the order given. *Master* at least one example of each type. Select your own examples if you prefer them to those given. Read them as if you were actually experiencing the emotion the lines suggest

and as if you were glad of the privilege of expressing it to sympathetic and friendly listeners whom you find in the audience. The reader must understand clearly and apply faithfully the general principles underlying the oral interpretation of a lyric.

Consider how the interpretation of a lyric *resembles* and how it *differs* from, the interpretation of the other forms of literature that have been studied.

4. Chapter XV, *Orations, Speeches, Addresses.* Master the subject matter concerning this form of oral expression, and apply the knowledge gained to the interpretation of the examples given, or to other similar examples of your own selection.

Consider how the oral interpretation of an oration *resembles*, and how it *differs* from, the other forms of literature that have been studied.

5. Study *The Play*, from the last part of Chapter XXV, *Dramatic Literature.* Prepare the lines given in the text or make your own selection of other lines. Follow given instructions carefully.

Two new points enter into the interpretation of lines from a play that have not been met with in the four forms of literature considered up to this time. They are:

1. impersonation,
2. an imaginary listener.

While it is not necessary for the reader of plays to impersonate characters as an actor does, nevertheless, a certain amount of *suggestion* of impersonation, which will reveal the essential qualities of a character, is imperative.

In the selections studied up to this point the reader has spoken *directly to the audience.* In reading a play, he must represent a character, or characters, and speak to one or more *imaginary* listeners who must be as real in the imaginations of both reader and audience as if they were there in person, and they must be talked to and considered in every way as if they were actually present.

Master the interpretation of several different individual speeches from individual plays. The *essential* qualities of the character speaking must be revealed and the imaginary listener must be made as real as the lines require.

Consider how the interpretation of lines from a play *resembles*, and how it *differs* from, the interpretation of forms previously studied.

The next step in the oral interpretation of lines from a play should be the use of *dialogue*, in which the reader speaks for *two* characters. First, one of them is speaker and the other one becomes the listener, then the process is reversed and the first speaker becomes listener and the first listener becomes speaker.

The transition from one character to another must be wholly blended with the scene. The changes from one to the other must be made in the person of the characters, not in the person of the reader. After the technique of reading dialogue has been mastered the number of characters represented may be increased. It is not advisable to attempt the representation of more than three or four characters in one scene until considerable experience in reading dialogue or "trialogue" has been gained.

Perhaps no form of oral interpretation of literature requires the aid of an accomplished teacher more than does the oral interpretation of scenes from plays. The student should receive considerable aid from what he has studied in the text up to this time, but only the most unusual and gifted student could dispense with the assistance of an adviser and critic.

The five forms of literature thus far considered,—the *story*, the *ballad*, the *lyric*, the *oration*, and the *play*—, represent the most fundamental forms of expression, as far as oral interpretation of literature is concerned. The interpretation of these five forms should be fairly well mastered before the interpretation of additional forms is undertaken.

The remaining forms of literature may be studied in any order which best suits the needs of those studying. The *principles* given for the *interpretation of each form* should be carefully *studied* and *applied* to the actual work of interpretation, until the highest possible degree of perfection has been obtained.

It is probably advisable to use the extracts from long works of literature which are given in the text until students have learned how to make such extracts themselves. Then actual practice in cutting and abridging long selections should be encouraged.

REMINDERS

In the study of *each individual selection*, reference should be made to the chapters dealing with *sounds, stress, grouping, pauses,* and *rhythm,* until the correct and lawful use of these factors of expression has become habitual.

Remember that correct *application* of the basic principles of the oral interpretation of each form of literature to *one* good representative example of that form, will give the reader the *key* to the right interpretation of *all* selections belonging to that form. In this way the doors to our priceless storehouse of literature may be unlocked and the trained reader may bring its treasures to eager multitudes that have no time to get them for themselves, and to other multitudes that did not know such treasures existed, but whose lives will be greatly enriched and beautified by the ultimate knowledge and possession of them.

CHAPTER II

ORAL INTERPRETATION OF LITERATURE

Literature

Literature is "a general term which in default of precise definition, may stand for the best expression of the best thought reduced to writing." *"Encyclopaedia Britannica."*

Literature is one of the most human of all branches of study, and is the most democratic of the fine arts. Its *subject matter* deals with the personal thoughts, emotions and experiences of mankind, its *medium of expression is words*, a medium which we all use every day of our lives in expressing our own thoughts and emotions and in gaining our experiences; consequently, literature speaks a language which we all know and understand, and it deals with activities which, as a very general rule, we can comprehend and which we have often actually experienced in our own lives.

Some Literature Requires Oral Interpretation

Sir Richard Paget says that speech
"is the basis of the arts of literature, poetry and song."

Human Speech, Harcourt, Brace and Company, Publishers.

The highest enjoyment of much literature can be obtained *only by hearing it* because the vital parts of its beauty and emotional effect are *rhythm, melody* and *tone-color*. These are produced by carefully chosen *sounds* and *words* arranged in particular *patterns* which can be fully and properly revealed *only* by means of the *voice*. Silent reading of much literature from the printed page, especially dramatic literature and all forms of poetry, is inadequate in the extreme. It is not necessary for the reader to have an audience; he may read aloud for himself. It is the vocal interpretation that is important.

One may gain a clearer understanding and a deeper appreciation of a piece of literature by listening to one fine oral interpretation of it* than could be gained by a great amount of study of the same selection by other methods.

While all forms of literature are greatly enhanced by good oral interpretation, *dramatic and poetic literature must have oral interpretation* to bring out their special significance and beauty, just as musical compositions must have instrumental or vocal interpretation to bring out *their* special significance and beauty. *Literature and music both make use of the harmony of sounds, carefully chosen and combined, for the expression of feeling and mood.* But literature has more than this, it has certain combinations or groups of sounds which express distinct and definite *ideas*. These can be *fully revealed* only by proper stress, subordination, word grouping, intonation, rhythm, tone-color, pitch, and other qualities belonging *exclusively* to the human voice and to human speech.

One may be a thorough student of many different phases of literature such as its history and development, its influence upon mankind, its different forms, its rhythms and metres, its various classifications of prose and verse, and yet know nothing at all of the actual oral interpretation of literature.

"A girl . . . . may have learned the names of a long list of English authors, the dates when they were born and when they died; the names of the works of each author and the qualities of his style which are set out in a text-book, and still she may not be able to tell a story to a child so as to interest or help him, . . ."

From *Everyday Problems in Teaching*. By M. V. O'Shea, Copyright 1912; used by special permission of the Publishers, The Bobbs-Merrill Company.

The fact that one is a great *writer* of literature does not

---

*See *The Confessions of a Browning Lover*, by John Walker Powell, Abingdon Press, New York, 1918.

necessarily mean that one is also a great *oral reader* or *interpreter* of literature. It is not sufficient for the oral reader to know literature thoroughly, or even to be able to write it masterfully, he must *also* know *how to read literature aloud* in a manner that will reveal its purpose and significance.

"It is well known that the higher forms of literature cannot be appreciated by young people except when read aloud, and that the reading aloud enriches the appreciation of even discerning minds."

The Oral Study of Literature, Algernon Tassin. F. S. Crofts and Company, Publishers.

"The adequate rendering of the thought of the printed page makes demands on the voice such as oral composition and ordinary class room speaking rarely make. For in reading literature, not ideas alone are to be stated but imagination and spirit are to be revealed as well. Without these poetry becomes dry as dust, and prose vain 'bibble-babble.' "

A Hand Book of Oral Reading. Emerson Lee Bassett. Houghton, Mifflin Company, Publishers.

". . . the younger Dumas pointed out how an effect made in the theater is sometimes so unlike any produced by a good narrative read at the fireside, that a spectator seeking to recover, by means of the printed page, the emotion that had stirred him as he saw the piece performed is sometimes 'unable not only to find the emotion again in written words but even to discover the place where it was. A word, a look, a gesture, a silence, a purely atmospheric combination, had held him spell bound.' "

From *The Development of the Drama*, Brander Matthews, p. 341. Charles Scribner's Sons, Publishers.

WHAT IS AN INTERPRETER?

To Interpret:—
"To tell the meaning of; to expand, to translate orally into intelligible language. To show by illustrative representation."
Webster's Collegiate Dictionary.

An *interpreter* is a go-between, an agent, who reveals the meaning, motives and feelings of one person—or persons—to others as accurately, fully and impartially as possible without changing them by his own thoughts, feelings or opinions, although he may clearly show his own reactions to them.

WHAT IS AN INTERPRETER OF LITERATURE?

An interpreter of literature is an agent between the author of the literature and the listener. *He is the spokesman for the author.* His function—and his privilege—is to turn the *silent written word* into the *audible spoken word*, to transform the mere pictured representation of a word into the real living animated word for the benefit of someone else, and at the same time to reveal his own understanding and appreciation of the author's meaning and motives through his technical use of these words, aided by the proper use of his voice, his facial expression and his whole bodily response.

THE TERMS 'INTERPRETER' AND 'READER'

The terms *interpreter* and *reader* are used interchangeably in this text to designate *the person who is speaking the lines of the literature* whether he is reading them from a book or manuscript, or reciting them from memory, and whether the lines were written by himself or by another.

THE GOOD ORAL READER IS A REFLECTOR OF THE AUTHOR'S THOUGHTS AND MOODS

The reader's speech, voice and body must become as mirrors through which his hearers see and understand the author's meaning, moods, and motives, whatever they may be.

It has often been said—and will be said again—that when one gets a selection clear in one's own understanding, the *manner of expression* will take care of itself, that there is no need of learning *how to read*, that one will do so intuitively, and that to try to learn how to read consciously, simply engenders artificiality and affectation. If untrained readers will actually get up before an audience and try to read a selection, giving it its full intellectual and emotional significance in a pleasing and interesting manner, they will be able to test the truth or falsity of this statement. In the great majority of cases untrained tongues and hands and feet will get in the way and will call attention to themselves instead of doing what their owner wants and expects them to do. They will not obey him, and therefore will become hindrances and stumbling blocks that only *interfere* with, instead of *helping, the expression* of the truth and beauty that his mind fully comprehends and his heart desires to portray. Often a shy and diffident person fully comprehends the inner meaning of a selection, while one with 'the gift of gab' only half comprehends it, but the latter will be given greater credit for knowledge because he can more nearly *express* what little he knows. The voice and speech and body are the *only agents* that can bring out and into being what is in the mind. Occasionally an individual *may* bring it out *naturally* but to each one who does, there are many thousands who must be thoroughly trained to do so.

The *manner of expression*, or, the *technique of expression*, must be carefully *studied* and studiously *applied* in all other arts,—in the practical arts as well as in the fine arts—: it scarcely seems possible that the art of the oral interpreter of literature should be an exception to a universal law that has stood the test of all the time that man has known.

Each reader may *discover* a fine and efficient technique for himself, and this is a most valuable thing but it takes a lifetime to do it. The would-be artist will save the majority of his lifetime for *application* and *accomplishment* and will not have to devote it all to *rediscovery*, if he will take advantage of what has been discovered by other artists in other lifetimes. He should make use of as much of this as will serve his purpose and discard that which will not, using his own discoveries to replace the inferior or outgrown or inadequate ones of his forbears. By this process he will make practical use of the priceless heritage that comes to him from the past and at the same time will make his own equally priceless contribution to the present and the future.

An art is the outgrowth of many minds and many hearts through many lifetimes of toil in choosing the essentials and eliminating the superfluous. No one person has a monopoly on it. Every real artist in every line gratefully accepts all the help he can get from his predecessors and humbly, though surely, makes his small but vastly important contribution to the artists that are yet to come. Thus progress is made through the ages, and pigmies though we be, we may stand on the shoulders of the giants who came before us and the giants who are with us now, and because of their help in lifting us up, our outlook is wider than theirs. It is only the *pigmy of the mind* who prefers to stand on his own small feet and on his own level, and limit himself to the little he can see therefrom, when he might stand on the shoulders of a giant, even an old fashioned one, and gain a wide vision of the stars. From this vantage point he will be able to see that there are *new things* to be done and *new ways* that they may be done and it is his obligation and his privilege to *do* them.

CHAPTER III

THE AIM AND QUALIFICATIONS OF THE ORAL INTERPRETER OF LITERATURE

The Aim of the Oral Interpreter

THE aim of the oral interpreter of literature is *to interpret adequately, for the pleasure and profit of others, the finest thoughts and deepest emotions of the great writers of all time.* It is indeed a tremendous undertaking; he who would succeed must approach the task with profound humility and sincerity, and must attempt to accomplish it only after long, serious and thorough study along many lines. It is not a task for the novice, the dilettant, or the uncultivated.

He who would be a true interpreter of literature must love literature for its own sake, he must study and assimilate it, and he must study what those who know say about it. He must love its meanings and its moods enough to inspire him to master the technique of *how to interpret them,* or, the *technique of oral expression.* Only by means of this technique will he be able to give full, adequate and satisfactory expression to his appreciation and understanding of the literature, and to the author's true meaning, mood, and purpose.

Instruction is Only a By-Product of the Oral Reader's Art

While the purpose of the oral interpreter of literature is to interest and entertain his listeners by a revelation of truth and beauty through his chosen medium, giving them a wider knowledge and appreciation of literature and life, awakening a greater love for the beautiful, extending their sympathies, understanding and experience, he may and usually does, instruct as well as entertain them. But *instruction is the by-product of his work* and must come as a result of the excellence of the work itself, not as a separate and distinct end to be achieved. The mission of all art is the revelation of truth and beauty in universal language; the art of the oral interpreter of literature is no exception to this ancient and time-honored rule.

*The Qualifications of the Oral Reader

The subject of *how to interpret literature orally*, constitutes the *technique of oral expression*. This requires a distinct and comprehensive course of study in itself which should be undertaken along with, or previous to, the study of *the forms of literature* that are best suited to *oral interpretation*, and the study of the basic principles which determine the general manner of such interpretation.

To be master of the technique of oral expression the reader must have certain *personal qualities*, natural or acquired, together with thorough *training* along many different lines. It is not possible to touch upon all of these subjects in this text—nor would it be advisable if it were possible—but some of the important and pertinent ones are outlined or discussed; others are only mentioned, still others are, of necessity, entirely omitted.

Personal Qualities of the Reader

The true interpreter of literature must have certain *abstract, intangible* qualities, either native or acquired. Some of these are:

---

*In the annual verse-speaking contest, or, festival, at Oxford, the contestants are graded as follows, under the heading, *Verse Speaking and Dramatic Art*.

TECHNIQUE 50	ARTISTRY 50
Breathing, Tone and Pitch, Enunciation } Vowels and Consonants,	Imagination, Concentration on central idea,
Phrasing, Rhythm, Pace	Vocal Expression, Relation of mind and body, Characterization.

1. A highly developed imagination.

2. That intangible but essential quality known as dramatic instinct.

3. Deep and sympathetic understanding of human nature, its frailties as well as its strengths.

4. A keen sense of rhythm and time, and of the melody and harmony of sounds.

5. A pleasing and gracious personality.

6. The ability to sense the reactions of his listeners, to respond to them, and to quietly but surely open the doors to the chambers of their imaginations and lead their thoughts away from themselves and their individual personal problems into the realm of more universal things suggested by the literature that he is reading.

THE GENERAL TRAINING OF THE READER

The reader's study of *tangible, concrete, technical* subjects should be extensive. He should have:

1. A good general knowledge of dramatic and poetic literature.

2. Some acquaintances with poetics.

3. The ability to discover an author's meaning and motives with a large degree of accuracy.

4. A special acquaintance with the particular forms of literature that are best suited to oral reading, and the general relation these forms bear to each other.

5. An understanding of the basic principles that determine the way each individual literary form should be read in order to bring out its particular purpose, its meaning, and its moods, to the best possible advantage without calling attention to himself or his methods.

6. He should have a good technical knowledge of the best way to use his *tools*, which are his own voice, speech and body. This technical knowledge should include:

7. A working knowledge of the science of phonetics as it is applied to the art of the production of speech sounds, pronunciation, articulation and word grouping. This will enable him to speak so that he may be *understood*.

> "We must learn to regard language solely as consisting of *groups of sounds*, independently of the written symbols which are always associated with all kinds of disturbing associations chiefly historical. . . . The first requisite is a knowledge of phonetics, or the form of language. Phonetics alone can breathe life into the dead mass of letters which constitute a written language. . . . Pronunciation, it is now generally admitted, can only be taught on the basis of scientific phonetics. . . . Phonetics alone enable us to analyze and register the various phenomena of stress, intonation and quantity, which are the foundation of word division, sentence structure, elocution, metre, and, in fact, enter into all the higher problems of language."

Collected Papers. Henry Sweet.
Clarendon Press, Oxford.

> ". . . further very important elements in proper expression are *Stress* and *Intonation*, which are phonetic problems. Therefore, phonetic training in the widest sense is an indispensable part of the preparation of those who wish to learn to read with feeling and intelligibility."

The Teaching of Reading, Henry Cecil Wyld. p. 12.
John Murray, London, 1924.

> "Language was long ago resolved into its alphabetic elements, and its Parts of speech . . . we teach a child its leters and their union into words: surely then, there is no cause why a clear perception of the varieties of stress, of time, and of intonation, and the power of knowingly employing them in curent uterance, should not be acquired in a similar elementary maner.

The art of reading-well consists in having all the constituents of speech, both alphabetic and expressive, under
complete comand. . . .

Notwithstanding we are all taut the alphabet, we are
not taut the true elements of speech: . . .

Let the first lesson consist of a separate, an exact, and a
repeated pronunciation of each of the thirty-five elements,
thereby, to insure a true and easy execution of their un-
mingled sounds: the pupil being careful to pronounce, not
the alphabetic sylable of the school, but the pure and indi-
visable vocal element; however unusual and uncouth that
sound may in some cases, be to his ear.

It may be asked if a careful pronunciation of words, in
which these elements, combined with others, must still be
heard, would not give the necessary exactnes and facility? I
believe it would not. When the elements are pronounced
singly, they may receive an undivided energy of the organic
efort, and therewith a clearnes of sound, and a definite
outline, that make a fine preparative for distinct and forcible
pronunciation in the compounds of speech."

From *The Philosophy of the Human Voice Together With a
System of Principles By Which Criticism in the Art of
Elocution May be Rendered Intelligible, and Instruction,
Definite and Comprehensive*, p.p. 483-4.
By James Rush, M. D.
The Library Company of Philadelphia, Publishers. 1893.

8. An understanding of the general principles and
significance of the intonation of his language.

9. A well developed speaking voice—full, clear, musical
and vibrant—which is varied as to pitch, volume, tempo and
quality and which is capable of expressing innumerable
shades of meaning and emotion. This will enable him to
speak freely, and forcefully enough to be *heard* in all situations, to give the proper vocal coloring to literature, and it
will make his speech pleasing to his listeners.

"The just interpretation of the author's meaning, which is
the highest attainment of a good reader or reciter, is a matter
of the intellect and the emotions. Before due expression can
be given to the ideas, emotions or passions contained in a

piece of prose or verse, these must first be apprehended by the mind and sympathies of the reader . . . the instrument of expression is the voice, so that Voice training is essential . . . ."

The Teaching of Reading, p. 11. Henry Cecil Wyld.

10. A highly trained ear capable of *judging* his own speech and voice.

11. A disciplined, obedient and expressive body; proper bodily poise and carriage; a good walk and good standing and sitting positions.

> One may be lame or otherwise physically handicapped and yet carry oneself with dignity and poise.

12. A thorough understanding of platform deportment and etiquette.

13. The ability to *subordinate himself* to the literature and its demands.

The technique of the oral reader of literature must harmonize with the technique of the writer of literature if the readings are to be true and adequate. Since the reader is the agent or the spokesman for the author the less conspicuous he is, personally, the better. Nevertheless in the capacity of agent he is important, and he should devote himself wholly to the performance of that task. His whole mind, spirit, voice and body, his sympathy, appreciation and enthusiasm, should be given freely and unselfishly, but inconspicuously, to the interpretation.

READINGS SHOULD SOUND NATURAL AND SPONTANEOUS

No matter what may be the nature of a selection, the reader should give the lines as if they were the expression of his own, or, of a character's original thoughts and feelings which are springing spontaneously and freshly from the mind and heart for the first time, even though they **may have** been repeated a thousand times. There must not be the slightest possible trace of their having been committed to memory, or that they are being read from a book. The reader should *talk* to his listeners, as if in conversation with them, maintaining natural and original genuineness and sincerity. He may express joy, sorrow, vengeance, despair, madness, love, enthusiasm, exhaustion, hysteria, rage, indifference, or any other mood or emotion of man, but he must express them so that they *seem* to be original, spontaneous and natural, although in reality they have been chosen discriminately and are being expressed according to a definite plan. The reader should reveal the *awakening* of each idea he expresses, the *relation* of one idea to another, and their continuous *unfoldment and progression,* together with the *feelings they arouse* and *the results they bring about.* He *must think the lines* as he reads them, and should *respond* to them as well; this can be done only when he has made the thoughts and moods of the author entirely his own.

The *listener* should be able to *see, or be aware of,* the birth of each new thought in the *reader's* mind, and should feel its nature, and the effect it has upon the reader's mind and heart.

Choose Essentials Only, in Artistic Expression

In the oral interpretation of literature—as in all other artistic expression—the artist must be able to distinguish between essentials and non-essentials. If the oral reader should actually *do* all that is done in natural speech and behavior, the essentials would be all mixed up with the non-essentials as they are in real life, and the result would be photographic imitation, not art. Art *chooses and idealizes significant things* and presents a picture of life with the *essentials left in and the non-essentials left out.* To choose and to omit wisely and effectively, to know with certainty what *is* essential and what is *not* essential, is the obligation of the artist.

"The highest problem of all art is to produce by illusion the semblance of a high reality. But it is a false endeavour to push the realization of the illusion so far that at last only a commonplace reality remains."

Poetry and Truth, Vol. II, Goethe
Bell and Sons, London.

Do Not Confuse the Means with the End

The end the oral reader wishes to gain must not be confused with the means by which he gains it. To be sure, the *means*—which is the technique—must be mastered before the *end* can be wholly attained, *but the means is important only as it brings the end about: it is not important in itself.* The *means* should be more and more completely *concealed* as the *end* is more and more nearly *accomplished,* until finally, *the means must be so completely submerged in the end* that there *seems* to be no special means at all. When this point is reached, speech, voice and action will seem to be wholly spontaneous and original.

Good reading will always *appear* to be perfectly free and natural. The words should flow from the lips of the reader with perfect ease, smoothness and sincerity and with apparent natural, original spontaniety, as if not a single thought had been given to *how* the reading should be done. The greatest art is to *conceal art* and to make the expression appear to be wholly natural and unstudied. To accomplish this end in the art of the oral interpretation of literature—as in all arts—requires long and serious study along many lines.

CHAPTER IV

SIGNIFICANCE OF SOUNDS AND WORDS
IN LITERATURE

"Literature is the interpretation of life through the medium of words."

New Methods for the Study of Literature, Edith Rickert, Chicago University Press, Chicago, 1928.

"We must choose our words, not only for elegance but for sound." Dante.

"The stuff of language is words, and the sensuous material of words is sound; if language, therefore is to be made perfect, its materials must be made beautiful." . . .

Interpretation of Poetry and Religion, George Santayana. p. 252.
Charles Scribner's Sons, Publishers, 1921.

"Poetry doesn't live completely except in sound, for sound is part of its meaning." Gordon Bottomly.*

EVERY great writer chooses the words for his writings as carefully as a great musical composer chooses the notes for a symphony. The great writer considers *each sound*, each *shade of sound*, its *quality, pitch* and *duration;* he carefully plans the *combinations of sounds* and considers their special fitness for the places they are to fill; he arranges them with the utmost care, forming illusive patterns of wondrous and intricate design. He knows full well what each sound will do to add to the balance and beauty, the unity and harmony, of the composition as a whole; he knows that some sounds will give an effect of lightness and crispness,—others will give

---

*This statement was taken by the author, verbatim, from one of Mr. Bottomly's talks at Rhodes House, Oxford, when he was a judge at the verse-speaking contest in the summer of 1933.

a sense of dignity and fullness of tone; he knows that some sounds will suggest delicacy and daintiness,—others will suggest abruptness and finality. He lovingly and understandingly considers each individual sound and the combinations of sounds that are to form syllables and groups of syllables, and they dance or skip or ripple for him as he wills. He can make them move in solemn procession and slow, or clash and clang in notes of danger and alarm. They whisper the secrets he wishes to tell; they sing and ring like birds and bells, or thunder and boom like waves and guns. He studies sounds and words as a painter studies his colors, for they are the stuff his art is made of and he must choose them with infinite care.

> "When the poet makes his perfect selection of a word he is endowing the word with life."

> "The emotion of poetry expresses itself in rhythm and . . . the significance of the subject-matter is realized by the intellectual choice of the perfect word."

> *The Lyric*, pp. 54 and 64 respectively.   John Drinkwater. Martin Secker, London, Publisher.

In speaking of a paragraph from *"Suspiria de Profundis"* by De Quincy, J. H. Gardiner says:

> "It is not so much what the words mean that moves you as their vague and mystical suggestion, and even more the haunting rhythm and the strange melody of the *sounds.*"

On pages 167 and 168, respectively, in the same text Mr. Gardiner says:

> ". . ., in description more than in any other kind of writing you need a musical and expressive rhythm. I have spoken of the way in which a natural glow of style gives the personal quality to exposition. Here in addition to that I mean the *pure musical quality of sounds.* . . . Generally as in music the exact workings of cause and effect are recondite: you can only say that the rhythm and the quality of the *vowels and consonants* affect your feelings by the direct stirring of your sensations. . . .

It is the highest achievement of Mr. Ruskin's style that it is able, by setting apt words in a style full of resonance and music, to express in words impressions which most men have to leave either to painting or to music; and to obtain this effect . . . without affectation and without losing its entire sincerity and sanity."

From *The Forms of Prose Literature.*
Charles Scribner's Sons, Publishers. 1912.

"Words have an individual and a relative value. They should be chosen before being placed in position. This word is a mere pebble; that a fine pearl or an amethyst. . . . For every sentence that may be penned or spoken the right word exists. . . . He who does not find them and fit them into place, who accepts the first term that presents itself rather than search for the expression which accurately and beautifully embodies his meaning, aspires to mediocrity, and is content with failure. The exquisite adjustment of a word to its significance; . . . the generous sympathy of a word with its surroundings, . . . are the twin perfections which constitute style, and substantiate genius. . . ."

From *Words* by Agnes Repplier
In *Essays in Idleness,*
Houghton Mifflin Company, Publishers.

When authors take such punctilious care in choosing the sounds and the words for their writings, a reader should never attempt or presume to interpret these writings for the pleasure and profit of others without himself having a thorough knowledge and appreciation of words and the sounds they are made of, and of the part they play in making literature beautiful, alluring and alive.

"Words have amazing powers. The world offers its treasures of money, power, and position to the skilful user of them. There are words for every occasion—words that thunder commands; words bristling with compelling force; words of zephyr-like delicacy; words of inspiration; words of romance; words to bend men's minds to your will; words to express every shade of meaning."

New York Times Book Review Section, Oct. 26, 1930. Page 25.

"You must get into the habit of looking intensely at words, syllable by syllable—nay, letter by letter . . . words if they are not watched will do deadly work sometimes."

Sesame and Lilies.   Ruskin.

EXAMPLE OF THE SIGNIFICANCE OF SOUNDS AND WORDS IN LITERATURE

DESERTION

So light we were, so right we were, so fair faith shone,
And the way was laid so certainly, that, when I'd gone,
What dumb thing looked up at you? Was it something heard,
Or a sudden cry, that meekly and without a word
You broke the faith, and strangely, weakly, slipped apart.
You gave in—you, the proud of heart, unbowed of heart!
Was this, friend, the end of all that we could do?
And have you found the best for you, the rest for you?
Did you learn so suddenly (and I not by!)
Some whispered story, that stole the glory from the sky,
And ended all the splendid dream, and made you go
So dully from the fight we know, the light we know?

O faithless! the faith remains, and I must pass
Gay down the way, and on alone. Under the grass
You wait; the breeze moves in the trees, and stirs and calls,
And covers you with white petals, with light petals.
There it shall crumble, frail and fair under the sun,
O little heart, your brittle heart; till day be done,
And the shadows gather, falling light, and, white with dew,
Whisper, and weep; and creep to you. Good sleep to you.

From *The Collected Poems of Rupert Brooke*, p. 107.
Used by permission of the Publishers.
Dodd, Mead and Company, Inc.

THE READER MUST BE MASTER OF THE USE OF THE SOUNDS OF HIS LANGUAGE IF HE IS TO INTERPRET ITS LITERATURE ADEQUATELY

A thorough knowledge and mastery of the sounds of his language and their use in words and groups of words, is absolutely necessary in order to enable the oral reader to *play fair* with the author and to truly and fully interpret the work of the author in the highest and best sense of the word.

The sounds of spoken English and general instructions **for** their production and use are given in the following chapter.

CHAPTER V

THE SOUNDS OF SPOKEN ENGLISH

ATTENTION has been called in the previous chapter to the very great *significance of sounds, and combinations of sounds,* and their effective use in all forms of literature. The oral interpreter of literature cannot even begin his study of oral interpretation until he has a fair knowledge of the sounds of English and the proper way to combine and use them. He can hope to *succeed* as an oral interpreter of literature only when he has fully *mastered* the correct production of the sounds and has learned how to combine them and use them to bring out all the qualities of the literature which they **and** the voice, alone, can reveal.

It is not possible to separate speech and voice. The perfection of each one depends upon the perfection of the other. *Sounds cannot be produced correctly until the voice is properly and adequately used.* A properly produced voice is wasted and unfulfilled unless the sounds which require that voice for their existence, are correctly formed in the mouth. The training of speech and voice must be done at one and the same time if the best results are to be obtained.

While it is not possible to give full information concerning the production and use of the sounds of English in this text, the most fundamental points can be pointed out which will be of service while the student is giving the subject wider study. A bibliography which should assist the student in his study is given at the end of the chapter.

SPEECH

Speech is the expression of thought and emotion by means of articulate sounds.

Speech sounds are produced by certain definite positions and movements of the speech organs acting upon the outgoing breath.

The correct positions and movements must be learned for each sound and practiced until the correct use becomes habitual.

"All spoken language is reducible to the concrete roots or bases, simple monosyllabic sounds. They are phonetic types, produced by a power inherent in human nature. Articulate speech is fabricated from these stems by man, guided only by innate laws, or by an instinctive impulse. . . . It is the use of articulate sounds that made man master of the tempest and the sea, master of lightning . . . and of all comprised in the material world. . . . There is no natural and intrinsic difference between the sounds of the brute and the words of man,—the difference is merely of application. . . . The lower animals are content in their operations. . . . Man is ever striving to improve or change his condition."

Science of Language. Part One. Max Müller.
Published by Scribner, Armstrong, and Company, New York, 1874.

The Speech Organs which are used to produce speech sounds are: the lips, lower jaw, tongue, teeth, upper gums, hard palate, soft palate, and vocal cords.

Breath is the stuff speech and voice are made of, consequently, it is absolutely *imperative* that the supply of breath be adequate, that *it be taken, in the proper way* and *at proper intervals*, and that it be *properly controlled* and *directed*. One of the greatest causes of harsh, unpleasant, and inadequate voices, and of indistinct speech, is *insufficient supply* of breath.

The Human Voice and Speech Machine,
or,
The Human Musical Instrument

We may well think of voice and speech as having two parts, *the spiritual part* and *the mechanical part*. The spiritual part is one of the "clouds of glory" that came with us, which no man giveth and no man taketh away. That always was and always will be ours, and it is peculiarly and sacredly individual. All we can do about it is to train the mechanical part to work one hundred percent perfect so that it will in no way *interfere* with the full use and beauty and individuality of that great spiritual possession.

We can study and analyse the mechanical parts of voice and speech; and train ourselves to make very serviceable and beautiful use of them. They will never perform their full service in the world until they *are* trained and trained well.

There are four parts to the speech and voice mechanism.
1. The motor,
2. The vibrator,
3. The resonator,
4. The articulator.

The *motor* is made up of the breathing apparatus; the lungs, the muscles of respiration, the diaphragm. The function of the motor is *to supply power* for the production of sound waves, and for the proper expulsion and control of air in the production of all sounds, whether voiced or voiceless.

The *vibrator* is made up of the larynx in general, but chiefly of the two vocal cords, or bands, or lips, which *produce sound waves* when the motor has been properly used and controlled and the breath properly directed on its outward journey.

The *resonator* is made up of the cavities of the mouth, nose, and pharynx especially, but the entire body acts as a resonator. The function of the resonator is to *reinforce or amplify the sound waves* which have been set in motion by the vocal cords.

The *articulator* is made up of the lips, lower jaw, tongue, teeth, upper gums, hard palate and soft palate. Its function is to *shape and mould* the outgoing breath,—voiced or unvoiced,—into different forms and patterns by its various positions and movements, which make what we know as the individual sounds of a language.

The two extremes of this mechanism—the motor and the articulator—can be definitely, directly, and consciously trained. The other two parts—the vibrator and the resonator

—perform their functions excellently as a result of the excellent performance of the motor and the articulator.

The basic purpose of speech is communication.

In order that speech may *fulfill* its basic purpose of communication it must be:

1. mutually *intelligible* between speaker and listener,
2. spoken *loudly* enough to be *heard,*
3. *articulated clearly*, and the
   words must be *grouped* and
   stressed in such a way that it
   can be *understood.*

In order that speech may be pleasing to the aesthetic sense of the hearer it must be:

1. pleasing in its quality,
2. expressed in a pleasing manner,
3. devoid of slovenliness, pedantry,
   artificiality, and affectation.

PHONETICS,
OR,
THE SCIENCE OF SPEECH SOUNDS AND THE ART OF PRONUNCIATION

The sounds of English, or of any other language, can be studied to the greatest advantage by the use of the science of phonetics, as it is applied to the art of pronunciation.

Phonetics gives all practical details concerning the positions and movements of the speech organs in the production of sounds, and the proper means of combining the sounds in connected speech. *It is necessary for the oral reader to know how to produce and combine the sounds of his language correctly and to practice doing so until the correct use has become habitual.* Only by so doing will he be able to get the full service and beauty out of the language.

In his text *The Teaching of Reading in Training Colleges*, published by John Murray, Albemarle Street, W. London,

Henry Cecil Wyld, in speaking of the superiority of the phonetic method of correcting speech errors and dialects, over other methods, says (pages 4 and 5):

"In the face of the problems it would be amusing, if it were not saddening, to find people still gravely discussing, both in conversation and in published works, whether Phonetics is of any use in this connection. The answer of experience is clear and categorical, and it is this: Unless you employ Phonetic methods, and apply them systematically, you will never have satisfactory results in your attempts to 'improve' the pronunciation of the Primary Teacher. . . . In asserting the necessity of Phonetic method in overcoming these difficulties, I wish to make the statement as strong as possible. As a result of considerable experience of teachers and of those who train them, I unhesitatingly assert that I have never known a person competent to form an opinion who doubted that Phonetics was essential. I have never known anyone who had a sound elementary knowledge of Phonetics, derived from proper training, and not merely from going more or less carefully through several books on the subject—anyone, indeed who had any pretence to be called a practical phonetician—who was not thoroughly convinced of the value of the Phonetic method. . . .

The dissentient voices raised against Phonetics are not from those who know, who are well trained themselves, who have applied Phonetic method patiently and skilfully, . . . but from persons who, possibly through no fault of their own, are not trained, who are quite ignorant of the subject, who have never tried it, who have never bestowed any serious thought upon the matter, and who are, therefore, not qualified to speak."

". . . it is important that the teacher should have a sufficient knowledge both of vocal and phonological method, and of phonetics. A large part of the confusion which exists in the teaching of spoken English arises from lack of ear-training, lack of practice in phonetic transcription and ignorance of the nature of vowel resonances." Elsie Fogerty.

The Speaking of English Verse. p. 166.
E. P. Dutton and Company, Publishers. 1923.

Classification of Speech Sounds

Vowels and Consonants

The two principal classes of speech sounds are vowels and consonants.

Each individual *vowel* sound is given its distinguishing characteristics by the positions of the tongue, jaw and lips as the vocalized breath passes out of the mouth.

There are fifteen English vowels.

Each individual *consonant* sound is given its distinguishing characteristics by *the place of articulation, the manner of articulation, and the presence or absence of vibration in the vocal cords.*

There are twenty-four English consonants.

All consonants may be divided into two classes: 1, voiceless, 2, voiced.

A *voiceless* consonant is one having no vibrations of the vocal cords, hence no *tone*.

A *voiced* sound is one in which there is vibration of the vocal cords.

There are nine voiceless and fifteen voiced consonants in spoken English.

Diphthongs

A *diphthong* is formed by the *blending* together of *two vowel sounds* in such a way that they *lose their individual identity* and are spoken in one syllable. The sounds are blended in such a way that it is not possible to say where the first one ends and the second one begins.

There are nine diphthongs in English.

Affricates

An *affricate* is formed by the blending together of *two*

consonant sounds in such a way that they *lose their individual identity* and are always spoken in the same syllable.

There are two affricates in English.

PHONETIC LETTERS

There are not enough *letters* in the Roman Alphabet to represent the *sounds* of the languages that use the Alphabet. Great confusion and uncertainty as to the accepted pronunciation of words has arisen as a result of this. To obviate this difficulty and assist in the study of all spoken languages The International Phonetic Alphabet was devised in which there is one and only one letter for each sound. The phonetic letters for the English sounds are given before the following specimen words which contain the sounds. It is necessary for students to learn these letters. The specimen words should be used in connection with the *Descriptive Charts of Vowels and Consonants.*

PHONETIC LETTERS FOR THE ENGLISH CONSONANTS AND SPECIMEN WORDS CONTAINING THEM

p^h	*po*p		s	his*s*
$p_|$	u*p* there		z	bu*zz*
b	*b*a*b*e			
m	*m*u*m*		ʃ	hu*sh*
ʍ	*wh*ale		ʒ	rou*ge*
w	*w*ail			
			ɹ	roa*r*ing
f	i*f*			
v	li*v*e		j	*y*es
θ	brea*th*		k^h	*c*oo*k*
ð	brea*the*		$k_|$	loo*k* there
			g	*g*a*g*
t^h	*t*o*t*		ŋ	si*ng*

t₁	what man		
d	deed		
n	none	h	he
l	will	ɦ	aha
		t₁ʃ	church
		dʒ	judge
		m̩	prisms
		n̩	often
		l̩	sparkle

Consonants
Stop-Plosives

In producing the sounds p b t d k g, the position of the organs of articulation is taken and held a second which constitutes the *stop;* then the position of the organs is quickly released and the air is emitted suddenly causing the *plosive.*

p t k are the *voiceless* stop-plosives.

b d g are the *voiced* stop-plosives.

Aspirated and Unaspirated p t k

When the voiceless stop-plosives, p t k, are used before a *vowel*, a *diphthong*, or a *pause*, they are spoken with a slight puff of breath and are called *aspirated* stop-plosives. The aspirated form is indicated thus: pʰ tʰ kʰ

When p t and k are used before *another consonant* within a breath group, either in the same word or in the following word, the puff of breath is omitted and the sounds are called *unaspirated* stop-plosives.   They are indicated thus: p₁ t₁ k₁

When the voiced stop-plosives b d g, precede a pause they have what is known as an *off-glide*. The plosive is obvious. In all other positions the plosive must blend into the following sound. Often there is very little of the plosive but the position of the organs and a slight voiced sound. Note the difference between the sound of d in the words *red* and *redman*, of b in the words *tub* and *subject*, and of g in the words *rag* and *rag-weed*.

Nasal Continuants

In producing the voiced sounds, m n and ŋ (so*ng*) the soft palate is lowered and the *air is emitted through the nose* in a continuous stream until the sound is finished. There must be *no* off-glide. Keep the organs of speech in the position for the sound until after the sound is stopped at the vocal cords.

Lateral Continuant

In producing the voiced sound l, the point of the tongue must touch the upper front gums directly behind the upper teeth and must be held in position while the air is emitted in a continuous stream over the sides of the tongue. There must be *no* off-glide.

Fricative Continuants

The positions of the organs of speech for the fricative continuants are such as to leave only a narrow channel through which the air must be forced in a steady stream by the speech motor. This causes *audible friction,* hence the name *fricative* continuants. Some of them are voiceless and some are voiced. There must be *no* off-glides. The fricative continuants are:

f v θ (*th*in) ð (*th*en) s z ʃ (hu*sh*) ʒ (rou*ge*)
ɹ (*r*ed) h ɦ ((a*h*a)

Glides

In the production of the sounds ʍ (*wh*ere), w, and j (*y*ou), we begin with one sound and then glide easily off it, hence the name *glides*. These sounds occur in English only at the beginning of syllables.

Affricates

The affricates have been explained on p. (34). They are:
tᵢʃ, *voiceless,* as in *ch*ur*ch*.
dʒ, *voiced,* as in *j*ud*ge*.

To produce these sounds place the tip of the tongue on the upper gums directly behind the front teeth and begin the first of the two sounds, then remove the *tip* of the tongue and finish with the second sound which is a continuant,

DESCRIPTIVE CHART OF

There are three different things that must be considered in the production of every consonant, since they determine exactly what the·

Place of

I		2	3		4		5	
Manner of Articulation ↓		Place I *Bi-labial.* Two lips articulating against each other		Place II *Labio-dental.* Lower lip articulating against upper teeth		Place III *Dental.* Tip of tongue on upper front teeth		Place IV-A *Alveolar.* Tip of tongue *touching* upper gums behind front teeth	
		v-s	v-d	v-s	v-d	v-s	v-d	v-s	v-d
b Stop-plosives		pʰ pǀ	b					tʰ tǀ	d
c Nasal continuants			m						n
d Lateral continuants									l
e Fricative continuants				f	v	θ	ð		
f Glides		ʍ	w						
g Affricates								tǀʃ	dʒ
h Vowel-like consonants			m / w						n / l
j Syllabic consonants (which may form a *weak* or unstressed syllable without a vowel)			m						n̩ l̩

k

Note: The double line marks the ends of the groups of consonants. Those following are repetitions. v-s indicates the sounds are voiceless, having no vibration of the vocal cords. v-d indicates the sounds

ENGLISH CONSONANTS

sound shall be. They are: 1. Its *place* of articulation; 2. its *manner* of articulation; 3. whether it is *voiceless* or *voiced*.

Articulation.

6						7		8		9	10
Place IV-B — *Alveolar:* Tip of tongue *free*, pointing toward, but *not* touching:						Place V — *Palatal.* Front of tongue articulating against *front* (or *hard*) palate		Place VI — *Velar.* Back of tongue articulating against *back* (or *soft*) palate		Place VII — *Glottal.* In the throat	
1 extreme *front* of upper gums		2 *middle* of upper gums		3 extreme *back* of upper gums							
v-s	v-d	v-s	v-d	v-s	v-d	v-s	v-d	v-s	v-d	v-s	v-d
								k^h k_1	g		
									ŋ		
s	z	ʃ	ʒ		ɹ					h	ɦ
							j				
					ɹ		j		ŋ		

are voiced, having vibration of the vocal cords. Aspirated p^h t^h k^h are used before a vowel, a diphthong and a pause. Unaspirated p_1 t_1 k_1 are used before another consonant within a breath group.

ENGLISH VOWELS

The positions of the *tongue, lips* and *lower jaw* must be considered in the production of every vowel, since they determine what the sound shall be.

The *tip* of the tongue rests behind the lower front teeth in *all* vowel sounds.

Front vowels have the *front* of the tongue arched in the *front* of the mouth.

Back vowels have the *back* of the tongue arched in the *back* of the mouth.

Mid vowels have the *middle* of the tongue arched in the *middle* of the mouth.

The *length* or *duration* of vowels is very important.

Two dots (:) placed after a letter indicate the sound is *long*.

DESCRIPTIVE CHART OF ENGLISH VOWELS WITH SPECIMEN WORDS

Front   Mid   Back

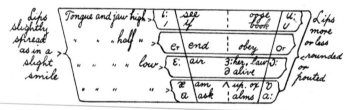

The mid vowels, ɜ: ə ʌ, and the last back vowel, ɑ:, have neutral, or, normal lip position.

SENTENCES CONTAINING THE VOWELS

Front vowels. i: ɪ eɪ ɛ(:) æ a
   Lee will let fair Anne pass.

Back vowels. u: ʊ oʊ ɔ: ɒ ɑ:
   Who could obey all honest fathers?

Mid vowels. ɜ: ə ʌ
   Twirl a thumb.

Phonetic Letters for English Diphthongs with Specimen Words

The diphthongs are grouped here according to the *second element* which is always *unstressed*. This is indicated by placing a curved line [ˇ], above the second letter.

Group 1. Diphthongs ending in unstressed ɪ

eᷠɪ̆	A	p*ay*	Pay my boy.
aɪ̆	I	m*y*	
ɔɪ̆	oy	b*oy*	

Group 2. Diphthongs ending in unstressed ʊ

oᷠʊ̆	Oh, g*o*	Go now.
aʊ̆	ow, n*ow*	

Group 3. Diphthongs ending in unstressed ə

ɪə̆	*ear,*	h*ere*	Here's their poor ore.
ɛə̆	*air,*	th*eir*	
ʊə̆	p*oor,*	y*our*	
ɔə̆	*oar,*	*ore*	

Length or Duration of English Sounds

There is nothing more important for the oral reader to know about sounds than when he may and when he may not lengthen them. The following rules should be learned and carefully applied.

Vowels

The vowels i: u: ɔ: ɑ: ɜ: are fully long:—

    a. in the stressed syllable of a word before a *pause.*

Ex. 'mi: ‖ me   'lɔ: ‖ law   'hɜ: ‖ her.

    'ju: ‖ you   'fɑ: ‖ far

    b. in the stressed syllable of a word before a *voiced sound,* either a consonant or a vowel.

Ex. 'si: d seed   'si:ŋ seeing.

iˑ uˑ ɔˑ ɑˑ ɜˑ are *half-long* in the stressed syllable of a word before a *voiceless* consonant.

Ex.   'iˑtʰ   eat   'sɔˑs   sauce   'fɜˑstʰ   first.

'djuˑtʰɪ duty   'lɑˑfɪŋ laughing

When the long vowels occur in the weak forms of words they are very short.

Consonants

All consonants are lengthened when they follow the short vowels ɪ eᴛ æ ʊ ɒ ʌ in a stressed syllable before a pause.

Examples.

| 'wɪn: ‖ | win | 'ɹæŋ: ‖ | rang | 'lɒs: ‖ | loss |
| 'seᴛz: ‖ | says | 'pʰul: ‖ | pull | 'lʌv: ‖ | love. |

The consonants m n ŋ l, are lengthened when they precede another voiced consonant in the same stressed syllable.

Examples.

| 'dʒeᴛɪ'm:z | James. | 'tᵢweᴛl:v | twelve, |
| 'hæn:d | hand. | bɪ'lɒŋ:z | belongs. |

Diphthongs

Each element of the diphthongs, eᴛɪ aɪ ɔɪ oᴛʊ aʊ, is half lengthened in the *last syllable* of a word when *stressed*, providing it is the *last sound in a stress group*, or a *breath group*, or, providing it is *followed by a voiced consonant*.

Examples.

1. 'tᵢɹeᴛɪˑ ‖   tray   4. ðə'tᵢɹeᴛɪˑ |'feᴛl: ‖

2. pʰɔˑtᵢɹeᴛɪˑ ‖   portray   The tray fell.

3. pᵢliːz 'pʰeᴛɪˑ ‖   5. 'tʰaᴛɪd ‖   tide

please pay   6. 'moᴛʊˑn ‖   moan

PRACTICE WORK

Practice the individual sounds before a mirror until they are mastered; then use them in the key words and the key-word sentences or in other words and sentences that will serve the same purpose. Practice the examples aloud, observing the beauty, force and significance of each sound. Choose your own extracts and practice them, making proper use of the sounds.

PHONETIC BOOKS FOR STUDY OR REFERENCE

Bases of Speech, The, by Gray and Wise. Harper and Brothers, 1934.

Directions for the Production of English Consonants, by S. A. Pray.

Effective Speech, by Gough, Rousseau, Cramer and Reeves. Harper and Brothers, 1930.

English Pronouncing Dictionary, by Daniel Jones. E. P. Dutton and Co.

First Principles of Speech Training, by Avery, Dorsey and Sickles. D. Appleton-Century Co., 1928.

Good American Speech, by M. P. McLean. E. P. Dutton and Co., 1935 edition.

Graded Objectives for Teaching Good American Speech, by S. A. Pray and Others, E. P. Dutton and Co., 1934.

Outline of English Phonetics. Third Edition, by Daniel Jones. Heffer and Sons, Cambridge, Eng., 1932.

Science and Art of Speech, The, by C. R. Walsh. Benziger Brothers, 1935.

Sounds of Spoken English, by Walter Ripman. E. P. Dutton and Co., 1920.

Speech for the Classroom Teacher, by D. I. Mulgrave, Prentice-Hall Inc., 1936.

Spoken Word in Life and Art, The, by Davis and Mammen. Prentice-Hall Inc., 1933.

Teaching of Reading, The, by H. C. Wyld. John Murray, London, 1924.

Voice and Speech Problems, by Raubicheck, Davis and Carll, Prentice-Hall Inc., 1931.

CHAPTER VI

DRAMATIC VALUES OF DIFFERENT SOUNDS

THERE are certain distinct characteristics to be found in different types of sounds that may be made use of to enhance the effectiveness, significance and beauty of oral reading. Like anything else in the world, this can be *overdone* or *underdone*. It must be done with judgment, understanding and good taste; obviousness must be completely avoided. All great *writers* of literature, particularly of verse, consciously or unconsciously, make use of the particular characteristics of sounds in order to make their writings effective and pleasing, and *oral readers* of these writings should also make use of them if they expect to fully *interpret* the author's meaning and mood.

It must be distinctly understood that the types of sounds do not stand *alone* or *function* alone. They are used, even though they are combined with others, to bear the chief burden of the expression of particular moods or motives or tempo.

In speaking of the English vowels, Albert Harris Tolman says that the vowels ɪ (little) eᴛ (met) æ (mat) ɛɹ (fair) eᴛɪ (mate)

> "are especially fitted to express uncontrollable joy and delight, gayety, triviality, rapid movement, brightness, delicacy, and physical lightness,"

while the sounds ʊ (wood) aʊ (cow) oᴛʊ (gold) u: (gloom) ɔ: (awe),

> "are peculiarly adapted to express horror, solemnity, awe, deep grief, slowness of motion, darkness, and extreme or oppressive greatness of size. The scale runs . . . from the little to the large, from the bright to the dark, from ecstatic delight to horror, and from the trivial to the solemn and awful . . . every English sound has some special expressive

45

force . . . a delicate use of sound symbolism is one of the innermost secrets of style."

From *The Symbolic Value of English Sounds.*
In *Views About Hamlet and Other Essays.*
Houghton, Mifflin and Company, Publishers, 1904.

There are many notable examples of writings in which the special use of particular sounds brings out the sense to excellent advantage.

Examples:

The Bells	Edgar Allen Poe
The Cataract of Ladore	Robert Southey
Song of the Chattahoochie	Sidney Lanier
Dover Beach	Matthew Arnold
Hiawatha	Henry Wadsworth Longfellow
Tarantella	Hilaire Belloc
The Song of the Banjo	Rudyard Kipling
The Golden City of St. Mary	John Masefield
St. Mary's Bells	" "
The Three Fishers	Charles Kingsley
The Bobolink	William Cullen Bryant
Angler's Reveille	Henry Van Dyke
The Listeners	Walter De La Mare
The Skater of Ghost Lake	William Rose Benét
Desertion	Rupert Brooke

The vowel-like consonants, w j l ɹ m n ŋ, *as a group,* will help to give a variety of melody, brilliance and delicacy to one's reading, but of these, the *nasal* consonants, m, n, ŋ, and the liquid consonant, l, seem to supply an *unlimited* amount of variety. They give beauty, force, power, lightness and darkness, height and depth, to the tone-color of speech. They may be made to contribute something to the expression of almost every mood, as well as every tone-color, and to help vivify the expression of thought. They may be used to give clear, ringing, bell-like tones that are as dainty and delicate as the finest notes of a flute or violin, or tones that are as

deep and sonorous as those of an organ. They can be made to
flutter or dance or twinkle or move in majesty. Poe's "Bells"
illustrates very beautifully the extraordinary variety of tone-
color they may give.

Examples:

> "How they tinkle, tinkle, tinkle,
> In the icy air of night."

. . . .

> "From the molten golden notes,
>   And all in tune,
> What a liquid ditty floats
> To the turtle-dove that listens, while she gloats
>   On the Moon."

. . . .

> "In the silence of the night
> How we shiver with affright
> At the melancholy menace of their tone."
> *The Bells.* Poe.

> "Others have had language teachers,
> Woods and waters my instructors,
> Homeless, friendless lone and needy
> Save in childhood with my mother."
> Epilogue of *Kalevala.*

The sound *w* lends itself well to the expression of moods
requiring low pitch and to the expression of solemn thought.

> "The wild wind whirls from leaf and limb."
> *The Phantom Skater.* William Ellery Leonard.

> "The waking wonder of the wide spread world."
> *The House of Rimmon.* Henry Van Dyke.

> "The mad old witch wife wailed and wept."
> *A Shepherd's Calendar.* Edmund Spencer.

Stop-plosive consonants, pb, td, kg, help to give **force**,
precision, decision, abruptness, distinctness, finality.

> "What a tale of terror, now, their turbulency tells:
>   In the startled ear of night
>   How they scream out their affright!
>   Too much horrified to speak,
>   They can only shriek, shriek,
>   Out of tune."
>
> *The Bells.* Poe.

". . . Passion and prejudice and propaganda impregnate public opinion until an atmosphere is created in which nothing can be seen in perspective. It has been fatally easy for our statesmen to prefer phrases to facts, to leave urgent issues unsettled and to attend conferences only to postpone decisions.'
P. W. Wilson.
The New York Times Magazine, Section 5, Oct. 4, 1931.

> "Rivers and Dorset, you were standers by,
> And so wast thou, Lord Hastings, when my son
> Was stabbed with bloody daggers . . .
>   (To Gloucester) . . . Stay, dog, for thou shalt hear me,
>   . . . Thou elfish-marked abortive rooting hog!
>
> From Queen Margaret's Curse. *King Richard III.* Shakespeare.

The *voiced consonants* b d g v ð z ʒ w combined with the long vowels i: u: ɔ: ɑ: ɜ: and the diphthongs eɪ aɪ ɔɪ oʊ aʊ help to give grandeur, dignity, sublimity, solemnity and majesty, to speech. They give it the *dark* colors, and express the deep and serious moods.

> "*Bloody the billows were boiling there
> Turbid the tide of tumbling waves
> Horribly seething with sword blood hot.*"
>
> "*Beowulf,*" lines 848-849-850. Gummere Translation.

Ghost.   "*I* am *thy* father's spirit,
> *Doom'd* for a certain term to *walk* the night
> And *for* the *day* confined to fast in fires
> Till the foul crimes done in my *days* of nature
> Are burnt and purged away."
>
> *Hamlet.* Shakespeare.

The *short vowels* ɪ eᴛ æ ᴜ ᴅ ᴧ will help to give daintiness, delicacy, lightness, crispness and alertness.

> "*E*ver that whirr*i*ng, that cr*i*sp sound th*i*n
> Like a str*i*ng pl*u*ck-pl*u*cked of a viol*i*n.
>
> . . . .
>
> Fl*i*t-fl*i*t—a phantom, with a stoop and a sw*i*ng . ."
> From *The Skater of Ghost Lake*. William Rose Benét.

> "*O*ne have I mark'd, the happ*i*est g*ue*st
> *I*n all th*i*s covert of the blest:
> Hail to Thee, far above the rest
> In joy of voice and p*i*nion
> Thou, L*i*nnet! *i*n thy green array
> Presiding Sp*i*r*i*t here today
> D*o*st lead the revels of the May;
> And th*i*s is thy dom*i*nion.
>
> . . . .
>
> Am*i*d yon t*u*ft of hazel trees
> That tw*i*nkle *i*n the g*u*sty breeze,
> Behold h*i*m perch'd *i*n *e*cstasies
> Y*e*t seeming st*i*ll to h*o*ver;
> There! where the fl*u*tter of h*i*s w*i*ngs
> *U*pon h*i*s back and body fl*i*ngs
> Shadows and s*u*nny gl*i*mmerings,
> That c*o*ver h*i*m all over."
> From *The Green Linnet*, By Wordsworth.

The *dipthongs* ɪə ɛə ᴜə ɔə, are the result of centuries of man's diminution of effort in sound production. They have come into being because man has followed the line of least resistance in producing them for a very long period of time, until now they are correct only when made with the least possible effort. They possess a quality which is particularly pleasing and seemingly illusive; that of giving a sort of *caress* to the utterance, expressive of tenderness and love.

> *F*airies are peer*i*ng over th*ere*.
> *F*ear no m*o*re, Montclair is y*ours*.
> *D*ear Mary, dem*ure* and f*air*.

"Here again, here, here, here, happy year!
Summer is coming, is coming, my dear."
                                    Tennyson.

"I would build that dome in *air*
That sunny dome! those caves of ice!
And all who heard should see them there,
And all should cry Beware! Beware!"
                                    Coleridge.

"Unto the pure all things are pure."
            The Bible, Epistle of Paul to Titus 1-15

"I'll make assurance double sure."
                                    Shakespeare.

The *lip-rounded sounds*, uː ʊ oꭨ ɔː ɒ oꭨʊ̆ ɔɪ ɑʊ̆ ʊꭥ ɔꭥ w, are an extremely important group. Perhaps because of the general shape of the mouth chamber which the lip-rounding gives, they have a very marked vibrant quality. This will help to give a feeling of warmth, sympathy, tolerance and kindliness to the utterance. They also help to express despair, despondency and grief. When fully mastered they will help to give to each speaker who uses them properly, that quality which has always been eagerly sought by all singers and speakers, and which is generally known as a "rich, round, resonant tone, full of warmth and color." It goes straight to the heart of the listener and awakens a genuine and sincere response.

Desdemona.   "I know not how I lost him."
              Othello. Shakespeare.

Hamlet.   "O, that this too too solid flesh would melt,
              Thaw, and resolve itself into a dew!"
              Hamlet. Shakespeare.

King Richard II.
              "Come, come, in wooing sorrow let's be brief
              . . . .

*W*e make *woe wa*nton *wi*th this fond delay,
*O*nce m*o*re; ad*ieu*; the rest let s*o*rrow say."
King Richard II. Shakespeare.
Act V, Scene I.

"Like the dull b*oo*ming b*o*lts of a cannon
the *w*ind s*we*pt the streets and the s*ho*res."
From *The Death Bridge of the Tay.*
Will Carlton.

"The *o*cean *o*ld,
Centuries *o*ld,
Str*o*ng as y*ou*th, and as uncontr*o*lled,
Paces restless t*o* and fr*o*,
Up and d*ow*n the sands of g*o*ld."
From *The Launching of the Ship.* Longfellow.

If the sounds of English are properly produced and carefully and faithfully practiced for perfection and beauty, they
will help to bring to the oral reader a rich and bounteous
harvest of success that will increase from year to year, as his
soul grows in understanding and his expression becomes more
full and complete, and more simple and sincere.

CHAPTER VII

GROUPS OF SOUNDS IN CONNECTED SPEECH
AND
THEIR SIGNIFICANCE IN THE ORAL INTERPRE-
TATION OF LITERATURE

SPOKEN English is made up of four different groups or combinations of sounds. These are:

1. Syllables.
2. Words.
3. Stress groups.
4. Breath groups.

A Syllable

A syllable is "an elementary sound or a combination of elementary sounds, uttered together, or with a single impulse of the voice. . . ." *Webster's Collegiate Dictionary.*

Formation of Syllables in Speech

The formation of syllables into words or into groups of words in English *speech* is often quite different from that in *written* English as indicated in most dictionaries. Oral readers of literature should familiarize themselves with these differences.

Combinations of Syllables

Syllables may be used separately, or they may be combined into groups forming *words, stress groups* or *breath groups.*

Stressed Syllables

When one syllable is spoken with greater *force* than others it is .called a stressed syllable. A stress mark (') is placed *before* the stressed syllable to indicate that it is stressed.

53

A Word

"A word is a spoken sign of a conception or an idea; a single component part of human speech or language." *Webster's Collegiate Dictionary.*

When we *write* we use *individual* words, and each one stands apart from the others as a separate and distinct thing. We do *not* use words as separate entities in most of our *speech.*   Only when one word is sufficient to express an idea do we speak in separate words.

Examples: When? Beware. Certainly. Stop. Come. Go.

When we use *two or more* words we run them together as we run syllables together in one word. We *may* continue this until we have used the supply of breath in the lungs, then we must *pause* to get more breath in order that we may continue.

"The first and most obvious necessity is the organic necessity of taking breath—we are unable to utter more than a certain number of sounds in succession without renewing the stock of air in the lungs, which unavoidably necessitates a pause. . . . Within these 'breath-groups' or phonetic sentences, there is no pause whatever . . . the words of a sentence run into one another exactly in the same way as syllables do. . . ."
Collected Papers. Henry Sweet.

Too much or *too little* of running words together is *equally disastrous*, both in life and in art.

We *write*, "Fourscore and seven years ago."

We *say* "'Four'scoren'seven'yearsa'go," as if it were one long word with five stressed syllables.

Examples of Word Separation and of Word Blending

We *write*, 1. It is nice and cool today.

2. "On the eighteenth of April in seventy-five."

3. "Tell me not in mournful numbers."

4. "The last time I remember using my knife."

    5. Good morning, Mr. Clifford.

    6. What are you doing over there?

We *say*,   1. Itsnicen'coolto'day.

    2. "Onthe'eighteenthof'Aprilin'seventy'five."

    3. "'Tellme'notin'mournful'numbers."

    4. "The'last'timeIre'memberusingmy'knife."

    5. Good'morningMr.Clifford.

    6. Whatareyoudoingover'there?

A Stress Group

"A stress group *must* contain *one* and *only one* stressed syllable, it *may* contain any number of unstressed syllables or none at all . . . a single vertical line, |, called a single bar, is placed *after* the group to indicate the end of the group. . . . A single bar does not indicate a pause."*

Examples:

    1. "'Still | have I 'borne it | with a 'patient | 'shrug."

    2. "'Old | 'Fezziwig | laid down his 'pen | . . ."

    3. "He is the very 'pine-apple | of po'liteness."

The stress group may be called the *logical foot of prose or verse*. It is *like* a *metrical* foot in verse, in that it has only *one stressed* syllable; it is *unlike* a metrical foot, in that it *may* have *any number of unstressed syllables. Like* a *metrical foot* in *verse*, and a *phrase* in *prose*, it expresses an idea, and it *may* express a complete thought.

Each stress group has:

    1. A *thought* value, great or small.

    2. A *rhythmic* value, great or small.

The Thought Value of Stress Groups

Each stress group supplies one link of thought in a chain of expression. The chain of thought in spoken English is made up of *stress group links*. Some of these links are made of

---

*From *Good American Speech*, by M. P. McLean, E. P. Dutton and Company, Publishers.

separate words but most of them are made of two or more words.

Every stress group adds something to that which precedes it or prepares for something that follows it, or, it shows the speaker's reactions to what he is speaking. One by one, the stress groups carry the thought of the expression to its fulfillment, as, step by step, we walk to a destination. Each stress group should mark a step in advance, carrying the thought onward toward a definite goal. No matter how insignificant a stress group may seem to be, if it is in the text at all it has *some* importance, and it should be read in a way that will bring out this importance. If one stress group is inadequately given something is lost that may break the interest or lose the attention of the audience. If three or four such groups are badly given the interest of the audience may be lost *entirely.*

THE RHYTHMIC VALUE OF STRESS GROUPS

Each stress group makes up one pulse beat of the rhythm of spoken English, both in prose and in verse. It may be a very weak, or it may be a very strong beat, but it is an *essential* wave in a necessary series of waves. It may supply one of several small waves which, together, make a larger wave, or it may make up one single wave.

STRESS GROUPS ARE IMPORTANT

Since both the meaning and melody of spoken English are dependent largely upon the proper formation and use of stress groups, it behooves the oral reader of English literature to understand them thoroughly and to use them properly.

The three general points, *stress, number of syllables,* and *quantity,* or, *length,* have been considered in the *writing* of literature since the time of classical Greece, and they must be considered in the *oral interpretation* of literature. If they are not considered properly and adequately, we have wholesale *mutilation* of literature, not interpretation. The principles that govern the *oral reading* of literature must be in perfect harmony with those that governed the *writing* of it. They can never be divorced without disaster.

"Measure is a condition of perfection, for perfection requires that order be pervasive, that not only the whole before us should have a form of its own, but that every part should have a form of its own, and that those parts should be co-ordinated among themselves, as the whole is coordinated with the other parts of some greater cosmos."

Poetry and Religion by George Santayana.
Charles Scribner's Sons, Publishers.

The Breath Group

A breath group *must* contain at least *one stressed syllable,*— it may contain *several stress groups.* It *must* be followed by a *pause* where a breath *may* be taken. One should breathe only during a properly placed pause, but it is not necessary to breathe during every pause.

The breath group might be called the *pause foot* of prose and verse, since it is determined by pauses, which, in turn, are made because of meaning, mood or situation, and because of the physical necessity of taking breath.

Two parallel vertical lines, ‖, called a double bar, are used to indicate the end of a breath group where the pause must be made.

Length of Breath Groups

A breath group may contain only one sound.

'Ah (ɑ:) ‖ 'sh-sh (ʃ) ‖ 's-s-s- (s:)

It may contain only one *syllable.*

'Yes ‖ 'No ‖ 'Why? ‖ 'Nine ‖ 'You ‖ 'I ‖ 'Look ‖

It may contain *one word* of more than one syllable.

'Robert ‖ Lemon'ade ‖ Cosmo'politan ‖ Sep'tember ‖

It may be of *medium* length.

"My 'father's 'brother ‖ but no more 'like my 'father ‖ Than 'I ‖ to 'Hercules." *Hamlet.* Shakespeare.

It may be very long.

> "There 'ought to be a 'law a'gainst a man's 'sister ever
> 'entering his 'house after he's 'married." ‖
>
> *How He Lied to Her Husband.* George Bernard Shaw.

The *limit* to the length of a breath group in oral reading is
determined by several factors and may differ greatly with
different people, or with the same person at different times.
The one absolute limit is the number of syllables that can be
spoken with one breath, but this limit should never be reached
in reading.

Breath Groups and Pauses

Since the breath group is preceded and followed by a
pause, it can be studied best in terms of the pause, which is
the subject of Chapter VIII.

A Stressed Syllable an Essential Part of Separate Words, Stress Groups, and Breath Groups

Since a stressed syllable is an essential part of *every*
separate word, every stress group, and every breath group,
stress becomes one of the most important factors in oral reading of literature, and therefore, deserves some especial
consideration.

Stress and Meaning

The *meaning* of English speech is brought out quite largely
by the use of stress applied to the particular syllable that best
conveys the speaker's thought, purpose, or wish, at the particular moment in which he utters it. This makes a very
flexible system of stress, which, in turn, makes a very flexible
spoken language, capable of expressing unlimited shades of
thought and emotion. While there are many technical means
of bringing out important points—intonation, pause, quality
of voice, volume, pitch, tempo, etc.—stress is used in combination with all of these and is, consequently, of tremendous
importance. Henry Sweet says:

. . . "force or stress is the most important element in the synthesis of speech sounds."

What Syllables Should be Stressed?

In any given selection the *first* syllable to stress is the one which—combined with the less important syllables that go with it—brings out the first important point, stated or implied. When a point has been stressed once it should not be stressed again unless there is a new reason for doing so. There are several reasons for repeating the stress on the same syllable.

(a) For the purpose of *contrast*.

Arthur to Hubert:
"I warrant 'I love 'you more than 'you do 'me."
King John. Shakespeare.

(b) To produce a *cumulative effect*.
"Leaping ' higher, ' higher, " higher."
The Bells. Poe.

(c) When the point which was stressed originally is *introduced anew* for a definite reason. There may be considerable time between such stresses.

Again quoting from *King John*, Arthur says:
"Must you with 'hot 'irons 'burn 'out my eyes?"

Twenty-three lines farther on Hubert answers:
"I have sworn to do it;
And with 'hot 'irons must I 'burn them 'out."

The *second* syllable to stress is the one that brings out the second important point.

The *third* syllable to stress is the one that brings out the third important point, or the one that shows the *relation* of the first two, or the reaction of the author regarding them, or, the one that shows what is to come. It is always the *new* idea, or the *relations* of old ideas, or the *contrasts* of ideas, or, the *reactions* of *author* or *characters* to ideas, that are stressed. Every stress must present something *new*,—an idea, a mood, a situation, their relations to each other, or the reactions they awaken.

Stress the syllables that bring out *essential* points in different ideas.

> "Her 'waggon-'spokes made of 'long 'spinners' 'legs,
> The 'cover of the 'wings of 'grass'hoppers,
> The 'traces of the 'smallest 'spider's 'web,
> The 'collars of the 'moonshine's 'watery 'beams,
> Her 'whip of 'cricket's 'bone, the 'lash of 'film,
> Her 'waggoner a 'small 'grey-'coated 'gnat,
> Not 'half so 'big as a 'round 'little 'worm
> 'Prick'd from the 'lazy 'forefinger of a 'maid;"
> *Romeo and Juliet.* Shakespeare.

Stress the syllables which show the *relation* of one idea to another.

> "'Speak the 'speech, I 'pray you,
> as I pro'nounced it to you,
> 'trippingly on the 'tongue:
> but if you 'mouth it,
> as 'many of your 'players 'do
> I had as 'lief the 'town 'crier 'spoke my 'lines."
> *Hamlet.* Shakespeare.

Stress the syllables that show *the reactions of characters.*

> . . . . . . "'Adam, 'soon as he 'heard
> The 'fatal 'trespass 'done by 'Eve, a'mazed,
> As'tonied 'stood and 'blank, while 'horror 'chill
> 'Ran through his 'veins, and all his 'joints re'laxed;"
> *Paradise Lost.* Milton.

Stress the syllables that show *significant contrasts.*

> "With the 'blue a'bove and the ˌblue be'low"
> *The Sea.* Bryan Waller Procter (Barry Cornwall).

> ". . . . . .behold alone
> the woman . . . .

'fair, di'vinely 'fair, fit 'love for 'gods
. . . . a'pproached by 'hate,
'Hate 'stronger under 'show of 'love well 'feigned;"
Paradise Lost. Milton.

Stress the syllables that show the *reactions of author or speaker.*

"I could not 'eat, I could not 'sit 'still, I could not continue 'steadfast to 'anything. So I re'solved to go to 'bed.

For 'hours I lay in bed 'listening to the 'wind and 'water, i'magining, now, that I 'heard 'shrieks out at 'sea; 'now, that I dis'tinctly heard the 'firing of 'signal-'guns; 'now, the 'fall of 'houses in the 'town. Then I fell into the 'depths of 'sleep until 'broad 'day."
David Copperfield. Charles Dickens.

In order to enable the listener to follow the author's meaning and motives closely, clearly, smoothly, eagerly and without effort, it is necessary for the reader to observe certain *cautions* in the use of stress. Some of these cautions are:

I. STRESS A SUFFICIENT NUMBER OF SYLLABLES

If a reader fails to stress a syllable which should have been stressed, the audience misses a point: it may be that something new should have been introduced but was not because of failure to stress a particular syllable; it may be a contrast should have been made but was omitted, or, an important relation of one idea to another should have been indicated, but failure to stress a syllable properly, interferred with this. If a single stress which *should* be made is *omitted* one step in the progression of the thought is left out, leaving a *missing link in the chain of ideas* that reach the listener. If several stresses which should be made are omitted, the *chain of ideas ceases to be a chain* and becomes a disjointed, disconnected collection of more or less meaningless parts, in which the listener gradually loses interest.

2. Avoid Stressing the Wrong Syllable

It is not sufficient to stress the right syllable, it is just as important to avoid stressing the wrong one. Each stress brings something into prominence; if the wrong syllable is stressed the *wrong* thing is brought into prominence. It is imperative for the reader to keep the attention of his audience in a definite and clearly defined channel; a stress on the *wrong* syllable may, and very likely will, take it out of this channel and set it running into a different channel. It is always more or less difficult and it may be impossible to get the attention back again where it belongs.

Repeat the following sentence five times, stressing *only one* syllable, but a *different one*, each time. Observe how the whole meaning of the sentence changes as the position of the stress changes. This will show the very great importance of placing the stress in the right place when reading aloud, in order to bring out the particular shades of meaning desired.

1. I said he was *'wrong.*
2. *'I* said he was wrong.
3. I said *'he* was wrong.
4. I *'said* he was wrong.
5. I said he *'was* wrong.

3. Do Not Stress Too Many Syllables

If *too many* syllables are stressed it gives an effect of argument, excitement, aggressiveness, noise, self-defense or self-justification. It makes everything important and thus there are no relative values, no contrasts, no rests. It is like a painting that is all scarlet, or a song with nothing but high notes. *Too much* stress is as monotonous as *too little* stress and is far more tiring to the listeners.

4. Use Different Degrees of Stress

The full expression of the lights and shades, the heights and depths, of the meaning and moods of a selection, requires the use of *different degrees of stress*. Also, the *rhythm and melody of English prose and verse are produced very largely*—some scholars say *wholly—by the use of a variety of stress* on syllables that are spoken in different stress groups and in different breath groups.

VERY STRONG STRESS

Very strong stress is used in exceptionally forceful or emphatic utterance; it is *indicated* by placing two stress marks before the syllable receiving the extreme stress.

> "He woke to hear the sentries shriek
> To "arms! they 'come! the 'Greek! the "Greek!"
> From *Marco Bozzaris*. Fitz-Greene Halleck.

> "In 'God's 'name, "no!"
> *The Victory of Truth*. Carlyle.

> "De'tested 'kite! thou "liest."
> *King Lear*. Shakespeare.

STRONG STRESS

When a word of one syllable stands by itself in ordinary speech, it is given a strong stress:
> 'No. 'Yes. 'Whom? 'What?

When a word of more than one syllable is spoken by itself, at least one syllable is given a strong stress in all cases:
> 'Mother. In'spire. Om'nipotent.

Some words have two syllables with strong stress:
> 'Black'bird. 'Un'harmed. 'Ding-'dong.

SECONDARY STRESS

Some words have a syllable with a secondary stress in addition to the syllable with strong stress. This is indicated thus:

ˌCavaˈlier. ˌLamenˈtation. ˌMetroˈnomic.

A word in a sentence may have a secondary stress:

> "And ˈthen, I ˌgrant, we put a ˈsting in ˌhim."
> *Julius Caesar.* Shakespeare.

Individual word stresses may be *retained,* or they may *disappear*—depending upon the meaning the reader wishes to convey—when the words are used in connected discourse. Some speakers use very slight stress, only*; this makes their speech insipid, uninteresting and lacking in significance. It is extremely trying and irritating to an audience, and it does an unforgivable injustice to an author, because it gives little or no meaning to his lines. There is only one thing that is worse than the constant use of very weak stress and that is a constant use of stress that is too strong.

Mark the Stressed Syllables When Studying a Selection

Since adequate expression of the meaning and shades of meaning of a selection is greatly dependent upon the position and degree of stress given to syllables, the reader will need to study each selection with these points in mind. He will be obliged to determine *where,* and *how heavily,* the stress should fall. When this has been determined it is well to *indicate the stress on the page* by placing proper stress marks before the syllables to be stressed** so that the lines may be repeated in the same way often enough to form the right habit of expression, thus making the use of the correct stress automatic. Then the mere mechanics of stress can be, and *must* be, forgotten, submerged in the expression of meaning and mood.

---

*Among them may be found a few persons who are well known on the stage today, but whose failures far outnumber their successes.

**It is advisable to have special, inexpensive books for study so that they may be marked with a clear conscience.

ACCEPTED WEAK FORMS OF SOME WORDS RESULT FROM VERY WEAK STRESS

Repeat the sentence, *I said he was wrong,* two different times, *stressing* the word *was* the first time and leaving it *entirely unstressed* the second time, and notice the marked difference in its pronunciation in the two cases. It is two entirely different forms of the same word: the *stressed* one, ('wɒz:), is called the *strong form;* the unstressed one, (wəz), occurring in a very weak position, is called the *weak form.* The two forms differ from each other in pronunciation as much as *will* and *well, tan* and *ton,* or *book* and *beak,* differ from each other, because they have two entirely different vowel sounds. There are several short words in English that have strong and weak forms; most of them are included in the following list.

WORDS WHICH HAVE STRONG AND WEAK FORMS

a	but	*had	is	*should	*there
*am	can	*has	must	*sir	*to
an	could	*have	not	some	was
*and	do	he	of	than	we
are	does	*her	or	that	were
as	*for	him	shall	*the	*will
at	from	his	she	them	*would

These weak forms of words are so universally and naturally used in spoken English, both standard and dialectal, that most poeple have never noticed them, yet the rhythm and meaning of all spoken English is tremendously influenced by the use of them as they are combined with strong syllables.

Since weak forms of words are universally used (in English) in natural and spontaneous speech, it is necessary to use them in the oral reading of our literature in order that it,

---

*Has more than one weak form. See pp. 243-244-245 *Good American Speech*—McLean. E. P. Dutton and Company, Publishers.

too, may sound natural and spontaneous, and in order to help to produce the proper rhythm.

The use of weak forms of words, like anything else, can be carried too far and overdone, or not carried far enough and underdone. If carried too far it gives an effect of careless, slovenly speech; if not carried far enough it gives an effect of artificiality, affection, pedantry and 'over-correctness.'

SENTENCES FOR PRACTICE OF WEAK FORMS

Read the following sentences making proper use of the weak forms. The words that should be given weak forms are printed in smaller type.

"He was my friend, faithful and just to me."

"For in the very torrent, tempest, and, as I may say, the whirlwind of passion, you must acquire and beget a temperance that may give it smoothness."
Hamlet. Shakespeare.

"'Tis not in our stars dear Brutus
But in ourselves that we are thus and thus."
Julius Caesar. Shakespeare.

"The quality of mercy is not strain'd,
It droppeth as the gentle rain from heaven
Upon the place beneath."
Merchant of Venice. Shakespeare.

"I shall know why, when time is over,
And I have ceased to wonder why;
Christ will explain each separate anguish
In the fair schoolroom of the sky."
From *The Poems of Emily Dickinson.*
Little, Brown and Co., Publishers.

"A public man is bound to represent his constituents, but he is no less bound to represent them when, on a great moral question, he feels that they are taking the wrong side."
From *The Use and Abuse of Property.* Theodore Roosevelt.

CHAPTER VIII

*GENERAL PAUSES IN ORAL READING

"Pauses or rests, in speaking and reading are a total cessation of the voice during a perceptible . . . space of time." *Murray's English Dictionary.*

Pauses may be long, short, or medium in length, but in all cases they break the flow of syllables into various lengths, units or sections. These sections are called *breath groups* in this text.

WHY SHOULD ONE PAUSE IN READING?

1. To separate one thought from another. This is the *logical* pause.

"You may think me a fanatic to-night ‖ for you read history ‖ not with your eyes ‖ but with your prejudices."
Toussaint L'Ouverture. Wendell Phillips.

2. To give the speaker opportunity *to think.* This might be called a *thought pause.*

"To be ‖ or not to be ‖ that is the question."
Hamlet. Shakespeare.

3. To give the speaker opportunity to *breathe.* This is the *breath pause.*

"Speak the speech, I pray you, ‖ as I pronounced it to you ‖ trippingly** ‖ on the tongue."
Hamlet. Shakespeare.

The logical pause and the breath pause *usually* coincide.

---

*A short double bar (‖) may be used to indicate an extremely short pause; a pause so short that the listener is unaware of its existence, but which enables a speaker to bring out an important point adequately.

**There are some special pauses that must be made in reading poetry which are considered in Chapter XVII.

4. To give the *listener* opportunity to follow, or to consider, what the reader has said.

"Gimme the Axe ‖ lived in a house ‖ where everything is the same as it always was."

How They Broke Away to Go to the Rootabaga Country.
Carl Sandburg.

5. Because something happens which interrupts the speaker's thought and takes his attention away from what he is saying, momentarily or permanently. This interruption may come either from *within* the speaker himself—one train of thought may cross the track of another and stop it temporarily or completely—or it may come from *outside* the speaker. In either case the interruption may come *at any time*, it may even come in the middle of a phrase or word. This is the *dramatic pause*.

"A king of shreds and patches ‖
    (the ghost enters)
Save me, and hover o'er me with your wings,
You heavenly guards."
Hamlet. Shakespeare.

Dowden says that a dramatic pause expresses:
"surprise or sudden emotion leaving a gap in the verse,—a gap through which we feel the wind of passion and of song."

6. To permit the *speaker* and the *audience* to *relax* for a moment. When there is a definite break in the thought of a reading—especially in those of some length—it is often advisable for the reader to make a brief pause to relax the attention of his audience and himself. This allows those in the audience to look away for a moment or to change their positions. The reader will need to make such a pause with the greatest watchfulness. He should not release the attention of the audience too completely or he will find it difficult to get it back again without interruption of the reading

as a whole. Such a pause should not be too obvious. This may be called a *relaxation pause.*

> "Then he tugged at his rein in the moonlight,
>   and galloped away to the West." ‖

(Relaxation pause should be made here)

> "He did not come in the dawning,
>   he did not come at noon;"

The Highwayman. Alfred Noyes.
In *Collected Poems*, Frederick A. Stokes Company, Publishers. Copyright, 1906.

Mark Places Where Pauses Should be Made

It is apparent that the first thing for a reader to do is to study a selection carefully to discover the author's meaning and motives. Having done this to the best of his ability he should indicate on the page, by the use of double bars—or by some other means—the places where pauses should be made, and he should *make them in these places every time he reads the selection in practice* until ultimately, he makes them there without giving any thought to it at all. It should be remembered that *in full and artistic oral interpretation of literature pauses must be carefully and systematically planned; they cannot be made at random,* any more than they can in the rendering of a musical composition or in executing a dance. But they must be fixed in their places during one's *practice:* a performer can have no time to think about them during performance.

Frequency of Pauses in Reading

Pauses are made very much more *frequently* in natural, spontaneous vocal expression than is commonly believed to be the case. But if oral reading of literature is to be made to sound like the natural and spontaneous expression of human beings like ourselves, pauses must be made in accordance with the basic laws that govern their usage in our natural and spontaneous speech.

When we speak slowly and deliberately we pause very often; when we speak rapidly we pause much less often and many of the pauses—sometimes all of them—are much shorter. The faster we speak the shorter the pauses, but *their importance increases with their brevity and infrequency.* One may read as fast as a human being can utter sounds and yet not become excited or get out of breath or lose poise, at the same time making his meaning perfectly clear, keeping the rhythm flowing properly and smoothly, providing he produces the speech sounds correctly, places the stresses properly, and makes correct use of stress groups and pauses, and of weak forms of words.

The *rate of speed* must not be allowed to change the proper form of the expression in any way. The correct *pattern of meaning and rhythm* must be maintained in all cases, whether the reading is prose or verse, logical or emotional, fast or slow. Reading is like music and dancing, in that its patterns must be kept intact with all proportions right, whether they are enlarged or reduced in size, or increased or decreased in tempo.

Pauses Should be Timed

All pauses in oral reading should be timed more or less accurately. In lyric verse the timing should be more definitely measured than in prose. Pauses must be timed to bring out the rhythm of the verse without losing the sense, and to bring out the sense without making the rhythm too pronounced or too obvious. In order to do this the reader should have a *dramatic sense or instinct* and a good *sense of rhythm,* which will carry him safely beyond the place where mechanical and logical methods cease to function, and to help him discover and bring out that intangible but exquisitely alluring swing of the verse, which the poet half conceals and half reveals by his skillful arrangement of sounds and syllables.

> "The wind was a torrent of darkness ‖ among the gusty trees ‖
> The moon was a ghostly galleon ‖ tossed upon cloudy seas ‖"
> *The Highwayman.* Alfred Noyes.

In the reading of *prose* the reader's dramatic sense and sense of rhythm and time must again be relied upon to determine the *length* of the pauses. They must be the proper length to make the *meaning clear* and must be made in harmony with, and must help to *maintain, the general mood, tempo and rhythm of the expression.*

> "He rose up hastily ‖ and found himself ‖ he knew not how ‖ seated on the bed. ‖ He remained for some time in that attitude ‖ lost in thought ‖ . . .All at once ‖ he stooped down and took off his shoes ‖ and put them safely upon the mat in front of the bed. ‖ "
> *Les Misérables.* Victor Hugo.

When pauses are too long or too frequent a reading drags and becomes monotonous, the interest of the audience wavers or is completely lost, the thought of the selection either does not move forward at all or it moves in jerks, the emotion is weak or dissipated, the performance lacks smoothness and continuity, life and vigor, and becomes disjointed, slow, dull and uninteresting.

When pauses are too short or too far apart the listeners find it difficult to follow the thought the reader is expressing. They get behind, as it were, and soon are lost in a maze because what has just been said, and what is being said, are so close together that they are all mixed up in the listener's mind. The reader is in danger of losing his own poise and composure; he seems to be in a hurry, not having given himself opportunity to think properly or to breathe properly. This, in turn, effects his pronunciation, his articulation and his voice, making them less clear, less pleasing and less efficient. The inevitable result of all this is confusion, inadequacy and fatigue on the part of the reader, and confusion, impatience or boredom on the part of the listeners.

PAUSES MUST BE FILLED WITH MEANING

The *voice* of the reader stops when a pause is made but, except in a relaxation pause, his *thought* must be even more active and alert than when he is speaking.

In some pauses the reader carries the thought on from point to point, making distinct and definite progress, and the thought of the audience follows with keen interest and deeply concentrated attention although the reader's voice is silent.

"So, on the bloody sand, ‖ Sohrab ‖ lay dead: ‖
And the great Rustum ‖ drew his horseman's cloak ‖
Down o'er his face, ‖ and sate by his dead son."
Sohrab and Rustum. Matthew Arnold.

Tense Pauses

In some pauses the reader must hold the attention of his audience in suspense as in a vice, with silence more compelling and more authoritative than speech. The listeners await something, they know not what, with every nerve tense, every muscle motionless but taut, all thought and emotion stopped, dead-still in their tracks, as it were, awaiting the signal to go. The reader should be able to hold them thus, breathless and motionless, as long as the drama requires it, by the intense fire of his thought. There is nothing in the whole realm of oral expression that is more dramatic or more compelling than such a pause.

"Adam, ‖ soon as he heard
The fatal trespass done by Eve ‖ amazed, ‖
Astonied stood ‖ and blank, ‖ while horror chill ‖
Ran through his veins . . . ."
Lines 887-890, Book IX. *Paradise Lost*. Milton.

"Then listening ‖ till those armed steps were gone, ‖
Rose the pale Queen, and in her anguish ‖ found
The casement: peradventure, so she thought, ‖
If I might see his face, and not be seen.
And lo ‖ he sat on horseback at the door."
From *The Idylls of the King*. Tennyson.

"So, ‖ struck with dread and anguish, ‖ fell ‖ the fiend."
Line 576, Book IV. *Paradise Regained*. Milton.

"Till now ‖ on the stroke of midnight ‖
  Cold on the stroke of midnight ‖
The tip of one finger touched it ‖
The trigger ‖ at least ‖ was hers!"
From *The Highwayman.* Alfred Noyes.
Frederick A. Stokes Company, Publishers. Copyright, 1906.

EMPTY PAUSES

While there is nothing more dramatic than a pause that
is packed to the utmost with fire of thought and emotion,
there is nothing so deadly for a reader or for an audience as an
empty pause, a pause that *says nothing.* It does not say *I must
think for a moment,* or, *you may rest for a moment,* or, *just wait
till you hear what comes next!* or, *I have completely finished,* nor
does it say anything else. Such a pause is very difficult and
embarrassing for those in an audience, and they instantly
assume that the reader has forgotten his lines. If the reader
has forgotten his lines and cannot recover them without delay
he should say so honestly and without shame or confusion.
Since the audience is composed of human beings like himself
they will appreciate both his dilemma and his frankness, and
as long as the reader himself is not disturbed, the audience
will not be embarrassed. The reader will be free to do whatever is necessary in order that he may proceed without having
created an unpleasant situation. Honest confession of the
short-coming of having forgotten lines is much better than
subjecting an audience to the torture or the banality of an
empty pause.

SENTENCES, PUNCTUATION MARKS AND PAUSES

Sentences and punctuation marks are the harmless looking traps that have caught many a potential reader of real
merit and have held him fast in a vice of misunderstanding
and obsolete conventions until he perished.

Punctuation marks were adopted for use in *writing.* While
they are, of course, of inestimable service to the oral reader in
his study of texts, they have in a great many cases, become
his iron shackles when he attempts to read aloud.

When we were children most of us were taught to pause in our reading every time we came to a punctuation mark, and at no other time, no matter how far apart or how close together the marks happened to be. We were also taught that the "voice should fall or rise" in strict accordance with certain of these marks. Sometimes all of this was right, but quite often a great deal of it was wrong. Obedience to these early, inadequate teachings has brought about ever-increasing confusion and uncertainty for the reader, and monotony and unnaturalness in his reading.

Originally a comma indicated a very short pause, a semi-colon indicated a slightly longer pause, and a period indicated a final and complete pause. But times and customs are continually changing. Punctuation marks are used less than they once were, and there is very wide variation in their use. Some writers use many, others use few, consequently they are a very unreliable and inadequate guide to the oral reader. Nevertheless, the habit formed in childhood, of pausing, and using a rising or falling intonation, only at sight of some one of them, still persists, and many an otherwise intelligent person will sacrifice sense, melody and beauty, in reading both prose and verse, in slavish recognition of the presence or absence of punctuation marks.

One can never learn to read aloud intelligently, pleasingly and naturally, until one follows a more reliable, accurate and consistent guide to the use of pauses and intonation glides than that furnished by punctuation marks on a printed page. Breath groups and pauses, whose length and location are determined by the sense, the mood and the rhythm of the lines must, for the oral reader, take the place of sentences divided into sections by punctuation marks, that are often too close together or too far apart or too lawlessly placed, to be trusted to bring out the meaning or the melody of the lines. Even if a *writer* follows the most hard and fast rules regarding punctuation marks they still remain very inadequate guides to the *oral reader*.

Extracts for Observation

The following extracts have been chosen at random to show how inadequate punctuation marks can be as guides to pauses, intonation glides and rhythm. The punctuations are given exactly as they appear in the printed texts from which they were taken. Read the extracts aloud pausing *always* and *only* where there are punctuation marks, and observe what happens to the meaning and to the rhythm.

1. "By the margin, willow-veil'd
    Slide the heavy barges trail'd
    By slow horses; and unhail'd
    The shallop flitteth silken-sail'd
    Skimming down to Camelot."
    The Lady of Shallot. Tennyson.

2. "Poetry turns all things to loveliness; . . . It transmutes all that it touches, and every form moving within the radiance of its presence is changed by wondrous sympathy to an incarnation of the spirit which it breathes; its secret alchemy turns to potable gold the poisonous waters which flow from death through life; . . ." Shelley.

3.   "I have heard
    That guilty creatures sitting at a play
    Have by the very cunning of the scene
    Been struck so to the soul that presently
    They have proclaim'd their malefaction;"
    Hamlet. Shakespeare.

4. "The clouds that gather round the setting sun
    Do take a sober colouring from an eye
    That hath kept watch o'er man's mortality;"
    Ode On the Intimations of Immortality. Wordsworth.

Exercises for Practice

The following extracts are punctuated exactly as they were in the books from which they were taken. Study each one to determine where pauses should be made and mark these places by the use of double bars, or by some other means.

Read the exercises aloud *making* all pauses as indicated. If, in the reading, it is discovered the pauses have not been placed properly, erase the old marks and add new ones. Continue the oral reading, making the pauses as indicated. They *must* be made in accordance with a plan; they cannot be made at random, in one place at one reading and in different places at other readings.

Hortensio to Petruchio:

"And tell me now, sweet friend, what happy gale
Blows you to Padua here from old Verona?"

Petruchio:

"Such wind as scatters young men through the world
To seek their fortunes further than at home
Where small experience grows."
The Taming of the Shrew.   Shakespeare.

"It ceased; yet still the sails made on
A pleasant noise till noon,
A noise like of a hidden brook
In the leafy month of June,
That to the sleeping woods all night
Singeth a quiet tune."
The Ancient Mariner.   Coleridge.

"It is for us, the living rather to be dedicated here to the unfinished work they have thus far so nobly carried on. It is rather for us to be here dedicated to the great task remaining before us, that from these honored dead we take increased devotion to the cause for which they gave the last full measure of devotion; that we here highly resolve that these dead shall not have died in vain, that the nation shall, under God, have a new birth of freedom, and that the government of the people, by the people, and for the people, shall not perish from the earth."
The Gettysburg Address.   Lincoln.

"Below the surface of the lake
The dark vault lies wherein we lay.
We heard it ripple night and day;

Sounding o'er our heads it knocked;
And I have felt the winter's spray
Wash through the bars when winds were high
And wanton in the happy sky;
And then the very rock hath rocked,
And I have felt it shake, unshocked,
Because I would have smiled to see
The death that would have set me free."
The Prisoner of Chillon. Lord Byron.

"For, as all flesh must die, so all,
Now dust, shall live. 'Tis natural;
Yet hardly do I understand
Here in the hollow of my hand
A bit of God Himself I keep,
Between two vigils fallen asleep."
This Quiet Dust. John Hall Wheelock.
Charles Scribner's Sons, Publishers.

"Tristram laid
His hand on Gouvernail's enduring shoulders
Which many a time had carried him for sport
In a far vanished childhood, and looked off
Where patient skill had made of shrubs and rocks
Together a wild garden half way down
To the dusk-hidden shore."
From *Tristram,* p. 27. E. A. Robinson.
By permission of The Macmillan Company, Publishers.

5. "A knave; a rascal; an eater of broken meats: A base,
proud, shallow, beggarly, three-suited, hundred pound,
filthy, worsted-stocking knave; a lily-livered, action-
taking knave, a glass-gazing superserviceable, finical
rogue."
King Lear. Shakespeare.

6. "My own, confirm me! If I tread
This path back, is it not in pride
To think how little I dreamed it lead
To an age so blest that, by its side,
Youth seems the waste instead?"
By the Fireside. Browning.

7. "I walk down the patterned garden-paths
   In my stiff, brocaded gown"

   . . . .
   "Tripping by in high-heeled, ribboned shoes."

   . . . .
   "For the lime tree is in blossom
   And one small flower has dropped
   upon my bosom."
   *Patterns. Amy Lowell.

8. "This erring mortals Levity may call;
   Oh blind to truth! The Sylphs contrive it all."
   The Rape of the Lock, Lines 101-102. Alexander Pope.

9. "Her long with ardent look his eye pursued
   Delighted, but desiring more her stay:"
   Lines 397-8. Book IX *Paradise Lost*. Milton.

*Used by special permission of the Publishers, Houghton, Mifflin
Company.

CHAPTER IX

RHYTHM AND METRE

RHYTHM

Rhythm is "movement marked by the regulated succession of strong and weak elements, or of opposite or different conditions." *Murray's English Dictionary.*

RHYTHMIC movement is a natural and universal thing. It deals with *time*, breaking it up into more or less evenly *measured units* by various means. Tides flow and ebb, hearts throb and rest, seasons come and go, and the night ever follows the day, in endless repetition of definite changes, varying here and varying there and thus avoiding monotony, but never breaking the law that governs their orderly sequence. It may take a second or a century to complete the cycle of movement, but completed it will be, sometime, somewhere, and a similar one will swing into its place.

RHYTHM AND SPOKEN LANGUAGE

Rhythm is a natural characteristic of all *spoken language*, consequently it is a dominant characteristic in our literature, prose as well as verse.

"In all literary expression there are two kinds of emphasis, the emphasis of sound and the emphasis of sense. The difference between those who have and those who have not the true rhythmic instinct is that, while the former have the innate faculty of making the emphasis of sound and the emphasis of sense meet and strengthen each other, the latter are without that faculty. . . . Perhaps the very origin of the old quantitative metres was the desire to make these two kinds of emphasis meet in the same syllable . . . in the English language at least, no really great line can be written in which the emphasis of accent (poetic accent) the emphasis of quantity and the emphasis of sense do not meet in the same syllable."

Encyclopaedia Britannica. Vol. 2. p. 637. Thirteenth Edition.

The Natural Rhythm of English Speech

Stress on some syllables and the *weakening and crowding together* of other syllables which belong with the stressed one, are basic factors in producing the natural rhythm of English speech.

The English language is characterized very dominantly by its particular use of stressed and unstressed syllables and this must be considered, primarily, in the oral reading of English prose as well as verse. The tune or melody of the language is produced and maintained largely by its relation of stressed and unstressed syllables and by the "rhythmic recurrence" of the stress. The *number of unstressed syllables may vary greatly but the oral reader must fit them into the proper rhythm* and the proper time interval. When the number of unstressed syllables is too small he must compensate for this and fill out the rhythm by a properly timed pause, or by the *proper* lengthening of a sound that may be lengthened.

The crowding and weakening of unimportant syllables is just as important in maintaining the rhythm of spoken English as the strengthening of important syllables, and it is very much less generally understood. The oral reader should continually bear this fact in mind. Parodoxical as it may seem, it is nevertheless true, that the crowding and weakening of unimportant syllables makes a reading very much easier to understand than it is when the syllables are separated and strengthened. This is due, of course, to the fact that we learned our spoken language that way and we hear it used that way all about us in daily conversation.

The Rhythm of English Prose

The rhythm of English prose is comparatively free and is usually inconspicuous, but it is present just as surely and inevitably as it is in verse. Prose rhythms are more subtle than those of verse and the ear must be more discerning to catch them. Properly produced, however, they represent an excellent musical sense and a high degree of refinement in both the author and the oral reader.

Although the rhythm of English prose is more inconspicuous than the rhythm of verse, it is, nevertheless, quite marked, but this fact is not generally recognized. One may easily discover it, however, in almost any book, magazine or newspaper one may pick up. Sometimes our prose has rhyme as well as rhythm although this is far less frequent. In *A Study of Poetry* (Houghton, Mifflin Company, Publishers), Bliss Perry calls attention to a remarkable example of rhymed and rhythmic prose. He says:

> "There has seldom been a more curious example of accidental coincidence than in this sentence from a prosaic textbook on 'The Parallelogram of Forces.' 'And hence no force, however great, can draw a cord, however fine, into a horizontal line which shall be absolutely straight.' This is precisely the 'four-stressed iambic' metre of *In Memoriam,* and it even preserves the peculiar rhyme order of the *In Memoriam* stanza."

If the preceding quotation—or any other piece of rhythmic prose—is written in lines as verse is written, the rhythm is more apparent. The capital letters usually used at the beginnings of lines of verse may be omitted if one so desires, in order to keep the continuity of the thought more apparent to the eye.

> "And hence no force, however great,
> Can draw a cord however fine,
> Into a horizontal line
> Which shall be absolutely straight."

Examples of Rhythmic Prose from Newspapers and Magazines

The first four are from the *New York Times* (chosen at random on widely different dates).

> "It was not until he reached his hotel in New York that he learned
> > the flowers of many summers had 'blossomed on the grave
> > in Oyster Bay."

> From *"Dinner with Roosevelt's Moroccan Friend."*
> By Jean McPherson Kitchen. Magazine Section, Feb. 1st, 1931.

"Calvin Coolidge on his way from his
childhood home in Vermont, to
Washington, to take up his duties
as President,
  *had gone to the cemetery by the roadside
  and prayed at the grave of his mother.*"
  May 9, 1932.

"Upon him
is the indelible impress of England,
not the England of pomp and circumstance
but the England
*which plows its land with oxen
and its Seven Seas with Ships.*"

  S. J. Woolf, in speaking of John Masefield.
  Magazine Section, page 4. Column 1, Paragraph 2.
  Jan. 22, 1933.

". . . the watcher of the recent river aspects—
has found it befitting
*so vast a shrine of beauty.
to which this austere winter
has opened its dazzling portals.*"

  Eliot White, in "*Letters to the Editor,*" March 12, 1934,
  in speaking of the resemblance between the ice
  on the Hudson and "the famed billowing floor
  of St. Mark's Cathedral in Venice."

"When the fog settles on the river,
the prisons become medieval castles
and the tugs prehistoric monsters
poking blind noses
through the steamy mist.
*And all up and down the river
their calls answer one another
and their toots and their blasts and their horns
are mellowed,
saddened into placeless timeless cries
of uncertainty and pain.*
  And at night, against the black window panes
triangles of disembodied light

red, green and blue
slip silently evenly by."

From *East River*, by Robert Littell.
The World, New York City, Aug. 27, 1930, p. 9.

"Back! Back, everybody!
A clear road for His Highness
the Temple Elephant
and for the troupes of whirling dancers
yet to come!"

. . . .

So tense is the excitement
when the head of the column draws near
that we almost forget to snap our cameras
and press the trigger of the 'movie' machine."

From *The Perhahera Procession of Ceylon.*
By G. H. G. Burroughs in *The National Geographic
Magazine*, July 1932, p. 99.

EXAMPLES OF FORMAL RHYTHMIC PROSE

" *He would fain set it down forever,*
engrave it on a rock if he could."
Sesame and Lilies. Ruskin.

" *No idlest word thou speakest*
but is a seed cast into time
and grows through all Eternity."
Sincerity in Speech. Carlyle.

"*All these told out the seconds*
in an intricate chorus of tickings."
Markheim. Stevenson.

"*But that vast fog ocean*
lay in a trance of silence,
nor did the sweet air of the morning
tremble with a sound."

"it was but a morning spring
and would now drift out seaward
whence it came."
Robert Louis Stevenson, in his essay, *The Sea Fogs.*

"The next year we saw three great (ice) bergs,

. . . .

in supreme and mighty indifference
they greeted us and passed by."
Russell Owen, in *South of the Sun.*
The John Day Company, Publishers.

"I would swear
that the very milestones had ears—
and that Harmer-hill
stooped with all its pines
to listen to a poet as he passed."
My First Acquaintance With the Poets. William Hazlitt.

". . . poetry . . . .
. . . *which breathes the free air of wild nature and moves*
with the prance of a horse."
History of English Literature, p. 326, Halleck.
Copyright. American Book Company, Publishers.

"*Yet—he did laugh once.*
It did happen once,
he lifted his head and face to the sky
and let loose a long ripple of laughs."
From *What the Six Girls With Balloons*
Told the Gray Man on Horseback. Carl Sandburg.
Harcourt, Brace, and Company, Publishers.

RHYTHM AND PROSODY

Rhythm as applied to prosody is a "kind of metrical movement as determined by the relation of long and short or of
stressed and unstressed syllables in a line." *Murray's*
English Dictionary.

The Rhythm of English Verse

The rhythm of English verse is produced largely by the *fairly* regular or measured recurrence *in time* of stressed syllables in a line. The stressed syllable *may* stand alone: when it does so, a measured pause often follows it. Usually one unstressed syllable, or more than one, precedes or follows the stressed one in fairly regular order. It is the repetition of such patterns which gives the effect of "strongs and weaks," or, "longs and shorts," producing the *metrical feet.* The stressed syllables may contain either *long* or *short* vowels.

> "Although a poem be not made by counting
> syllables upon the fingers, yet 'numbers'
> is the most poetical symbol we have for
> verse, and 'measure' the most significant
> equivalent for beauty, for goodness, and
> perhaps for truth. Those early and pro-
> found philosophers, the followers of
> Pythagoras, saw the essence of all things
> in number. . . ."
>
> *Poetry and Religion.* George Santayana.
> Charles Scribner's Sons, Publishers.

Metre

Metre is "any specific form of poetic rhythm, its kind being determined by the character and number of the feet or groups of syllables of which it consists." *Murray's English Dictionary.*

The more or less fixed rhythm of verse is usually called metre, although the terms *rhythm* and *metre* are used quite interchangeably by many writers. In his *Handbook of Poetics*, (Ginn and Company, Publishers). Gummere says:

> ". . . Metre; Rhythm means pretty much the same thing,—
> 'a flowing,' an even measured motion."

Kinds of Metrical Feet

Iambic. A metrical foot consisting of two syllables, the first one short or unstressed, the second one long or stressed. Example: *a'lone*.

"The 'day is 'dark and 'dreary." Longfellow.

TROCHAIC. A metrical foot consisting of two syllables, the first one long or stressed, the second one short or unstressed.

Example: '*Sister*.

"'Rock of 'ages, 'cleft for 'me,
'Let me 'hide my'self in 'thee."
Rock of Ages. Augustus Montague Toplady.

DACTYLIC. A metrical foot consisting of three syllables, the first one long or stressed, the last two short or unstressed.

Example: '*beautiful*.

"'Backward, turn 'backward, O 'Time, in your 'flight,
'Make me a 'child again 'just for to'night!"
Rock Me to Sleep. Elizabeth Ann Akers.

ANAPESTIC. A metrical foot consisting of three syllables, the first two short or unstressed, the last one long or stressed.

Example: *sere'nade*.

"Do you 'know you have 'asked for this 'priceless 'thing,
As a 'child might 'ask for a 'toy?"
A Woman's Answer. Elizabeth Barrett Browning.

SPONDAIC. A metrical foot consisting of two syllables, both long or stressed. This is used only in combination with other metrical feet. In itself it is non-metrical.

Example: '*black'bird*.

"Come 'out, come 'out where the 'red 'leaves 'fall."
A Ballad of the Road. Constance D'Arcy Mackay.

"Our 'times are in 'His 'hand
Who 'saith, 'A 'whole I 'planned,
'Youth 'shows but 'half, 'trust 'God:
    'see 'all, nor be a'fraid!' "
Rabbi Ben Ezra. Browning.

There are many other metrical feet that are sometimes used. The *Encyclopaedia Britannica* lists them as follows:

Tribrach—short, short, short.
Molussus—long, long, long.

Amphibrach—short, long, short.
Amphimacer—long, short, long.
Bacchuis—short, long, long.
Antibacchuis—long, long, short.
Choriamb—long, short, short, long.
Pyrrhic—short, short (non-metrical).

THE TRAINED EAR MUST BE THE FINAL JUDGE OF RHYTHM

There are various theories concerning the use of metrical feet in verse, as to whether they should be used rigidly or freely. Such theories are the concern of the writers of verse much more than of the readers of verse. The business of the oral reader is to read what is already written so that it *sounds* right to the cultivated ear and is in harmony with the author's meaning and purpose. He may know all of the theories of metre in the world and never achieve this end, or he may know nothing about them and yet read very well. While the trained oral reader should have a general understanding of the use of metrical feet in verse, and of the prose rhythm of his own language, to help and guide him in his study, he should never lose sight of the fact that the oral reading of literature must be governed ultimately, not by the number of metrical feet in a line of verse, or by any other *mechanical* means, but by the effect the reading has upon the *discriminating and discerning ear*, and upon the *aesthetic* sense.

The ear of the oral reader should be highly trained and sensitive, capable of catching all *shades of sound* and all *degrees of stress, measuring pauses* with accuracy, definitely directing the *intonation* and all *changes of pitch* of the voice and every *change* in the *quality, volume, rhythm* and *tempo*.

The people in an audience always judge a reading by the way it *sounds;* they are not at all interested in the way the effect is produced. They like it or they do not like it, that is all that they know and all that they care to know, and all that the reader cares to have them know. When one goes to hear an opera or a symphony orchestra one goes to enjoy the music not to discover and analyze the methods by which the music is produced. Audiences, as such, are not interested in the technique of any art, and the performer who allows the attention of his audience to stray to the technical points in his performance has not yet arrived at artisthood.

CHAPTER X

INTONATION

Intonation: "The rise and fall in the
pitch of the voice in speech."
The *New Merriam Webster Dictionary*.

THE intonation of a language may be said to be the tune
or melody that is produced as the voice glides from one
pitch to another. A breath group constitutes an intonation
group, and English intonation can be studied—as far as is
known at present*—to the best advantage by studying it in
breath group units.

There seems to be a *basic principle* underlying the characteristic tune of each language. When this basic principle is
observed and its workings understood, one should be able to
apply the principle in a variety of ways.

In reading literature, particularly poetic and dramatic
literature, *one must have complete mastery over one's own
intonation*. Countless different shades and qualities of
thought can be revealed *only* by means of certain definite
kinds of tonal movements. The greater the reader's understanding and mastery of these, the greater will be his success
as a reader.

"Proper intonation which is so important an element in
expressive reading, must be systematically studied. This can
only be done satisfactorily by means of oral instruction. The
various tones, rising, falling, level, and the compound tones,
must be guided by ear, and applied to certain typical passages which the student should learn by heart. . . .

*See *Übungen im englischen Tonfall* by H. Klinghardt and G. Klemm:
Cöthen, Otto Schulze, 1920, for the first and most complete scientific
work on the subject of English Intonation. There is no English trans-
lation of this text but, *"Good American Speech,"* by Margaret Prendergast McLean, E. P. Dutton and Company,—contains a brief summary of
the subject matter and many of the English examples from Klinghardt's text, the use of which was personally authorized by Klinghardt.

A student who has learnt by heart a few typical passages, as rendered by a good reader, so that every note of intona-ation, every stress, each characteristic pronunciation can be accurately produced, will serve as a model upon which he may shape his own reading aloud with the greatest profit.''

Henry Cecil Wyld.
In *The Teaching of Reading*, p.p. 74-75.
John Murray, Albermarle St. W. London, Publishers. 1924.

KLINGHARDT'S MARKINGS OF ENGLISH INTONATION

The simple basic principle of English intonation can be represented most effectively and accurately by the use of Klinghardt's intonation markings.

A horizontal line called the *measuring line* is used to represent, in a very general way, the average pitch of the speaker's voice. Because of typographical problems, the height of this line is indicated in this text by "em"—dashes. *Heavy dots* are used to represent the *stressed syllables* in any given breath group, and *light dots* are used to represent the *unstressed* syllables. In every intonation group there must be as many dots as there are syllables in the breath group it represents. Rising or falling *glides* on certain individual syllables in a group are among the outstanding characteristics of English intonation. These glides almost invariably occur on stressed syllables. Klinghardt represents them with slightly curved lines rising up from, or going down from, the dots which represent the stressed syllables on which the glides occur. *An up-glide represents a rising tone; a down-glide represents a descending tone.*

In *simple logical* breath groups, English intonation usually begins above the medium pitch of the voice on the first stressed syllable and moves in a general direction downward to the last stressed syllable on which the glide usually occurs. Examples.

'Students are 'happy at 'school.

'Are students 'happy at 'school?

Intonation Patterns and Their Significance

1. A simple *falling* intonation, or, a *down-glide* indicates:
   a thought completed,
   a statement made,
   a command given,
   a decision reached,
   that the will of the speaker is dominant.

A falling intonation is usually—but not always—used when a question is asked with a question word, such as, *what, when, where, why, which, who, whom, whence, wherefore*. It *may* occur, particularly in dramatic utterances, anywhere within an intonation group, wherever the thought or emotion requires it, but it usually occurs on the last stressed syllable.

2. Simple *rising intonation* or *up-glide* indicates:
   unfinished thought,
   reasoning,
   simple surprise,
   simple doubt or uncertainty,
   deference to the will of the hearer,
   a question asked without a question word.

3. *Level intonation* indicates:
   suspended thought,
   incomprehensible thoughts,
   awe,
   vastness,
   wonder,
   grandeur,
   limitlessness,
   numbed senses,
   deep, controlled, submerged emotion.

4. *Circumflex* intonation is a combination of rising-falling or falling-rising, or it may be up-down-up, or down-up-down, or up-down-up-down, or down-up-down-up, or it may be even more elaborate and complicated. Circumflex intonation indicates combinations and complexity of thoughts and moods, such as:

> sarcasm,
> scorn,
> incredulity,
> complicated surprise and doubt,
> belief and disbelief combined,
> subtlety of mind and mood.

The *length* of the intonation glides and the *range* from high to low pitch, or from low to high, is determined by the vigor and significance of the thought, upon the nature and vitality of the mood, upon the type of character speaking, and upon the size and the acoustics of the hall in which one speaks. As expressions become more forceful and positive, the length of the glides usually increases. In extremely forceful expressions the glides may be very long and the movement of the voice from pitch to pitch either very rapid or very slow. But apparently the *basic principle* does not change in any case. Sometimes an individual word is held on a level pitch for a considerable time, or the pitch of a group of words may be approximately level.

EXAMPLES OF SIMPLE, UNEMOTIONAL PATTERNS

1. Intonation on separate words.

'No —♩   ♩—   'yes —♩   ♩—   'why —♩   ♩—

'nothing —♩.   ♩˙—

2. Stressed beginning and ending with a glide on the last syllable.

Down-glide

a. a statement made.

'Men and 'women 'usually tell the 'truth.

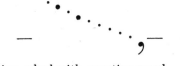

b. question asked with question word.
'Why do 'men and 'women tell the 'truth?

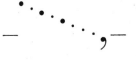

Up-glide

a. incomplete thought.
'Men and 'women tell the 'truth. . . .

b. question asked without a question word.
'Will 'men and 'women tell the 'truth?

3. Unstressed beginnings.

In *all* cases the unstressed syllables which precede the first stressed one seem to have *approximately equal stress*, and to be spoken on *approximately the same pitch*, which is approximately the medium pitch of the speaker's voice. Klinghardt represents this by placing small dots of equal size, equal distance from the measuring line, either a little above or a little below it.

Men and women 'usually tell the 'truth.

Do men and women 'usually tell the 'truth?

4. Unstressed endings.

Unstressed *endings* which follow an up-glide *differ* from those which follow a down-glide.

After a Down-glide

When an unstressed ending follows a down-glide the syllables are spoken on approximately the same pitch as that on which the glide ended. There is often some variation in the *degree* of stress, but unless it is sufficiently strong to be marked as secondary stress, the dots representing the unstressed ending are about of equal size.

Men and women 'usually tell the 'truth about things.

After an Up-glide

When an unstressed ending follows an up-glide the voice continues to rise until the group is finished. This is indicated by placing the dots representing the syllables in a slanting line which follows the general direction of the curve representing the up-glide.

Do men and women 'usually tell the 'truth about things?

5. Intonation moving down by degrees.

In this variety of intonation the unstressed syllables which follow a stressed one are spoken on the same pitch as the stressed one, which makes the pitch move down, as it were, by steps rather than on an incline.

'Only those who 'loved him
under'stand what it 'meant.

6. Broken intonation groups, called *slight jointing*.

When the pitch of one syllable is raised *above* that of the syllables immediately preceding or following it, it brings it into *greater prominence*. The higher it is raised the more prominent it becomes. When a *simple intonation pattern is broken* in order to bring some syllable, other than the first stressed one, into greater prominence than it would have if it remained in the simple unbroken line, it is called *slight jointing*. The syllable that is to be raised may be underlined *once* if it is to be *as high or less than as high* as the first stressed one, and it may be underlined *twice* if it is to be *higher* than the first stressed one. It is possible to indicate many different degrees of importance of syllables by this means but three will serve as illustrations.

'Men and 'women 'usually tell the 'truth.

'Men and 'women 'usually tell the 'truth.

'Men and 'women 'usually tell the 'truth.

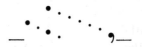

7. *Blending* of intonation groups.

The term blending should explain itself. It is a *combination of two or more groups* used to express a unit of thought. The first group—or groups—, has an up-glide on the last stressed syllable, which indicates the thought is going on, and the last group has a down-glide on the last stressed syllable. A *wavy line* may be placed under the syllables which move *upward* in tone, either stressed or unstressed. The sign, ⌇, is placed between the two groups to indicate blending.

'Men and 'women ⌇ 'usually tell the 'truth.

'Men and 'women ⌇ usually pre'fer
to tell the 'truth.

In the second example the syllables, *us-u-a-lly*, *pre*, become the unstressed beginning of the second group.

8. *Binding* of intonation groups is the same as blending except that there is a pause between the two groups, whereas, in blending there is no pause between them.

'Men and 'women ‖ 'usually tell the 'truth.

Simple Exercises to Practice for Intonation Glides

Practice the following words with a good singing tone giving them with down-glides and up-glides until proficiency has been attained in each; then try the circumflex intonation, down-up, up-down, down-up-down, up-down-up; then make them as elaborate as is needed.

me	pay	come	love
you	why	won	breathe
law	no	sing	judge
far	boy	bell	nothing
sir	now	buzz	

Examples Showing a Wide Variety of Applications of the Principles of Intonation*

Simple greeting. Good 'morning.

Simple question. Are you 'ready?

Simple statement. Not 'yet.

Indecision, uncertainty. 'Yes ‖ I 'think 'so.

Incredulity. "'Martha, ‖ 'not 'coming?"

Sarcasm. "Hath a 'dog, 'money?"

*Klinghardt did *not* use the compound intonation curves which are used here to indicate various kinds of compound, or, circumflex tones.

"'Is it 'possible that a 'cur ||
can 'lend 'three 'thousand 'ducats?"'

Defiance. "'Traitor! || to 'whom? || to 'thee?"

Affirmation, with long glide.
"'Ay || 'every 'inch || a 'king."

". . . he 'sets me 'free ||
this 'one 'long 'day."

Examples of Down-glides

Oswald to Kent:
"'What 'dost thou 'know me 'for?"

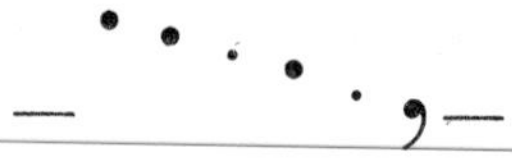

Kent.

"A 'knave; || a 'rascal

An 'eater of 'broken 'meats.

a 'base, 'proud, 'shallow, 'beggarly

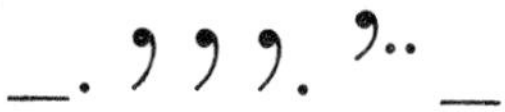

'three 'suited, 'hundred 'pound

'filthy, 'worsted stocking 'knave."

From *King Lear*. Act. II Sc. I Shakespeare.

"But a 'great 'cry,

'audible,

even a'bove the ˎwind and ˎwater

'rose from the 'shore;

the 'sea,

sweeping 'over the ˎwreck,

made a 'clean 'breach,

and carried 'men, 'spars, 'casks,

'planks, 'bulwarks,

'heaps of such 'toys

into the 'boiling 'surge."

From *David Copperfield*.   Charles Dickens.

Oliver to his brother, Orlando:
    "'Now 'Sir! ‖ what 'make you 'here?

Orlando:

    "'Nothing

I'm not 'taught to make anything.

I'm helping 'you to 'mar that which 'God ˎmade.

From *As You Like It*. Act. I Sc. I Shakespeare.

Queen Katherine to Cardinal Wolsey:
    "'Therefore ⌒ I 'say a'gain

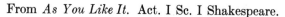

. I 'utterly ab'hor

'yea, from my 'soul

re"fuse you for my 'judge."

From *King Henry the Eighth*. Act. II Sc. IV Shakespeare.

King Lear to Gloster:
    ""Vengeance! "Plague! "Death! || Con"fusion.

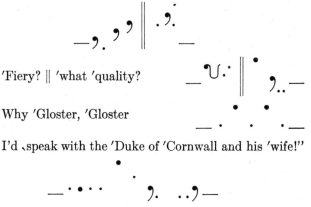

    'Fiery? || 'what 'quality?

    Why 'Gloster, 'Gloster

I'd ₍speak with the 'Duke of 'Cornwall and his 'wife!"

From *King Lear*. Act. II Sc. III Shakespeare.

    Judith (as she defiantly throws great pieces of wood into the fire):

    "'There! and "there!

    'There's your 'penny'worth || 'burning.

    And a'nother! and a'nother and a"nother."

From *Granite*. Clemence Dane
William Heinemann, Ltd. London, 1926.

Nicky to his mother:
"'Mother ‖ 'don't go on like 'that ‖ its 'useless.

'We've a'rrived at a 'crisis

wher'ever we 'go—what'ever we 'do

we 'can't e'scape from it."

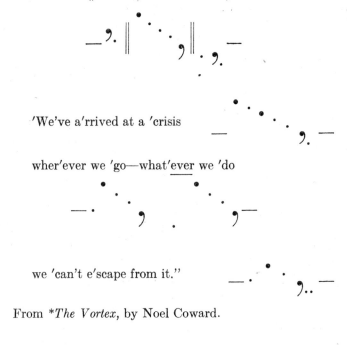

From *The Vortex*, by Noel Coward.

EXAMPLES OF UP-GLIDES

"'He that formed the 'eye ‖ shall he not 'see?"

"He that formed the 'ear ‖ shall he not 'hear?"

"Can 'curses ⌡ 'pierce the 'clouds ‖ and 'enter

'heaven?"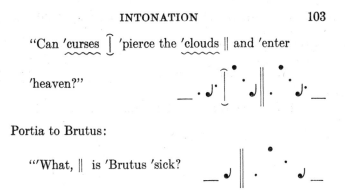

Portia to Brutus:

"'What, ‖ is 'Brutus 'sick?

And 'will he 'steal out of his 'wholesome 'bed,

to 'dare the 'vile con'tagion of the 'night,

and 'tempt the 'Rheumy and un'purged 'air

to 'add unto his sickness?"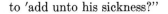

From *Julius Caesar* Act. II Sc. I Shakespeare.

Brutus to Cassius:

"'What ‖ shall 'one of 'us

that 'struck the 'foremost 'man of 'all the 'world

but for su'pporting 'robbers

shall 'we 'now

con'taminate our 'fingers with 'base 'bribes

and 'sell

the 'mighty 'space of our 'large 'honors

for so much 'trash

that 'may be 'grasped 'thus?"

From *Julius Caesar* Act. IV Sc. III Shakespeare.

EXAMPLES OF INTONATION THAT IS LARGELY, NOT WHOLLY,
LEVEL

"'O that 'this 'too, 'too 'solid 'flesh ‖ would 'melt,

'thaw ‖ and re'solve it'self into a 'dew."

From *Hamlet*. Act. I Sc. II Shakespeare.

"'I am thy 'father's 'spirit,

'doom'd for a 'certain 'term‖ to 'walk the 'night.

And for the 'day ‖ con'fined to 'fast in 'fires

till the 'foul 'crimes ‖ 'done in my 'days of 'nature

are 'burnt ‖ and 'purged a'way."

From *Hamlet*. Act. I Sc. V Shakespeare.

"On 'her that I 'loved of 'yore

'Robe upon 'robe ‖ I 'cast.

On 'her that I 'hated ‖ 'sore.''

From *Electra*. Sophocles.

"And 'on a 'sudden ‖ 'lo ‖ the 'level 'lake

And the 'long 'glories ‖ of the 'winter 'moon."

From *"The Passing of Arthur"* in *The Idylls of the King*. Alfred Tennyson.

Discover the Right Intonation for the Following Quotations

"The tremendous sea itself,
when I could find pause to look at it,
in the agitation of the blinding wind,
the flying stones and sand,
and the awful noise,
      confounded me.
As the high watery walls came rolling in
and tumbled into surf,
I seemed to see a rending,
and upheaving,
      of all nature."
From *David Copperfield*. Charles Dickens.

Quotations having many marked rising tones some of which have the combined falling-rising movement.

Medea speaks to the Chorus about King Creon:
  "Dost dream I would have grovelled to this man
  Save that I won mine end, and shaped my plan
  For merry deeds?"
From *"The Medea"* of Euripides. Sir Gilbert Murray, Translator.

Petruchio to Grumio:
  "Think you a little din can daunt mine ears?
  Have I not in my time heard lions roar?
  Have I not heard the sea, puffed up with winds,
  Rage like an angry boar, chafed with sweat?
  Have I not heard great ordnance in the field,
  And heaven's artillery thunder in the skies?
  And do you tell me of a woman's tongue,
  That gives not half so great a blow to ear,
  As will a chestnut in a farmer's fire?"
From *"The Taming of the Shrew."* Act I Sc. II Shakespeare.

Intonation with a slight upward tendency which shows, in the following example, a desire on the part of the speaker to be sociable, agreeable and casual, while trying to hide a deep and lasting sorrow.

Mrs. Frazier speaks of her husband to Miss Austen, her neighbor:
  "He'll be dead ten years this coming November.
  Yes.
  Yes, he died the twenty-third of November.
  He was injured on the second
  in an automobile accident.
  I was telling Mr. Craig about it.
  So, you see,
  the melancholy days
  have really a very literal significance for me.
  Every year,
  as soon as November comes around
  I just pack up my things
  and go out to Dayton, Ohio.

I have a married daughter living out there.
She makes all manner of fun
of my annual pilgrimages to Dayton.
She says
instead of being in England now that April's there,
with me,
it's in Dayton now that November's there—
We have great fun about it.
But I must go somewhere;
I couldn't stand it here:
I have too many memories."

From *Craig's Wife*. George Kelly.
Little, Brown and Company, Publishers.

Intonation that has no positive glides either up or down, because of grief and physical weakness, yet it is not level intonation.

Queen Katherine to Capucius:
"I thank you, honest lord. Remember me
In all humility unto his highness;
Say his long trouble now is passing
Out of this world; tell him in death I bless'd him,
For so I will.—Mine eyes grow dim.—Farewell,
My lord.—"

From *King Henry the Eighth*, Act. IV Sc. II Shakespeare.

Intonation with no clear cut glides either up or down, and with pitch nearly level within a breath group. Variety is gained by speaking different groups on different levels. It shows mystery and incomprehensible things.

"When at last no answer came
nor any sign from their totems,
they pulled out of the bag
those golden gods
that Loma gave not up except in flames
and when all her men were dead.
They had large ruby eyes
and emerald tongues.
They set them down upon that mountain pass,

the cross-legged idols
with their emerald tongues;
and . . . bowed them down and prayed
in their desperate straits
in that dank ominous night
to the gods that they had wronged,

. . . .

and the gods all laughed,
all four,
and wagged their emerald tongues;
the Indians saw them
though the night had fallen
and though the mist was low."

From *The Loot of Loma*. Lord Dunsany
In *Last Book of Wonder*.
John W. Luce and Company, Publishers.

Circumflex intonations, denoting sarcasm, scorn, deceit,
fawning, showing-off.

The Poet's wife, to the Old Lady who lives at Land's End.:
   "We've not been married very long.
   Of course it pained me to leave him.
   But I was so wearied with social pleasures
   that he wanted me to rest;
   and what was I to do?
   I was even growing bored,
   not being as fresh as he
   to such fullness of life.
   But you can know nothing of that,
   here at the end of things.
   You've never seen the world?"

From *Will o' the Wisp*. Doris Halman.
Walter H. Baker Company, Publishers.

Shylock to Antonio:
      "Shall I bend low,
      and in a bondman's key,
      with bated breath
      and whispering humbleness,
      say this:

"Fair sir,
you spet on me on Wednesday last;
you spurned me such a day;
another time
you call'd me dog;
and for these courtesies
I'll lend you thus much moneys."

From *"The Merchant of Venice."* Act. I Sc. III Shakespeare.

Cassius to Brutus, speaking of Caesar:
"This man is now become a god;
and Cassius must bend his body
if Caesar carelessly but nod on him.
He had a fever when he was in Spain
and when the fit was on him.
I did mark how he did shake:
'Tis true, this god did shake.
His coward lips
did from their colour fly;
and that same eye,
whose bend doth awe the world,
did lose his lustre.
I did hear him groan;
ay, and that tongue of his,
that bade the Romans mark him,
and write his speeches in their books,
Alas! it cried,
Give me some drink Titinius,
as a sick girl."

From *Julius Caesar.* Act. I Sc. II Shakespeare.

Satan speaks to the Son of God:
"Then hear,
O Son of David, virgin born.
For Son of God
to me is yet in doubt:
Of the Messiah I have heard
foretold by all the prophets.
Of thy birth,
at length announced by Gabriel

with the first I knew,
and of the Angelic song in Bethlehem field,
on thy birthnight,
that sung thee Saviour born.
From that time
seldom have I ceased
to eye thy infancy,
thy childhood, and thy youth.
Thy manhood last, though in private bred;
till at the ford of Jordan,
whither all flocked to the Baptist,
I, among the rest,
though not to be baptized,
by voice from heav'n
heard thee pronounced
the Son of God beloved.
Thence forth,
I thought thee worth my nearer view,
and narrower scrutiny,
that I might learn
in what degree or meaning
thou art called the Son of God."

From *Paradise Regained*. Book IV Lines 500-517. Milton.

CHAPTER XI

TERMINOLOGY
AND
GENERAL SUGGESTIONS FOR PREPARING A
SELECTION FOR ORAL INTERPRETATION

TERMINOLOGY

THE terms *reader,* and, *interpreter*—as has been previously stated—are used to designate the person who is speaking the author's lines whether he is actually reading them from a book, or has committed them to memory, and whether they were written by himself or by another.

The term *speaker* designates the person for whom the reader becomes the mouthpiece.

In *My Last Duchess,* (Browning) the reader speaks for the Duke of Ferrara,

In *Mandalay,* (Kipling) he speaks for a British soldier,

In *Highland Mary,* (Burns) he speaks for the author.

The terms *listener and listeners,* are used to designate the person, persons or object, real or imaginary, to whom the speaker in the literature speaks.

In *John Anderson, My Jo,* (Burns) a wife speaks to her husband; therefore, he is the listener.

In *To a Skylark,* (Shelley) the author speaks to a skylark; consequently, an imaginary skylark is the listener.

The term *audience* designates the person or persons *for whom* the reading is given. It may or it may not be given directly to the audience depending upon the nature of the selection.

Stories as a whole, and orations, are given directly *to* the audience. Plays and monologues are given *for* the audience.

The term *impersonate* is used in accordance with the following definitions:

"To invest with personality. To assume or *act the person or character of."
Webster's *New International Dictionary.*

"To represent under the form of a person. To take into or unite with, one's own person or character. To appear or *act the character of; represent the person, character or *actions of." *The New Standard Dictionary.*

Suggestions for Preparing a Selection for Oral Interpretation

All suggestions made concerning the oral interpretation of selections apply to selections that are ready to be used as readings assuming that all necessary cutting, abridging and arranging has been done.

It has been stated previously that there are certain general principles to be applied in the interpretation of all forms of literature, but there are countless different ways of applying them. Each student will eventually discover for himself the *method of application* that is best for him. However, such discovery comes only with years and experience. Unless one has some suggestions or guide to follow *in the beginning* there is danger of losing a great deal of valuable time and of wasting a great deal of energy and priceless enthusiasm while one is discovering one's own best method. General suggestions are, therefore, given for the sake of students who have no idea how to begin to study a selection preparatory to reading it aloud before an audience for purposes of artistic entertainment.

Get the Thought of Each Selection

It cannot be stated too often or too emphatically that *the first and most important thing to be done is to get the author's meaning and purpose.* It will seem to the casual observer that

---

*The italics are the author's.

this is an obvious thing and that anyone with ordinary common sense will do it without fuss or feathers. Theoretically this is all right but it very seldom works out in practice. In his *Oral Study of Literature*, p.p. 1-2 and 28, Professor Algernon Tassin says:

> "What is wrong is that students do not know how to read. They do not get the meaning of the printed page. What is needed is systematic laboratory work in the science of reading. . . . always keep in mind the purpose of the author. To depart from it is to be ineffective as well as confusing."

The great majority of students must have very definite help in learning how to prepare a selection to get the most out of it within a reasonable limit of time, and to be ready to *give out* to others the riches they have gleaned, so that the others may understand and appreciate them with their minds and hearts.

SUGGESTIONS FOR A PLAN OF PROCEDURE

There are, of course, many other, and undoubtedly better, methods of procedure than those given here and as soon as they have been discovered or formulated they should be adopted and the old ones discarded.

1. Read the selection silently from beginning to end *without interruption*, to get a concept of it *as a whole*.

2. Look up all necessary words, references and notes.

3. Read the selection silently again several times simply for the enjoyment of it.

4. Read the selection *aloud* as if to *interest* an audience but there should be no audience. This will help to clarify the author's meaning in the reader's mind more than many silent readings will do and will help to keep the thought moving ahead, step by step, and unfolding in proper sequence.

5. Give a *brief* general outline of the selection *aloud in your own words.* Read it again to test the correctness of your outline. Repeat this process as often as necessary until you can give the *essential* points in proper sequence, briefly, and in *your own words.*

6. (a) Copy the lines of *all* selections *except lyrical poetry,* on sheets of paper as large as that used for typewriting, *placing only one main breath group on a line.* If there are very short breath groups closely related in thought, two or perhaps three such groups may sometimes be written on one line.

(b) Underline the words which are to be stressed because a line is seen at a glance more readily than a stress mark.

(c) Place a single bar after every stress group and a double bar after every breath group.

(d) Decide upon the weak forms to be used and if need be write them in the line.

(e) When this is completed satisfactorily read it over and over many times, silently and aloud, always from the copy you have made, following your own plan. If you can improve upon your first plan do so, but indicate the improvements upon the page. At every reading, *think the thoughts* as you express them, giving them the proper quality, tempo, volume, etc.

(f) Copy lyrical poetry as the poet has written it but indicate all stresses, stress groups and pauses on the page.

7. Repeat the oral readings *at various intervals of time* remembering that it is your task to make the literature clear and interesting to *someone else,* consequently, **it must be clear to you first.** When the selection *as a*

whole is clearly understood, you may begin a more intensive study of its parts. Usually there are different steps in the unfoldment of the thought, or the emotion, or the action, of a selection (except perhaps in very short ones) and these may be studied separately for a time, but ultimately they should be put together again to retain their proper relation to each other and the proper *unity* of the selection as a whole.

8. Make your readings sound as if you were talking, *not* as if you were "reciting," except in cases of chants or other unusual types of expression which *require* the recitative style of delivery.

> "The reader is taking the place of the writer and simply talking what he has to say. Literature is talk made permanent."
> Introduction to *The Oral Study of Literature*, p. 21, Algernon Tassin.

9. The thought in the selection may be of any conceivable nature; the mood may be gay or sad, beautiful or ugly; the tempo may be fast or slow; the volume may be great or small, but the reading must *seem* to be spontaneous and original expression with the fire of mind and heart behind it.

10. It takes time to prepare a selection well because the understanding and appreciation must grow, and growth always takes time. Undue haste is a grave mistake.

Do Not Commit Words to Memory Mechanically

By reading a selection from the page silently and aloud, endeavoring to keep the thought and purpose clear, and to make them clear and interesting to others, by unfolding thought after thought, action after action, in their proper relation to each other, and in their proper sequence, showing your own understanding and appreciation of them, you will soon fix the selection in your memory as a living and vital *experience* and it will *remain* there as such. Not a single moment will need to be given to the slavish committing of words to memory. However, the lines must be repeated *accurately each time* they are read from the page or they will neither fix themselves correctly nor well. The constant dropping of the water finally wears away the stone, leaving its indelible imprint, but it must always drop *in the same place* if the imprint is to be made quickly, clearly, and definitely.

Committing words to memory mechanically is a great waste of time and effort and brings about the least desirable results.

QUESTIONS THE ORAL READER SHOULD BE ABLE TO ANSWER

There are certain questions that the oral reader should be able to answer concerning his readings. Some of the questions will apply to some selections while others will apply to other selections. Some of these questions are:

1. Who is supposed to be talking, or—in more technical terminology—who is the *speaker*?

   Different people speak and act differently and the interpreter must know whom he is supposed to represent if his reading is to ring true.

2. To whom is the speaker talking, or, who is the *listener*? We talk to different people differently, sometimes very differently.

3. What is the *relation* between speaker and listener? Are they friends, enemies, strangers or mere acquaintances; are they equal or different in social position, intelligence, ability, etc?

4. Is the *place* of any importance? If so, what is it? Is it a church, a moonlit beach or a department store, etc. ?

5. Is the *situation* of any importance? If so, what is it? Is it humorous or serious, common-place or unusual, etc?

6. Is the *time* of any importance? If so, what is it? Is it a certain time of day, of year, of life, or of history; is it the time of Agamemnon, of Caesar, of Oscar Wilde or of John Drew? Try reading the lines of Lady Teazle as if she were a modern girl in pajamas, or the lines of *Carcassonne* as if a young man were speaking them, and observe how all that they stand for is lost.

7. Is the *purpose* of the speaker dominated by:
   (a) a *mental* or *intellectual* impulse? Does he wish to outline, define, analyze, explain, instruct, consider, reflect, compare, etc?
   (b) an *emotional* impulse? Does he wish to help, comfort, win, soothe, inspire, console, beautify, ennoble, persuade, etc? Does he wish to express joy, fear, sorrow, sympathy, love, regret, disappointment, desire, etc?
   (c) an impulse concerned with *action*? Does he wish to depict action, to arouse or compel others to act, to stop action, to command, denounce, etc?

THREE GENERAL CRITICISMS OF READERS

Readers are frequently—and often justly—criticised because:

1. They have gained an *intellectual* understanding of a selection only, and omit the emotional element which makes it sound something like a lesson in mathematics.

2. They let the *emotion* dominate and submerge the thought which makes the selection lack proper form and meaning.

3. They speak with more *force* or *loudness* than the selection requires which makes it seem bombastic and noisy and distorts its whole significance and purpose.

If a reader will analyze each selection carefully so that he is able to answer the preceding questions he will *know* when the lines require didactic, explanatory or analytic expression; when to *express*, when to *suppress*, and when to *eliminate*, emotion; when to speak *quietly* and when to use *volume*.

BE PREPARED TO COVER THE FIELD OF LITERATURE

The preceding list of questions may seem like an imposing array of details when one is preparing a sonnet or a simple three stanza poem for delivery. But this text is concerned with the oral interpretation of *all* literature that is suitable for oral presentation, and some of these questions must be answered for every selection, though it be but one line in length; therefore, it is necessary to make note of all of them in order to cover the whole field.

PART TWO
CHAPTER XII

LITERATURE FOR ORAL INTERPRETATION; ITS SUBJECT MATTER, FORM, AND CLASSIFICATION

The Subject Matter and the Form of Literature

THERE are two factors to be considered especially, in the study of literature which is undertaken here.

1. The *inner thought and feeling* which will be called the *subject matter*.

2. The *outward expression* of the thought and feeling which will be called the *outward, or, the external form*.

Fine and noble thoughts and feelings are expressed intuitively and naturally in fine and noble form, while ordinary prosaic thoughts and feelings are expressed naturally in ordinary prose form. *In natural expression there is harmony between the nature and quality of the thought and feeling to be expressed and the manner of expressing them.* This may be stated as a general law of expression.

A Law of Natural Expression

The nature and quality of the subject matter *determines*, in a general way, what the outward form of the expression shall be.

Man has many different kinds of thought and emotion which he expresses in language, hence there are many different forms of natural expression. Each one of these forms expresses something which no other form can express so well. *From these natural forms of expression by means of spoken language man's artistic forms of literature have developed.*

". . . the investigator who has examined a piece of literature simply in order to know what it is . . . is now compelled to take a wider view; and seeking to know whether there be not certain principles common to all literature and derived from the general mind of humanity. . . .

That there are such laws or principles applying to the various forms of literature, in whatever age and in whatever clime produced, is certain. . . ."

From *New Studies in Literature*.   Edward Dowden p.p. 450-451.

Kegan Paul, Trench, Trübner and Company, Publishers.

Origin of the Forms of Literature

Most of the forms of literature are innate in man.   They are *not invented* by him, he *discovers* them within himself. For example, man rejoices over some victory of his tribe, his country, or his football team, he chants and sings and dances to celebrate the event, and *ballads* are the outgrowth of his spirited and vigorous enthusiasm; his soul overflows with appreciation of the glory of a sunset, the haunting note of a bird, or the fidelity and charm of a loved one, and this over-flow of feeling takes expression in a *lyric* of nature or a lyric of love; his soul is torn with anguish, his needs are beyond the aid of man, he makes a reverent and fervent appeal to God and we have *prayer*.   No one has to tell man how or when to do these things, he cannot help doing them, they are instinctive and natural.

When man idealizes his natural forms of expression and carefully chooses his manner of expression we have artistic forms of expression.   Such expressions by means of language, duly recorded and preserved, have become our literature.

The Basis of Classification of Literature for Oral Interpretation

Since there is such a vast amount of literature that *might* be studied it is absolutely necessary to classify it in order that it *may* be studied advantageously.   The classification should be made according to the needs of the one studying. The oral reader of literature will find it profitable to base his classification of literature upon *its dramatic significance in oral interpretation*, since the literature that is best suited to oral interpretation is that which has special dramatic significance, not "just any" literature, however great or remarkable it may be,

> "not history or science or philosophy, not what remains on the general level, but the great division of literary art which is the expression of emotional life . . ., the exceptional, the extraordinary, the powerful, the unexpected, that soars far above the general level."
>
> *Life and Literature*, by Lafcadio Hearn.
> Used by permission of the Publishers.
> Dodd, Mead and Company, Inc.

What Constitutes Dramatic Significance in Literature?

There are countless factors that give literature dramatic significance. Some of the most tangible of these are:

1. Interesting and entertaining *subject matter*.

2. *Beauty of language* and of the arrangement of sounds and words into delightful patterns which have particular *melody* and charm when read aloud.

3. Genuine and concentrated *emotion* which makes a strong appeal to the *heart* of man.

4. Interesting *characters* depicted.

5. Interesting, perplexing and exciting *situations* building up to a definite climax.

General Classification of Literature Suitable for Oral Interpretation

All literature that has *no* special dramatic significance should be eliminated at once. That which remains for consideration and study will include both prose and verse and may be classified in a general way, as follows:

1. Stories of practically every kind.
2. Many orations.
3. Many essays.
4. Lyrical poetry.
5. Narrative poetry.
6. Dramatic poetry.
7. Monologues.
8. Plays.

SOME SELECTIONS ARE NOT SUITED TO ORAL PRESENTATION

There are some individual selections even in so-called dramatic literature that are *not* suitable for purposes of entertainment, and therefore, they should never be used in that way. The good taste of the reader will have to be the guide in such cases.

WHO DETERMINES THE PROPER MANNER OF INTERPRETATION OF A SELECTION?

The above question may be answered briefly thus: *The selection itself determines it;* the *subject matter* which the *author* chose to use and his *manner of expressing* the subject matter.

"Be sure that you go to the author to get at *his* meaning, not to find yours, . . . And be sure also, if the author is worth anything, that you will not get at his meaning all at once. . . . The metal you are in search of being the author's mind and meaning, his words are as the rock which you have to crush and smelt in order to get at it. And your pickaxes are your own care, wit, and learning; your smelting furnace is your own thoughtful soul."

Sesame and Lilies. Ruskin.

There are definite, basic, fundamental principles underlying the *true* oral interpretation of each *form* of literature.

These principles are determined by the *subject matter and form of the literature itself—not by the reader*. The reader must *discover* them in the literature, he may not *invent* them. *The general manner of the oral reading of literature is determined by principle or law within the literature itself, not by chance. Each particular form of literature demands interpretation to suit itself—not to suit the whim or opinion of the reader.*

The Principle is Constant, its Application is Variable

The fundamental *principle* governing the oral interpretation of each form of literature *does not vary* but the *application of the principle varies endlessly* in accordance with the universal law that while *principles are constant, their application is variable.*

No two persons will ever read a given selection in exactly the same way—and no one wants them to—, no matter how earnestly they may try to do so, because no two persons will apply the principle in exactly the same way, but if the selection is read with true understanding of the author's meaning and mood the two interpretations will be *fundamentally* the same. The same individual will not read a given selection in exactly the same way at two different times, but if he reads it *according to principle* all the readings of the selection that he will give in a lifetime will be *fundamentally the same*, although his understanding and appreciation will ripen with time. No two human beings—as far as man knows—have ever looked exactly alike and yet we are all created according to *one fundamental principle or law.* We have a nervous system, a respiratory system, a circulatory system, a head, torso, and limbs, a given number of bones of certain shapes and sizes, arranged in a certain definite order; most people have two eyes, two ears, one nose, one mouth, hair and teeth, etc., yet we are all different because *the application of the principle is different* in each case.

Important Law to be Remembered

The principle itself gives constancy and universality to an expression; the different applications of the principle give endless variety and interest.

The oral reader of literature must know:

1. the *basic principles* which determine the general method of interpreting each form of literature he undertakes to read, and

2. *how to apply these principles* to a given selection in order to bring out the spirit and purpose of the literature while he himself remains in the background.

"You must know that it is no easy thing for a principle to become a man's own, unless each day he maintain it and hear it maintained, as well as work it out in life."
No. XXX, *The Golden Sayings of Epictetus.*
Translated by Hastings Crossley.

"Like Nature, art has its laws; the difficulty is to ascertain them."

Channels of English Literature, p. 19. W. M. Dixon.
J. M. Dent and Sons, Publishers.

Keys to the Oral Interpretation of Forms of Literature Having Dramatic Significance

The complete mastery of the right oral interpretation of *one* representative example of a form of literature will give the reader *the key* to the right general method of interpreting *all* selections having a similar form. When he has mastered the right oral interpretation of *one* representative example of each of the different forms of literature that are suited to oral interpretation, he will have *the key* to the right general method of interpreting *all* literature that is suited to oral interpretation. This makes it imperative for him to *study one example of each form with painstaking care and thoroughness*, giving full consideration to important details, and then he must blend and harmonize the details into a unified and finished whole.

FORMS OF LITERATURE NOT ALWAYS EASILY DETERMINED

Sometimes it is very difficult to determine to which form of literature a given selection belongs. In such cases a selection will have to be given special consideration and the interpretation given according to one's best understanding and judgment.

> "Literary compositions run into each other precisely like colours: in their strong tints they are easily distinguished; but are susceptible to so much variety and of so many different forms that we can never say where one species ends and the other begins." Lord Kanes.

Channels of English Literature, p. 18, W. M. Dixon.

CHAPTER XIII

PROSE AND VERSE OR POETRY.

Prose

The most familiar forms of literature are *prose* and *verse*, or, *poetry*. Prose is "straightforward or direct speech. The ordinary written or spoken language of man." *Century Dictionary*.

THE *aim of prose is service:* as a general rule it makes—or at least seems to make—its appeal to the *intellect*. It is *primarily* concerned with *what is said*— not with the *manner of saying it*. As man becomes more cultivated his prose becomes more elegant and refined, he chooses and arranges his words more and more thoughtfully and carefully. As a result of this care and discrimination a very high art of prose is developed in which the *manner* of expression is as important as the *matter:* the *way* it is expressed is as important as *what* is expressed. Good prose is, therefore, of value for two reasons:

1. because of the value and significance of its *subject-matter*.

2. because of the arrangement and beauty of its outward *form*.

Prose—as has been said previously—has a definite rhythm but it does not have metre except in rare cases.

"Prose *must* be rhythmical and it may be *as much so* as you will; but it *must not* be metrical."

Robert Louis Stevenson.

"The needful qualities for a fit prose are regularity, uniformity, precision, balance."
Essentials of Criticism. Matthew Arnold.

"Prose at its best has high qualities far beyond the ken of poetry. . . . One thing at least is certain, that prose however

fervid and emotional it may become, must always be directed
or seem to be directed by the reins of logic. Like a captive
balloon it can never really leave the earth."
Watts-Dunton in *Encyclopaedia Britannica.*

FORMS OF PROSE SUITABLE FOR ORAL READING

Some authorities classify prose for oral reading into
narrative, descriptive and *dramatic.* This is, of course, an
excellent classification but a slightly more detailed classification may be helpful to the student of oral reading. The detailed classification includes:

1. Stories of all kinds that may be used for oral reading.
2. Orations, speeches, addresses.
3. Prose plays.
4. Prose monologues.
5. Selected essays.

STATEMENT

In order to simplify the consideration of different forms of
literature, plays and monologues that are written in prose and
those that are written in verse are discussed under the head
of *Dramatic Literature.*

VERSE OR POETRY

"Absolute poetry is the concrete and artistic expression
of the human mind in emotional and rhythmical language."
Watts-Dunton in the *Encyclopaedia Britannica.*

"Poetry is that one of the fine arts which addresses itself
to the feeling and the imagination by the instrumentality
of musical and moving words; the art which has for its object the exciting of intellectual pleasure by means of vivid,
imaginative, passionate, and inspiring language; usually
though not necessarily arranged in the form of measured
verse or numbers." *The Century Dictionary.*

"Poetry feeds and waters the passions instead of withering and starving them. " Plato.

"Poetry is an expression of life. To know poetry is to know life. . . . Poetry develops man's mental and spiritual nature. It awakens him to what life really is. . . . All that is best in life is the poetry of it."
The Teaching of Poetry in the High School, p.p. 171-5. Arthur H. Fairchild.
Houghton Mifflin Company, Publishers.

. . . poetry is metrical and euphuistic discourse, expression of thought which is both sensuous and ideal. Such is poetry as a literary form, but if . . . we think of poetry as that subtle fire and inward light which seems at times to shine through the world and to touch the images in our minds with ineffable beauty, then poetry is a momentary harmony in the soul amid stagnation and conflict,—a glimpse of the divine and an incitation to a religious life."
The Elements and Functions of Poetry, by George Santayana, In *Interpretation of Poetry and Religion*.
Charles Scribner's Sons, Publishers. 1924.

THE PURPOSE OF POETRY

It is quite impossible to say what the *purpose* of poetry is. It is much easier to mention some of the things it *does*, or seems to do.

Poetry reveals the universality of truth and beauty in a manner that is pleasing, appealing, convincing and sincere. It makes its primary appeal to the emotions. It is characterized by *the particular nature and beauty of its form*, due partially at least, to the careful choice of sounds and words, and to the arrangement of words into patterns. It has a more or less definite rhythm measuring intervals of time. Ruskin says poetry is:—

"the presentment, in musical form, to the imagination, of noble grounds for the noble emotions."

But poetry is more than all of this. It is a slightly open doorway through which one may catch glimpses of a soul, an ideal, struggling to be free and through which one sees reflected, that part of God that lies within himself. Poetry is a spirit, a dream, a desire; it is everything that we love, everything that inspires us and makes us happy: it is mother, sweetheart, moonlight, ideality, vision, ambition; it is music, dancing and song. Poetry is—just poetry. We know it when we hear it but it defies accurate description and analysis, it taunts and fascinates but *eludes* all captors.

Poetry Demands Oral Interpretation

It cannot be stated too often or too forcibly that poetry demands adequate *oral* interpretation to reveal its full beauty and significance just as a musical composition demands oral or instrumental interpretation. Many technical suggestions can be made that, if properly followed, will be of genuine service to the student, but these are only the *outward mechanics of interpretation,* and they must be completely concealed in the *real interpretation* that springs from *within the soul* of the reader. This technique is the *means* by which the oral reader is able to express his soul's understanding and appreciation. Technical study is absolutely essential in order that one may truly interpret poetry but this technique must be kept in its proper place which is in the back-ground, serving only as a *means to an end.*

All great artistic expression is made possible only because the artist has learned the technique of his trade and is willing to obey its laws in order to be free of hindrances to the revelation of the understanding of his soul. The prospective reader of great literature might well learn the two following quotations and use them as daily reminders that while *there must be laws in order that there may be freedom,* the *laws must not* be allowed to *become fetters* and defeat their own purpose by cramping and limiting the expression.

"Law alone can give us freedom." Goethe.

"Poetry read aloud as something sensuous and passionate cannot possibly conform exactly to a set mechanical pattern of rhythm and metre."
A *Study of Poetry*, by Bliss Perry.
Houghton, Mifflin Company, Publishers.

Different Ways of Classifying Poetry

There are many different ways of classifying poetry for the purpose of studying it for oral interpretation and there are advantages and disadvantages in each. There is no *one* right way, and probably there is no *best* way; there are only *good* ways. Certainly no pretense is made that the classification given here is anything more than one that has been tried out thoroughly and has proved to be very useful and helpful. A *general* classification is given first, followed by a more *detailed* classification. The principles underlying the oral interpretation of some of the many different forms of poetry are given under the *detailed* classification; however, there is much poetry that is not definitely covered by these classifications.

Broad General Classification of Poetry

1. Lyrical
2. Narrative
3. Epic
4. Dramatic

The division of poetry into epic, lyric and dramatic is very ancient. The epic narrated something, or, it told a story; a lyric was a song; a drama depicted characters actually living through a particular experience, speaking and acting in a way that represented life. Our understanding of these terms is the same today as it was then.

"To talk of dramatic poetry, epic poetry and narrative poetry is to talk of three different things—epic, drama and narrative; but each is combined with a fourth thing in common, which is poetry, which, in turn is in itself of precisely the same nature as the lyric. . . . The quality which is commonly said to be exclusively lyric is the quality of all poetry."

John Drinkwater. *The Lyric.* p. 30.
Martin Secker; London.

The *broad* classification of poetry into lyrical, narrative, epic and dramatic will be of service to the oral reader through his whole time of study—but particularly at the beginning and toward the end.

> First, it will be helpful because it is so general that it enables him to get a bird's eye view of his material which is always an extremely helpful thing to do.

> Second, toward the end of his special study it will be helpful because it permits a freedom which comes with knowledge gained and digested. When a much more' specific classification has been studied and thoroughly mastered, the specific forms will be recognized almost intuitively with a broad sweep of understanding. This ability will come, however, only after long and thorough study of details.

> Third, there are many selections, particularly those of modern writers, which are difficult to classify any more specifically than as narrative, lyrical or dramatic; when this is true there is, of course, no reason for trying to classify them otherwise. The detailed classifications that follow are given simply to help the reader over the difficult places that he must inevitably find in his path. Where there are no difficult places he will have no need of help.

CHAPTER XIV
THE STORY

"The story is a narrative of real or, more usually, fictitious events, designed for the entertainment of the hearer or reader; a series of traditional or imaginary incidents forming the matter of such a narrative." *Murray's English Dictionary*.

KINDS OF STORIES

THERE are a great many different kinds of stories, depending upon the nature of their subject-matter: some of these are:

Primitive Stories	Myths
Fairy Stories	Legends
Animal Stories	Heroic Stories
Historical Stories	Ghost Stories
Love Stories	Fantastic Stories
Dramatic Stories	Adventure Stories

Stories that teach special lessons, indirectly, as allegories, parables and fables.

Stories that are made from extracts from novels or other works of literature.

THE PURPOSE OF THE STORY

The purpose of all stories is to entertain. They appeal to the imagination. They *may* teach important lessons but these should be *by the way* and should not be allowed to interfere with the main purpose of entertainment. The less conspicuous and obvious such lessons are, the better.

Stories are suitable as a form of entertainment, for people of all ages, classes and nationalities, and for practically all occasions, consequently, they may be used very extensively by the oral reader.

The Speaker and The Listener

In the oral interpretation of a story the reader speaks *for the author directly to the audience* except when the dialogue of characters is introduced. In such cases the reader must speak for the characters as well as for the author, but such dialogue should—almost invariably—be made subservient to the *story as a whole*, and the changes from narrator to character and back again should be made so simply and so unobtrusively that the audience is entirely unaware of anything but the *unfoldment of the events of the story*. The reader's object is to interest his hearers in these events and to entertain them by recounting the events. In order to do this the reader must catch the attention of the audience at the beginning of the narration and hold it to the end, by making the happenings so real that his hearers follow them with unbroken eagerness. The reader should unfold the events of the story in *close and lively sequence* as if they were vivid and *actual experiences*, one thing following fast upon another and growing out of it, or related to it, in a way that keeps his hearers keenly anxious to know what is coming next.

The reader should so fully interest his hearers *in the story* that they lose themselves in it completely. They should have no idea what the reader is doing or how he is doing it, but they should follow the *story* so closely that they could tell it in their own words from beginning to end without omitting any of the *essential* parts.

Impersonation in Stories

When characters appear in stories and speak for themselves the reader should identify himself with them in thought, emotion and purpose. His facial expression, bodily carriage and positions, and his gestures, should all *suggest* the character when the character is speaking, but, as a very general rule, more than a suggestion of characterization or impersonation is not desirable, since there is great danger of

overdoing it and thereby getting away from the main purpose
of the story.

The *characters* in a story are almost invariably *incidental
to the plot* and should be suggested just enough to make them
play their part in the unfoldment of the plot in a natural and
convincing way, but not enough to take the listener's attention away from the plot to the characters themselves. Even
if the story is a character study the character is almost invariably revealed through the unfoldment of the plot.

As a rule, it is better to impersonate too little in a story—
or in any other form of literature—than too much.

THE RHYTHM OF STORIES

The rhythm of the story is, in a *general* way, the rhythm
of daily speech with its stressed syllables occurring at amaz-
ingly regular intervals and its unstressed syllables more or
less *crowded* around the stressed ones. But this *general*
rhythm is so affected by countless different influences brought
to bear upon it by the nature and quality of each story that
it gives to each one a *special* rhythm of its own. It is practically impossible to even hint at a way to find the subtle but
distinctive rhythm that lies within the lines and between the
lines of every well written story. Such a rhythm cannot be
brought out wholly by *tangible* means, only a spirit can catch
it, a spirit that is in harmony with the spirit of its *author*. The
rhythm is there and the *reader* must sense it, feel it, hear it,
live it, and then *reveal* it.

Contrast the delightful swing of Carl Sandburg's *Rootabaga Stories* with the equally delightful but vastly different
swing of Kipling's '*Just So*' *Stories*. Note the stately rhythm
of the stories of Victor Hugo and the modern gallop of those
of George Ade or Irvin Cobb. Each rhythm moves in harmony with the subject matter and its moods. The oral reader
should catch the pulse-beat of each story, regulate his step
to harmonize with it, and follow it in perfect time to the end.

SHORT EXTRACTS SHOWING THE RHYTHM OF STORIES

"It was a long, long way from here I saw them"
he went on,
"it would take years and years
to ride to where they are.
They were sitting together and talking to each other,
sometimes singing,
in a place where the land runs high
and tough rocks reach up.
And they were looking out across water,
blue water
as far as the eye could see.
And away far off
the blue waters
met the blue sky."

From *The White Horse Girl and The Blue Wind Boy*. In Carl
Sandburg's *Rootabaga Stories*.
Harcourt, Brace and Company, Publishers.

"When Carol had walked for thirty-two minutes
she had completely covered the town,
east and west, north and south.
    Main Street
with its two-story brick shops,
its muddy expanse from concrete walk to walk,
its huddle of Fords and lumber-wagons,
was too small to absorb her.
The broad, straight unenticing gashes of the street
let in the grasping prairie on every side.
She told herself
that down the street the leaves were a splendor,
the maples were orange,
the oaks a solid tint of raspberry,
and the lawns had been nursed with love.
But the thought would not hold."

From *Main Street*. Sinclair Lewis.
Harcourt, Brace and Company, Publishers.

MR. LOBEL'S APOPLEXY

"First let us introduce our principal.
Reader meet Mr. Max Lobel,

President of Lobel Masterfilms, Inc.,
also its founder, its chief stockholder and its general manager.
He is a short, broad, thick, globular man
and a bald one,
wearing gold-rimmed spectacles,
carrying a gold-headed cane
and using a private gold-mounted tooth pick after meals.

.   .   .   .

when he walks he favors his feet.
Mostly though,
he rides in as good a car
as domestic currency can buy in foreign marts.

.   .   .   .

Mr. Lobel has not always been in the moving-picture business.
Nobody in the moving-picture business
has always been in the moving-picture business—
excepting some of the child wonders
under ten years of age."
From *Sundry Accounts*, by Irvin S. Cobb.
Coypright 1922 by Doubleday Doran and Company, Inc.

"From either end of that narrow, terrible ledge
the third night was closing in;
It was dropping down on them
from the heights of the mountain
and slipping up to them
out of the abyss,
the third night since Loma blazed
and they had left it.

Three more days of tramping
should bring them in triumph home,
and yet their instincts said
that all was scarcely well.

.   .   .   .

Though in the heights
the fleecy clouds were idle,
yet the wind was stirring mournfully
in the abyss
and moaning as it stirred,

unhappily at first
and full of sorrow;
but as day turned away from that awful path
a very definite menace
entered its voice
which fast grew louder and louder
and night came on with a long howl.

. . . .

It seemed that the wind
was saying . . . some dreadful thing
in a tongue that they did not know,
They listened,
but they could not tell what it said."

From *The Loot of Loma.* Lord Dunsany
In *The Last Book of Wonder,* pp. 74, 75, 76.
John Luce and Company, Publishers. 1916.

Descriptive Narrative

In *reading* a story of description before an audience one may well heed the following advice given by J. H. Gardiner to the *writer* of stories.

"Your problem is rather to make other people know your impressions, and feel the feelings which are roused in you by what you are describing."

From *Forms of Prose Literature*, p. 166. Charles Scribner's
Sons, Publishers. 1912.

The Shipwreck (Abridged).

As the night advanced, it came on to blow harder and harder. I had been in Yarmouth when the seamen said it blew great guns, but I had never known the like of this, or anything approaching it.

The tremendous sea itself, when I could find pause to look at it, in the agitation of the blinding wind, the flying stones and sand, and the awful noise, confounded me. As the high watery walls came rolling in, and tumbled into surf, I seemed to see a rending and upheaving of all nature. The height to which the breakers rose and bore one another down, and rolled in, in interminable hosts, was most appalling.

In the difficulty of hearing anything but wind and waves, and in the unspeakable confusion, I looked out to sea for the wreck, and saw nothing but the foaming heads of the great waves.

A boatman laid a hand upon my arm and pointed. Then I saw it, close in upon us. But a great cry, audible even above the wind and water, rose from the shore; the sea sweeping over the wreck, made a clean breach, and carried men, spars, casks, planks, bulwarks, heaps of such toys, into the boiling surge.

From *David Copperfield*. Charles Dickens.

SIMPLE NARRATIVE WITHOUT DIALOGUE

Sir Claude and Lady Wyverne turned back and made their way to the inn, which was now shrouded in the deep shadows of the rapidly approaching night.

At dinner the only other person in the room was a very smart and handsome young Arab, who, the waiter told them, was an officer in the Spahis, and was stationed at Algiers, but who was now on leave and going to the home of his father, an important Caïd in the Zibans district. Lady Wyverne looked at the guest with interest. He wore a snowy turban and a red jacket, and between the white and the red his magnificent black eyes sparkled impudently, and his teeth gleamed as he smiled at the waiter, to whom he addressed a few words in excellent French. His face was extraordinarily expressive, brilliant but cruel and startlingly intelligent.

All through dinner Sir Claude was talking about Barbary Sheep. When dinner was over he cast a drowsy glance towards the young Spahi, who had just picked up a walnut out of a fruit-dish and was holding it delicately in his slim fingers. The Spahi looked demurely down. Sir Claude and Lady Wyverne rose and turned to leave the room. A sharp little sound rang through the room. Sir Claude turned. The Spahi had cracked the nut with his fingers and was smiling gently as he extracted the kernel. Sir Claude frowned and turned quickly to speak to Lady Wyverne but she had vanished from the room and he followed her.

The Spahi looked after them, got up, lit a cigarette, and strolled out into the little paved enclosure, above which the veranda projected. He leaned against a pillar and stood motionless staring toward the white road that wound away among the shadows toward the desert.

Sir Claude went to bed. Lady Wyverne tucked him up then at the familiar sound of his first snore, she went out on the veranda. The Spahi heard the rustle of her gown above him in the still night and smiled. Nobody was about. After a minute he moved away from the pillar, turned and stood motionless facing the veranda, but did not look up. Lady Wyverne watched him curiously. He puzzled her. The place puzzled her, the vast and unknown desert in which the man was born and bred. A sensation of awe crept over her and she began to wonder.

When a woman begins to wonder there is no limit to her mental journeyings. A voice startled Lady Wyverne. A voice, singing or rather murmuring a soft, uncouth almost weird tune. She listened leaning over the balustrade. By degrees the singing began to affect her almost painfully, to play upon her nerves. Who was the singer? She tried to locate the sound. It seemed to come from where the Spahi was standing. Was it really he who was singing—was this a serenade? She smiled, and took her arms from the rail. When she moved the Spahi moved too. He walked softly across the little court, lifted his head and showed Lady Wyverne his dark face with lips moving. He was the singer and now, almost insolently he sent the song to her.

Lady Wyverne was accustomed to admiration, even to worship, but this was a new experience. Almost before she realized what she was doing she had smiled at the Spahi. He stopped singing and smiled up at her. Then he spoke, as if to speak with her was the most natural thing in the world."

From *Barbary Sheep* by Robert Hichens, (abridged).
Methuen and Company, Ltd. London, 1911.

Combination of Narrative and Dialogue

Lady Wyverne and the Spahi were walking together slowly down the moonlit road between the towering rocks of the gorge that led to the Sahara. The night sky was a deep purple and the noise of the waters of the river was in their ears.

The Spahi was silent thinking of his departure tomorrow to the house of his father. He wore over his shoulders a great red cloak which swung gently to and fro as he walked on with the magnificent dignity and pride which are the birthright of the Arab race. Lady Wyverne glanced up at him sideways and his eyes flashed on her like fire. What a gulf was fixed between her and this man with whom she was adventurously walking through the savage solitude. And yet his cloak as it swung touched the skirt of her gown and she could see the fire sparkling in his eyes as he bent his head down when she spoke to him. She had a capricious desire to find some bridge across this gulf and to venture upon it.

"This was where we stopped last night," he said, "one step farther tonight Madam." He pointed with his hand outstretched and the red folds of his cloak flowing down from his arm. "The desert calls us Madam—listen." She listened like one in expectation of some distant voice from the far away that lay beyond the spaces her eyes could see. But in the deep silence of the night she heard only the murmur of the river flowing into the moving shadows of the palms. "There's no voice" she said.

"There is for me" he answered.

"But I am a son of the desert. I love it. I belong to it. It has no secrets from me. I have learned all its lessons."

(Lady Wyverne)	"Could I learn them too?"
(The Spahi)	"One can learn what one chooses to learn. I have learned to be a French officer."
(Lady Wyverne petulantly)	"You know as well as I do that men can do a thousand things women can't do."
(The Spahi)	"Even a woman can go a step further."
(Lady Wyverne)	"Oh well—I don't mind—but the atmosphere of the desert tires me."
(The Spahi)	"It gives life to me. That is the difference between us. I am awake and alive. You are dozing—and he— Milord, your husband—he is fast asleep. You could be awake as I am awake, you could be alive as I am alive if only"—he paused a moment and looked at her more intently—"if only you were not afraid of being alive and of feeling joy."

He seemed to tower above her. His great cloak made him look vast in the night—vast and enveloping. He was so close to her that she felt the warmth of his great red cloak and smelt the faint odour of some strange Oriental perfume that came from the folds of his scarlet and white garments. It suggested mystery and something else, a distant ecstacy that might be reached by going forward. The Spahi, watching her face in the moonlight, read with the swift certainty of the Arab, all that was passing in her mind. He laughed softly, "You are afraid Madam, very much afraid."

At this moment there was a shrill cry in the darkness of the gorge, that sounded half human, half animal. Lady Wyverne started and instinctively clung to the Spahi's arm. Instantly his arm and the warm folds of his cloak were around her. The cry rose up at once more shrill and nearer. Then out of the gorge into the moonlight on the road there came a man capering and running. His face was fair and pale, like the face of a Christ, with curling yellow-brown beard and vacant restless blue eyes. In his hands he held an enormous staff. "Allah! Allah!" he shrieked, whirling the staff round and round and then pointing it suddenly to right and left. Lady Wyverne cowered close against the Spahi. To her strung up imagination it seemed as if the gorge had suddenly let loose a crazy Messiah to point a finger of condemnation at her. The Spahi, keeping his arm round her protectingly said softly, "It's only the mad Marabout. He was a rich man who loved a dancing girl. One night the girl was murdered for her jewels. Since then he has been mad. By night he wanders, seeking the girl and calling upon Allah to assist him."

Suddenly the Spahi lifted his voice in a powerful cry—"Allah Allah"—Instantly the Marabout began once more to whirl his staff. He capered along the road toward the desert until he was lost in the night.

Then, Lady Wyverne, became *aware* of the arm about her. She moved quickly and it fell away. But as they walked back to the inn she still seemed to feel it, as one who has been touched by a powerful hypnotist seems to feel the magnetic hand long after it had been removed.

That night, as she lay awake, listening to the sound of the river passing on its way to the Sahara, she was troubled as she had never been troubled before. She was thinking of the perfume that clung about the folds of the Spahi's cloak;

of a revolver ready to protect her, an arm that felt like iron under a scarlet cloak, black eyes that were fierce as a hawk's or velvety with tenderness. What was this man? His manners were perfect even in their occasional impudence. Was his real nature gentle or barbarous? And his heart? Had he been cruel to women?

Suddenly Lady Wyverne got up, and went into her husband's room. She sat down on a chair by his bed and touched his long body with her little hand. He loved her, he would defend her against the world, he would lie down for her to tread upon if she desired it—and, there was no mystery in him.

From *Barbary Sheep*, by Robert Hichens.

EXTRACT WHICH DEPICTS AND VIVIFIES ACTION

The King
sat listening to the busy hum among the soldiery.
The voice of the soldiers was loud and cheerful.
Some were playing at games,
others spoke together of the approaching battle,
and several lay asleep.

Amid these careless warders
glided the puny form of a little old Turk,
poorly dressed
like a marabout of the desert.
When he approached
so nigh as to receive some interruption from the warders,
he dashed his green turban from his head,
showed that his beard and eyebrows were shaved
like those of a professed buffoon,
and that the expression of his fantastic and writhen features
was that of a crazed imagination.

"Dance, marabout,"
cried the soldiers,
"or we will scourge thee with our bow-strings."

The marabout,
as if happy to do their behests,
bounded from the earth,

spun his giddy round before them
with singular agility,
which made him resemble a withered leaf
twirled round and round
at the pleasure of the winter's breeze.
He flew here and there,
approaching,
almost imperceptibly,
to the entrance of the royal tent,
so that, when at length he sunk exhausted on the earth,
after two or three bounds
still higher than those yet executed,
he was not above thirty yards from the King's person.

"Give him water," said one yeoman.
The dervise *seemed* to drink the large flagon
to the very bottom.
When he took it from his lips,
he uttered with a deep sigh
"Allah kerim,"
or God is merciful.
There was a laugh among the yeomen,
so obstreperous
as to disturb the King,
who said angrily,
"How, knaves,
no respect,
no observance?"
All retreated in haste
leaving the dervise on the ground,
unable, it seemed,
to stir.

For the space of a quarter of an hour,
all remained quiet.
The King read and mused
at the entrance of his pavilion;
behind, and with his back turned to the same entrance,
the Nubian slave
burnished the ample pavesse.
But the Nubian had the advantage of a mirror,
which the surface of the highly polished shield afforded,
by means of which he beheld,

that the marabout raised his head
so as to survey all about him.
As if satisfied he was unobserved
he began to drag himself
nearer and nearer to the King.
He glided on,
imperceptibly,
serpent-like,
till he was about ten yards from Richard,
when,
starting on his feet,
he sprung forward
with the bound of a tiger,
stood at the King's back
and brandished aloft the poniard
which he had hidden in his sleeve.
But ere he could strike,
the Nubian
caught his uplifted arm
and dashed him to the ground.

Richard had arisen
and with little more surprise or interest
than an ordinary man would show
in brushing off and crushing an intrusive wasp,
caught up the stool on which he had been sitting
and exclaiming,
"Ha, dog!"
dashed almost to pieces
the skull of the assassin,
who uttered,
"Allah ackbar!"
—God is victorious—
and expired
at the King's feet.
From *The Talisman*. Sir Walter Scott.

Stories Not Listed Here

It seems superfluous to attempt to make a list of stories for the reader's use when there are hundreds of lists given in every library. These will give a far greater variety than could possibly be given here, and each reader can make his own choice according to his taste and his needs.

CHAPTER XV

ORATIONS, SPEECHES, ADDRESSES

An *oration* is an elaborate and dignified public discourse.

A *speech* is a formal discourse in public.

An *address* is a formal communication either written or spoken.

The three terms may be used synonomously.

> Note. The preparation of the subject matter of orations is a study in itself and is apart from the purpose of this text which is concerned only with the oral *delivery* of the forms of literature. Written orations must not be confused with *extemporaneous* speeches.

THE PURPOSE OF AN ORATION, SPEECH OR ADDRESS

THERE are many purposes of orations, speeches or addresses.

1. It may be to convince, to explain, to outline, to define, to clarify, etc., all of which appeal particularly to the *intelligence*.

    Example: *Eloquence*. Daniel Webster.

2. It may be to win, to inspire, to persuade, to comfort, to ennoble, etc., all of which appeal particularly to the *feelings*.

    Example: *The Character of Washington*. Edward Everett.

3. It may be to arouse others to *action*, to get something done, making a particular appeal to the desire *to do, to act*, to *accomplish something*, or it may be to *depict* and *make vivid* some *action* that has already taken place.

    Example: *Spartacus to the Gladiators*. Elijah Kellogg.

While there is a special and particular purpose in each speech which is distinctly individual, and which is unlike the purpose in other speeches, nevertheless the purpose of most speeches can be classed in a *general* way under the heads just mentioned.

THE SPEAKER AND THE LISTENER

An oration must be spoken directly to the audience. No matter who wrote it, it must seem to be the original, personal, and spontaneous expression of the one who is *delivering* it. In delivering an oration the interpreter *always* takes the place of the author. He should imagine himself to be speaking *at the time, in the place,* and *under the conditions* that the author had in mind when he wrote the oration.

IMPERSONATION IN ORATIONS

There can be no impersonation in orations, speeches or addresses, unless, perhaps, for momentary satire or humor.

THE RHYTHM OF ORATIONS

The rhythm of orations should be the rhythm of *daily speech* but this will be influenced by the particular mood of each oration, whether it be didactic, informative, persuasive, inspiring, consoling, or animated. But no matter what may be the nature of the thought expressed in an oration, or the nature of the emotion, or the occasion upon which it is given, the orator must *talk* to his audience and he must talk in a manner fitting the time, place and occasion, and the nature of the thought he is expressing.

SUGGESTIONS FOR THE DELIVERY OF AN ORATION

An oration may be:
1. read *wholly* from a manuscript,
2. it may be partially committed to memory with *occasional references* to the manuscript,
3. it may be entirely committed to memory.

Orations Read Wholly from Manuscript

It is extremely difficult for any one to read an oration or an address *wholly* from a manuscript and make it really interesting to his hearers. One of the most important points in the delivery of such an oration is the vital *personal contact* which the orator establishes with his hearers by looking directly into their eyes, watching their response to what he says, and governing his manner of procedure accordingly. If he is obliged to keep his eyes on his manuscript, practically all of this contact is lost, and no matter how excellent the subject matter may be he almost invariably loses the interest of his hearers and they become restless. The speaker's own reactions which are—or should be—revealed by his facial expression and his whole bodily attitude and bearing, are very largely, if not wholly, lost to the audience when his attention must be concentrated on the page of his manuscript.

To read an oration wholly from manuscript is the most *undesirable* and *least effective* way of presenting it to an audience.

Orations Partially Committed to Memory
with Occasional References to the Manuscript

There are many *very formal* occasions on which it is usually considered good form for the speaker to have the manuscript of his address before him, and to which he should refer occasionally, as a matter of form, if not of necessity. Such formal occasions are:

> Inauguration of Presidents,
> Laying of corner stones of public buildings,
> Dedications,
> Unveiling of important monuments,
> Funerals of important national characters,
> Baccalaureate addresses,
> Installation of pastors of great churches.

The reference to the manuscript at such times is intended to add dignity and importance to the occasion, as if to indicate that the proper care and consideration had been given to the preparation of the address. This, however, is only a matter of form which has developed into a custom; a custom which shows some signs of changing.

Even when the presence of the manuscript is necessitated by convention, it is well for the speaker to know the address as well as he would know it if the manuscript were absent; then his occasional references to it can be made where they will least interfere with his contact with his audience, causing little or no interruption. There are always points in an address at which the thought changes definitely, where a speaker may consult his manuscript without breaking the attention of his hearers.

ORATIONS WHOLLY COMMITTED TO MEMORY

An oration wholly committed to memory offers the *greatest possibilities* of *effective presentation* as well as very *great dangers of ineffective presentation.*

An oration—or any other piece of literature—should be so thoroughly committed to memory that the interpreter can entirely forget about the lines. The lines should be as completely and entirely his own as they would be if they were actually conceived in his own mind at the moment of utterance. He must *never* have to hesitate a second for a word; if he does, it interrupts the flow of thought, interferes with the expression of his purpose, taking the hearer's attention from *what* is said and centering it on the speaker's difficulty in saying it. The speaker's whole attention must be concentrated on *what* he is saying and *why* he is saying it. *How* he is to say it must have been completely mastered previously, so that it does not enter into his consideration at all while the speech is being delivered to an audience.

Only when the oration has been *completely committed to memory* and *wholly assimilated* is the speaker *free* to do his best and he *must* be free in order that he *may* do his best.

Dangers to Avoid in Delivering an Oration
Wholly Committed to Memory

Three of the outstanding dangers for the interpreter to avoid in delivering an oration which has been committed to memory are:

1. insincerity
2. unnaturalness
3. artificiality

These may be avoided by a thorough understanding of the meaning and purpose of the speech—which may be gained by heeding the *suggestions* given at the end of this chapter— by full sympathy with it, by absolute memorization of the lines, by sufficient practice to make the given lines *express* the *author's* meaning and purpose sympathetically, but as if they were original and spontaneous. The speech must flow clearly, distinctly, smoothly and pleasingly, without apparent or conscious effort. Very decided *conscious effort* is necessary in one's *preparation* in order that the final rendition may *seem* to be effortless and natural. The type of so-called oratory that is a *display of the orator's personal talents* is not true oratory and is intolerable under all circumstances and not worthy of any further comment. While the orator's personal talents are of the utmost importance, they must be used for service, not for display.

Preparation for the Delivery of an Oration

1. State its *purpose* in one or two sentences.
2. Note each step made in the *carrying out* of this purpose.
3. Note the *relative* force and *importance* of each step.
4. Where is the *climax?* or, what is the turning point in the argument?
5. Where does it begin to *go down* after the climax is reached?
6. Where does the *conclusion* begin?

7. What should be the *reactions of the audience* if the speech is producing the desired effect?
8. How may one *take the greatest advantage of these reactions* without the audience being aware of it?

EXTRACTS FROM ORATIONS

No. 1—The purpose is to explain, clarify, define, etc.

"Human sagacity
stimulated by human wants,
seizes first on the nearest natural assistant.
The power of his own arm
is an early lesson among the studies of primitive man.
This is animal strength;
and from this
he rises to the conception
of employing for his own use
the strength of other animals.
A stone
impelled by the power of his arm
he finds will produce a greater effect
than the arm itself:
this is a species of mechanical power."

From *Progress of the Mechanic Arts*, by Daniel Webster.
Delivered before the Boston Mechanics' Institution, 1828.
In *The World's Best Orations*, Editor, David J. Brewer.
Fred P. Kaiser, St. Louis, Mo. 1901. Volume 10, page 3856.

No. 2—The purpose is to inspire, ennoble, eulogize.

"I do not think I exaggerate when I say that never since God made Demosthenes has He made a man better fitted for a great work than O'Connell.

You may say I am partial to my hero; but John Randolph of Roanoke, who hated an Irishman . . . when he heard O'Connell, exclaimed, "This is the man, those are the lips, the most eloquent that speak English in my day." . . .

The wonder about O'Connell was that he could out-talk Corwin, he could charm a college better than Everett, and leave Henry Clay himself far behind in magnetizing a senate. . . . . He never took a leaf from our American gospel of compromise; he never filed his tongue to silence on one truth fancying so to help another; . . .

When I was in Naples I asked Sir Thomas Foxwell Buxton, "Is Daniel O'Connell an honest man?" "As honest a man as ever breathed" he said. . . .

Beside his irreproachable character, he had what is half the power of a popular orator, he had a majestic presence . . . and he had what Webster never had, the magnetism and grace that melts a million souls into his.

When I saw him he was sixty-five, lithe as a boy. His every attitude was beauty, his every gesture grace. . . .

It would have been a pleasure even to look at him if he had not spoken at all, and all you thought of was a greyhound. And then he had what so few American speakers have, a voice that sounded the gamut. I heard him once in Exeter Hall say, "Americans, I send my voice careering like the thunder storm across the Atlantic, to tell South Carolina that God's thunderbolts are hot, and to remind the negro that the dawn of his redemption is drawing near," and I seemed to hear his voice reverberating and re-echoing back to London from the Rocky Mountains. And then, with the slightest possible flavor of an Irish brogue, he would tell a story that would make all Exeter Hall laugh, and the next moment there were tears in his voice, like an old song, and five thousand men would be in tears. And all the while no effort—he seemed only breathing.

'As effortless as woodland nooks
Send violets up and paint them blue,' "

From *Oration on the Centennial of the Birth of O'Connell.*
    Wendell Phillips.

No. 3—The purpose is to arouse others to action.
Ye stand here now like giants,
as ye are!
The strength of brass
is in your toughened sinews,
but to-morrow some Roman Adonis
shall, with his lily fingers
pat your red brawn,
and bet his sesterces upon your blood.
Hark!

hear ye yon lion roaring in his den?
'Tis three days
since he tasted flesh,
but to-morrow
he shall break his fast upon yours.
If ye are beasts,
then stand here like fat oxen,
waiting for the butcher's knife!
If you are men,
follow me!
Strike down your guard,
gain the mountain passes,
and then do bloody work,
as did your sires
at old Thermopylae!
Is Sparta dead?
Is the old Grecian spirit
frozen in your veins?
O comrades!
warriors!
if we must fight,
let us fight for ourselves!
If we must slaughter,
let us slaughter our oppressors!
If we must die,
let it be under the clear sky,
by the bright waters,
in noble, honorable battle.

From *Spartacus to the Gladiators.* Elijah Kellogg.
In *Choice Readings*, p. 263, Robert McLean Cumnock.
A. C. McClurg and Company, Chicago. 1892.

EXTRACTS FROM A EULOGY

Nomination of U. S. Grant.
(Delivered at the Republican Presidential Convention at
Chicago, June 5, 1880)
". . . Ulysses S. Grant—
never defeated
in peace or in war
his name is the most illustrious
borne by living man.

His services attest his greatness,
and the country,—
nay, the world—
know them by heart.
His fame was earned
not alone in things written and said,
but by the arduous greatness of things done.
And perils and emergencies
will search in vain in the future,
as they have searched in vain in the past,
for any other,
on whom the nation leans with such confidence and trust.
Never having had a policy to enforce
against the will of the people,
he never betrayed a cause or a friend,
and the people
will never desert or betray him.
Standing on the highest eminence of human distinction
modest, firm,
simple and self-poised,
having filled all lands with his renown,
he has seen
not only the high-born and the titled,
but the poor and the lowly,
in the uttermost ends of the earth,
rise and uncover before him.
He has studied the needs and the defects
of many systems of government,
and he has returned
a better American than ever,
with a wealth of knowledge and experience
added to the hard common-sense
which shone so conspicuously
in all the fierce light that beat upon him
during sixteen years,
the most trying, the most portentous, the most perilous
in the nation's history.
         . . . assaults upon him
have seasoned and strengthened
his hold on the public heart,
and the name of Grant will glitter
a bright and imperishable star
in the diadem of the republic
when those who have tried to tarnish that name

have mouldered in forgotten graves,
and when their memories and their epitaphs
have vanished utterly.

. . . .

Roscoe Conkling.

From *Life and Letters of Roscoe Conkling, Orator, Statesman
and Advocate*. P. 596.
By Alfred R. Conkling. C. L. Webster Co., New York, 1889.

*EXTRACT FROM "THE WILL OF PEACE"
(Delivered before the Members of the League of Nations Non-
Partisan Association, January 10, 1927.)

. . . .

As a people
we seem just now
not to be able to grasp the fact
that it is given to us
to stand at one of the turning points of human history
and to watch the great procession of the ages
as it changes its line of march
and alters its objective.
One wonders
whether when Ancient Greece was passing,
the leaders of Greek thought and letters
knew that it was passing.
When the Roman Empire
was tottering to its fall,
did the men of light and leading
really understand
that a stupendous change was going on?
Did the men of the Renaissance
have any conception
of the period through which they lived
and to which they made such powerful contribution?
Did the political philosophers of England and France
of the 17th and 18th Centuries
realize
that they were teaching ideas and thoughts
that were to make a new political and social and economic
world?

---

*Reprinted with special permission of Dr. Nicolas Murray Butler,
author, and Charles Scribner's Sons, Publishers.

Do we know—
do we realize—
that the long process of nation-building
that has been going on in the western world
now for more than a thousand years
has come to a substantial end,
and that those nations—
built
many of them on strong and firm foundations,
others
still in the first flush of youth—
are seeking,
some of them in darkness,
for ways and means to clasp hands together
to make a new form of human unity,
of human cooperation,
of expression of human effort,
that shall destroy no nation
but enrich them all?
He must be blind and deaf
who cannot see and hear the signs of the times.
Locarno
from being only the name
of a little town by a mountain lake,
has become a significant symbol
that will take its place in the long list of names
that mark the progress of man's march,
first toward liberty,
then toward that fine and noble and lofty use of liberty
which is human cooperation
and international peace.

.   .   .   .

Nicholas Murray Butler.

EXTRACT FROM "THE MEANING OF THE DECLARATION
OF INDEPENDENCE."

(Delivered by the President of the United States at Independence Hall, July 4, 1914)

.   .   .   .

Have you ever read
the Declaration of Independence

or attended with close comprehension
to the real character of it
when you have heard it read?
If you have,
you will know that it is not a Fourth of July oration.
The Declaration of Independence
was a document preliminary to war.
It was a vital piece of practical business,
not a piece of rhetoric;

. . . .

it consists of a series of definite specifications
concerning actual public business of the day.
Not the business of our day,
for the matter with which it deals is past,
but the business of that first revolution
by which the nation was set up,
the business of 1776 . . .
        In one sense
the Declaration of Independence
has lost its significance . . .
Nobody outside of America
believed
when it was uttered
that we could make good our independence;
now
nobody anywhere
would dare to doubt that we are independent
and can maintain our independence . . .
Our independence
is a fact so stupendous
that it can be measured
only by the size and energy
and variety and wealth and power
of one of the greatest nations in the world.
But it is one thing to be independent
and it is another thing
to know what to do with your independence.

. . . .

What are we going to do
with the influence and power
of this great nation?

. . . .

My dream is
that as the years go on
and the world knows more and more of America
it will . . . turn to America
for those moral inspirations
which lie at the basis of all freedom;
that the world will never fear America
unless it feels that it is engaged in some enterprise
which is inconsistent with the rights of humanity;
and that America will come into the full light of day
when all shall know
that she puts human rights
above all other rights
and that her flag
is the flag not only of America
but of humanity.

. . . .

I do not know that there will ever be
a declaration of independence and of grievances
for mankind,
but I believe
that if any such document is ever drawn
it will be drawn
in the spirit of the American Declaration of Independence,
and that America
has lifted high the light
which will shine unto all generations
and guide the feet of mankind
to the goal
of justice
and liberty
and peace.

                        Woodrow Wilson

In *Modern Short Speeches.* Compiled by James Milton O'Neill.
The Century Company, New York and London, 1923.

COLLECTIONS OF ORATIONS OR ADDRESSES

The Forms of Public Address. Edited by George Pierce Baker.
Henry Holt and Company, New York, 1904.

The World's Best Orations. 10 volumes. Edited by David J.
  Brewster. Fred P. Kaiser, St. Louis, Missouri, 1901.
Classified Speech Models. William Norwood Brigance. F. S.
  Crofts and Company, New York, 1928.
Classified Models of Speech Composition. Compiled by J.
  M. O'Neill.
Modern Short Speeches. Compiled by James Milton O'Neill.
Contemporary Speeches. Compiled by James Milton O'Neill
  and Floyd K. Riley. The Century Company, New York,
  1926, 1923, 1930, respectively.
Modern Eloquence. 15 volumes. Edited by Thomas B. Reed.
  George L. Shuman and Company, Chicago, 1900.

BOOKS ON THE PREPARATION AND DELIVERY
OF A SPEECH

The Method of Argument. Charles A. Fritz.
Speaking in Public. Arleigh B. Williamson. Prentice-Hall,
  Incorporated, Publishers, 1931 and 1929 respectively.

CHAPTER XVI

THE ESSAY

"An *essay* is a short piece of prose, not attempting to treat its subject completely nor logically, but rather giving the author's opinions upon it; opinions which may or may not be serious, but which are set forth with a high degree of literary art. It usually reveals more or less of the personality of the author, and in this respect corresponds in prose to the lyric in poetry."

Types of the Essay. B. A. Heydrick.
Charles Scribner's Sons, Publishers.

". . . the personal note . . . becomes the final test for distinguishing the essay from its allied forms."

The Essay in American Literature. A. M. Conway.
Published by the Faculty of the Graduate School, New York University.

THE PURPOSE OF THE ESSAY

BRIEFLY, the purpose of the essay is to *teach*, to *inspire*, to *expound*. However, these cold and formal terms tell only partial truths about one of the most delightful of literary forms; it is about as adequate as saying a mother is one who feeds and shelters her young.

The essay may deal with any subject; history, religion, society, philosophy, nature, art, things, qualities, *anything;* it may treat the subject humorously or seriously; it may express opinions or beliefs; it does not, *as a whole*, tell a story but brief and thrilling *stories* or suggestions of stories may be extracted from it; *as a whole*, it is supposed to have little to do with *emotion*, but many touching and tender heart throbs run through its pages ready to reward the sensitive reader who can find and feel its pulse; theoretically, it has little, if any, *action*, and none of the *dramatic* element, but in *reality* it may recount vigorous action of great dramatic significance. Its *form* is *studied* and *artistic*.

Types of Essays

B. A. Heydrick in *Types of the Essay* (Charles Scribner's Sons, Publishers), lists them as follows:

The Personal Essay, Lamb, *Old China*.
The Descriptive Essay, Thoreau, *Brute Neighbors*.
The Character Sketch, Goldsmith's, *Man in Black*.
The Critical Essay, Ruskin, *What and How to Read*.
The Editorial Essay, Topics of the Times, *In Good Newspapers*.
The Reflective Essay, Emerson, *Self Reliance*.

Speaker and Listener

The interpreter speaks *for* the *author, directly to* the *audience*.

Impersonation in the Essay

There is no impersonation in the essay.

Rhythm of the Essay

The rhythm of the essay is the rhythm of careful, elegant, cultivated conversation.

The mood of each essay will determine whether the movement of the reading should be fast or slow, stately or vigorous, solemn or merry.

The Essay May be Used for Oral Reading

The essay offers an extensive and practically unexplored field of riches to the discriminating oral interpreter. Readers are very often misled by the fact that the purpose of the essay is *to teach, to inspire, to expound* and that its diction is elegant and literary; consequently they discard it bodily as a form of literature to be used for purposes of entertainment. This is unfortunate, for snugly nestling within a countless number of apparently severe and formal essays—reminding one of an unexpected cosy nook with comfortable easy chair and foot-stool, lamp and inviting book, which is tucked partly out of sight in a formal drawing room—are fascinating short stories, exquisite expressions of deep emotions or of moments of intensely dramatic action. It is these that the oral reader must seek and *extract from the essay as a whole,* and add as rich and interesting treasures to his repertoire. While they will *not be as universally popular* as some other forms of literature, they will be found of exceptional value for *special audiences* and special *occasions.* Such extracts have a particular charm of their own which is to be found in no other form of literature. Perhaps the best essays for this use are those which are written in a lighter vein, such as Charles Lamb's universal favorite, *Dissertation Upon Roast Pig.*

Excellent and entertaining lessons in natural history are to be found in some essays which will delight children as well as adults. Examples of these are *an experience with a loon,* and, *a battle of the red and black ants* from Thoreau's *Brute Neighbors.*

There can be no more pleasant way of giving to others brief and interesting glimpses of famous men than by reading extracts concerning them from such essays as Hazlitt's *My First Acquaintance With Poets,* which gives a not-to-be-forgotten impression of Coleridge, or Julian Street's *The Spirit of Theodore Roosevelt,* which gives a loving picture of the human side of a great statesman.

It would be difficult to find a more tender picture of the private life of a great writer than that which Charles Lamb gives of himself in his essay on *Old China.* By eliminating all except that portion of the essay which depicts the past and present life of Lamb and his sister Mary, one has made a reading which is a rare gem and which is quite certain to touch the heart strings of thousands of men and women who have had experiences similar to those recounted in the essay.

Nothing could be more fitting or more effective for certain occasions than short extracts from Emerson's *Self-Reliance* or Bacon's *Great Place*, or from countless other similar essays.

The use of extracts from essays for purposes of oral reading has many advantages for both reader and audience. One of these advantages is to be had in the *acquaintance it gives with excellent English*. Good essays offer the strongest proof that elegant and beautiful English may be—and should be—genuinely simple, direct and sincere. A thorough acquaintance with such essays cannot fail to develop in both reader and hearer a more refined taste in their personal use of their own spoken English and a keener appreciation of it in others. It will impress upon students better than dozens of lectures could do, the fact that elegant spoken English is not artificial, stilted, cold nor lifeless.

The Oral Interpretation of Essays

In his analysis of each essay that he studies the oral interpreter should give special attention to the particular *way* in which the author *brings out* his purpose, since in many cases, it is not the *purpose* of the essay that has value, but the delightful and individual manner in which the subject is treated. The reader must first discover for himself the delights and charms of each essay and then *lead* the audience to share and enjoy these *with* him. In reading an essay aloud the contact between speaker and listener must be very close and friendly,—held by a strong bond of mutual interest, understanding and appreciation—or there will be no contact at all. The reader will find it imperative to give very close attention,—*in his preparation, not* in his final reading—to the proper grouping of words and the proper use of weak forms of words, in order that he may *appear* to be talking in an unstudied, sincere and natural manner. If *time, place* and *situation* are significant they, also, should be given adequate attention in the preparation of the essay.

EXTRACTS FROM ESSAYS

From THE SPIRIT OF THEODORE ROOSEVELT

We, whom Theodore Roosevelt
used proudly and affectionately to call his "fellow Americans,"
have always listened with great relish
to characteristic stories of him.

As long ago as when he was Governor of New York
it was his practice
to go every Saturday afternoon for a tramp in the country
with Mrs. Roosevelt and the children.
And it was understood between them
that in the course of all such tramps
he would lead them to some physical obstacle
which must be overcome.
Sometimes
it would be merely the obstacle of long distance
over a difficult terrain,
calling for sustained effort in the face of fatigue,
sometimes it would be a wide brook
to be crossed in a difficult place,
and on one memorable occasion
there was a steep cliff of crumbling slate
to be ascended and descended.

The idea
that Colonel and Mrs. Roosevelt attempted to fasten in the
    children's minds
was that life frequently presents obstacles
comparable with those encountered on these walks,
and that it is the part of good manhood and good womanhood
squarely to meet and surmount them,
going through or over
but never around.
Sometimes,
as in the adventure of the Slate Cliff,
there was danger.

The bank,
soft and almost perpendicular,
at first appeared insurmountable,
but after an hour and a half
all but one of that day's walking party
had managed to climb up and down again.

The exception was Alice Roosevelt,
then a girl of sixteen,
who, having reached the top,
found herself unable to descend.

On this day Elon Hooker,
an old friend of the Roosevelts,
was with them.
Walking along the base of the cliff,
this young man found a stout tree
growing up beside it.
Climbing the tree,
and leaning out
and, seizing with one hand a hummock of slate
at the crest of the little precipice,
offered his arm as a bridge
over which Alice could step into the tree,
whence it would be no very difficult matter
to climb down to earth.

The hummock was less secure than it appeared.
As she stepped upon his arm
the slate to which he was holding
broke away
and his arm fell beneath her.
She managed to grasp a branch,
and to this she clung
until he succeeded in catching her
and drawing her safely into the tree.

On reaching the ground
they discovered that the fallen mass of slate
had struck the Colonel
fairly on the head,
laying open his scalp
from the forehead
to a corresponding point at the back of the skull.
Though the wound bled freely,
they were immediately reassured by his smile.
Finding a brook,
they washed the gash as best they could;
later
a surgeon took a dozen stitches in the Colonel's scalp;

and, when, some ten days after,
he attended the Republican National Convention
he was none the worse for the accident.
Few persons knew of it at all,
for it was characteristic of him
to avoid any mention of his injuries or ailments.
He had an aversion
for the discussion of bodily ills.
And still, when others suffered
physically or spiritually,
he was the most solicitous,
the gentlest,
the tenderest of men.
He has taken his last tramp
with his children and with us.
And the one thing he would ask of us is this:
That we go on without him.
That we be foresighted,
prompt, practical, honest,
resolute,
courageous.
So, in ourselves,
we make his spirit live.

In *The Most Interesting American.* Julian Street.
Used by permission of D. Appleton-Century Company, Inc.

From ON WEARING A HAT

There's a good deal to be said about wearing a hat.
And yet this humorous custom,
this ripe topic, of wearing a hat
has been sadly neglected, as far as I can make out,
by scholars, scientists, poets, composers,
and other "smart" people.
Man has been variously defined,
as the religious animal, and so on;
but also,
to the best of my knowledge and belief,
he is the only animal that wears a hat.
He has become so accustomed to the habit of wearing his hat
that he does not feel that he is himself out of doors without it.
Mr. Howells (I think it was)

has told us in one of his novels
of a young man who determined upon suicide.
With this intent he made a dash for the sea.
But on his way there
a sudden gust of wind blew off his hat;
instinctively he turned to recover it,
and this action broke the current of his ideas.
With his hat he recovered his reason,
and went home as alive as usual.

His hat has come to mean for man
much more than a protection for his head.
It is for him a symbol of his manhood.
You cannot more greatly insult a man
than by knocking off his hat.
As a sign of his reverence,
his esteem, his respect,
a man bares his head. . . . . .
We express great joy
by casting our hats into the air.
If I wish to show my contempt for you,
I will wear my hat in your house;
If I wish you to clear out of my house,
I say: "Here's your hat";
If I am moved to admiration for you
I say: "I take off my hat to you."
I greatly enjoy seeing you run after your hat in the street,
because you are made thereby excessively ridiculous,

. . . .

The English painter, Thomas Gainsborough,
gave his name to a hat. . . .
A hat worn tilted well back on the head
indicates an open nature
and a hail-fellow-well-met disposition;
while a hat decidedly tilted over one eye
is the sign of a hard character,
and one not to be trifled with. . . .
Upon assuming office
the cardinal is said to "take the hat."
When a man is conspicuously active in American political
    life
"his hat is in the ring." . . .

The hat-stands in our swagger hotels
make a great deal of money;
I know a gentleman
who affirmed that a hat which originally cost him three
    dollars
had cost him eighteen dollars
to be got back from hat-checking stands.

. . . .

    Our grandfathers wore "stove-pipe hats;"
and the hats of politicians
were one time frequently called "plug hats."
This male headdress, . . . books of etiquette sometimes say
you should not call a "silk hat"
but a "high hat." . . .
Intoxicated gentlemen in funny pictures
have always smashed their silk hats.

    The day in the autumn
fixed by popular mandate,
when the straw hat is to be discarded for the season
is hilariously celebrated in Wall Street
by the destruction by the affronted populace
of the straw hats
of those who have had the temerity or the thoughtlessness to
    wear them.

. . . .

And now and then somebody turns up
with the idea in his head
that he doesn't need a hat on it.

. . . .

    The modern hat can be traced back to the *petasus*
worn by the ancient Romans when on a journey.

. . . .

Not until after the Norman Conquest
did the use of hats begin in England.
A "hatte of biever"
was worn by one of the "nobels of the lande,
mett at Clarendom"
about the middle of the twelfth century . . .
The use of the scarlet hat
which distinguishes cardinals

was sanctioned in the thirteenth century
by Pope Innocent IV. . . .
Throughout medieval times
the wearing of a hat was regarded as a mark of rank and
    distinction.

. . . .

The Puritans
affected a steeple crown and broad-brimmed hat,
while the Cavaliers
adopted a lower crown
and a broader brim ornamented with feathers.
In the times of Charles II
still greater breadth of brim and a profusion of feathers
were fashionable features of hats,
and the gradual expansion of the brim
led to the device of looping or tying up that portion.
Hence arose
various fasionable "cocks" in hats. . . .
The Quaker hat
plain, low in crown, and broad in brim,
originated with the sect
in the middle of the seventeenth century.
The silk hat
is an article of recent introduction. . . .
    So much for hats.

From *Walking Stick Papers*, by Robert Cortes Holliday.
George H. Doran and Company, Publishers, 1918.
Reprinted by special permission of the author.

From THE AMERICAN IDEAL

    There is nothing the matter with Americans
except their ideals.
The real American is all right;
it is the ideal American who is all wrong.
It is the code and conception of life
imposed from above,
much more than the merely human faults and weaknesses
working up from below.

. . . .

The real, natural Americans
are candid, generous,
capable of a beautiful wonder and gratitude;
enthusiastic about things external to themselves;
easily contented
and not particularly conceited.
They have been systematically educated
in a theory of enthusiasm,
which degrades it into mere egotism.
The American has received as a sort of religion
the notion that blowing his own trumpet
is as important as the trump of doom.

. . . .

The Americans were never naturally boomsters
or business bullies. . . .
An egotistic heresy,
produced by the modern heathenry,
has taught them·
against all their Christian instincts
that boasting is better than courtesy
and pride better than humility.

. . . .

What should we think
in a private party,
if an old gentleman had written on his shirt front
in large fine flowing hand:
"I am the only well dressed person in this company."
What should we think of any person of taste and humour
who went about wearing a placard inscribed
"Please note quiet charm of my personality."
What should we say
if people gravely engraved on their visiting card
the claim to be the handsomest
or the wittiest
or the most subtly, strangely attractive people about town.

. . . .

Yet modern business,
especially in America,
does really enforce this sort of publicity
in public life,
and has begun to press it
even in private life.

But the point to be emphasized here is
that it is really pressed upon most of the Americans;
they are goaded and driven into this sort of public life;
large numbers of them
would have been perfectly contented with private life.

. . . .

The Americans are always excused as a new nation;
though it is no longer exactly a new excuse.
But in truth these terms are very misleading;
and in some ways
they have rather the atmosphere of an old nation.
In no nation in the world
are so many people
attached to a certain sort of old texts,
familiar quotations,
or the pieces of sentiment
that were written on the pink pages of Victorian albums.

. . . .

And people having that sentiment,
people inheriting that tradition
would not necessarily, on their own account,
have become believers
in selfish, sensational self-advertisement.
I suspect, as a matter of fact,
that there is rather less of such callous and contemptuous
    egoism in America
than anywhere else. . . . . .
A Frenchman
can be much more cynical and sceptical than an American;
a German
much more morbid and perverted than an American;
an Englishman
much more frozen and sophisticated with pride.
What has happened in America
is that a number of people
who were meant to be heroic and fighting farmers,
at once peasants and pioneers,
have been swept by the pestilence
of a particular fad or false doctrine;
the ideal
which has and deserves
the detestable title of Making Good.

The very words are a hypocrisy. . . . .
for they manage,
by one mean twist of words,
to combine the notion of making money
with the entirely opposite notion of being good.
But the abnormality of this notion can best be seen
in its heathen and barbaric appeal
to a brazen self-praise.
Selling the goods meant incidentally, of course,
lying about the goods;
but it was almost worse
that it meant bragging about the goods.

. . . .

Certain crudities in the American
are not so much a part of American crudity
as actually a part of American culture.
They are not mere outbreaks of human nature;
they are something systematically impressed upon human
    nature.

. . . .

But the point is
people are taught to be impudent and greedy,
not that they are naturally impudent and greedy.
As a matter of fact they are not.
And that is the whole paradox of the position.

. . . .

I have seen in the United States
young people . . . .
who actually pulled themselves together to be rude,
as normal young people
have always pulled themselves together to be polite.
They were shy in fact
and shameless on principle.
They would ask rude questions . . . .
they would use the most brazen methods
to induce somebody to see them,
and anybody who did see them
would pity them for their bashfulness.

. . . .

They were perfectly nice and normal people in themselves,

but they had never been left to themselves,
by those who were always telling them to assert themselves.
They were bounced into bouncing
and bullied into being bullies.
And the explanation
is the existence of this . . . false ideal,
that has been preached to everybody
by every organ of publicity and plutocracy:
the theory that self-praise
is the only real recommendation.

. . . .

The trouble with the false commercial ideal
is that it has made these men struggle against modesty
as if it were morbidity;
and actually try to coarsen their natural courtesy,
as other men stifle a natural crudity.
I do not think that bragging and go-getting
are American faults.
I hate them as American virtues;
I think the quarrel is not so much with the men
as with the gods;
the false gods they have been taught to worship
and still only worship with half their hearts.
And these gods . . . are stone and brass,
but especially brass;
and there is an eternal struggle
in that half-hearted idolatry;
for often,
while the gods are of brass,
the hearts
are of gold.

From *Sidelights*, by G. K. Chesterton.
Used by permission of the Publishers.
Dodd, Mead and Company, Inc.

NAMES OF A FEW ESSAYS
FROM WHICH EXCERPTS CAN BE MADE FOR READINGS

America on Wheels	Frances Warfield
An Inland Voyage	Robert Louis Stevenson
Jungle Peace	William Beebe
Locusts and Wild Honey	John Burroughs

My Last Walk with the School Mistress	Oliver Wendell Holmes
Old Friends	William Winter
Seein' Things at Night	Heywood Broun
Smart Novelists and The Smart Set	G. K. Chesterton
The Great Blizzard	Hamlin Garland
Adventures in Friendship. The	David Grayson
Mowing. Begin p. 175	(Ray Stannard Baker)
Travels With a Donkey	Robert Louis Stevenson
Through the Magic Door	Conan Doyle
Westminster Abbey	Washington Irving
The Condescention of Borrowers	Agnes Repplier

SOME ESSAYS OF THE FOLLOWING WRITERS MAY BE
ABRIDGED FOR READINGS

Repplier, Agnes	Halliday, Robert Cortes
Holmes, Oliver Wendell	Lamb, Charles
Thoreau, Henry David	Emerson, Ralph Waldo
Hearn, Lafcadio	Hazlitt, William
Mabie, Hamilton	Stevenson, Robert Louis
Van Dyke, Henry	Irving, Washington
Burroughs, John	Chesterton, G. K.
Leacock, Stephen	Morley, Christopher
Belloc, Hillaire	

CHAPTER XVII

LYRICAL POETRY

"Lyrical poetry is a general term for all poetry which is, or can be supposed to be susceptible of being sung to the accompaniment of a musical instrument. . . . It is . . . the personal thought or passion, or inspiration which gives its character to lyrical poetry, while the metrical form is also to be taken into consideration. . . .

Confusion of terms . . . led to considerable error. . . . A poem may be heroic, iambic, or elegiac, and at the same time in all senses of the word, lyrical. . . .

The ballad is heroic." *Encyclopaedia Britannica.*

"The quality which is commonly said to be exclusively lyric is the quality of all poetry."
From *The Lyric*, p. 30. John Drinkwater.
Martin Secker; London.

" 'Lyrical' it may be said, implies a form of musical utterance in words governed by overmastering emotion and set free by a powerfully concordant rhythm."
From *Lyric Poetry*. Ernest Rhys.
E. P. Dutton and Company, Publishers.

"The meaning of the word 'lyrical' has been broadened so as to imply frequently, a quality of poetry rather than a mere form of poetry."
From *A Study of Poetry*. Bliss Perry.
Houghton, Mifflin Company, Publishers.

The Ballad is a Form of Lyrical Poetry

BECAUSE the ballad usually tells a story, objectively, it is often called the *little epic*. But as it has a very definite rhythm it may be included in the forms of lyrical poetry according to the definition previously given. Unless these facts are made clear in the beginning, confusion of mind may arise concerning the proper classification of the ballad,

Lyrical Poetry Exclusive of the Ballad

Lyrical poetry *exclusive* of the ballad deals with the *emotions* of the *present*, the *author speaks for himself* in carefully chosen words which he arranges in definite patterns; it is subjective and highly imaginative; a *genuine* sincere expression of the author's *personal feeling;* it appeals to the heart and to the aesthetic sense. The careful choice and arrangement of words produces a constantly recurring rhythm.

"The natural form of expression which literature takes, . . . when it . . . passes beyond the normal powers of prose, is lyric poetry. When your feelings rise beyond a certain degree of stress, you need the stronger beat and vibration of verse; to express the highest joy or the deepest grief poetry is your natural instrument . . . beyond lyrical poetry you pass over into the realm of pure music, where sounds without any resemblance to articulate meaning speak directly to your emotions: sensation and emotion are one; and in music the sensation speaks directly to the depths of your soul. It is towards this end that description is always striving to attain. It can never go very far; but every now and then a man will come who will carry it a little farther, who will reduce to words—as Mr. Ruskin has done—some impression of vivid pleasure which has never been reduced to words before. It is only the great master that makes these advances; by studying his works you may perhaps come somewhere near the mark that he has set."

From *The Forms of Prose Literature*, J. H. Gardiner. p.p. 170-1 paragraph 43.
Charles Scribner's Sons, Publishers, 1912.

The Obligations of the Reader of Lyrical Poetry

The oral reader of lyrical poetry should be able to read any poem:

 1. so that the *meaning, mood* and *purpose* of the lines are perfectly clear to his hearers without impairing its poetic form:

2. so that the full *beauty, symmetry* and *rhythm* of the lines are properly maintained, without losing their meaning in excess of song.

"Those oral readers of poetry who have any appreciation of it as such, fall for the most part into two divisions: the one preserves nothing whatever but the metrical values and reads with a scansion repellent to sense and humanity; the other reads in a saccharine monotone equally devastating to humanity and sense. Both shear away the intended sense from the sound, just as the prosy readers shear away the intended sound from the sense."
From *The Oral Study of Literature.* p. 15. Algernon Tassin. F. S. Crofts and Company, Publishers.

It is the *form* of the expression that *makes it verse:* the form is essential to the very existence of the verse, and, therefore, it must be maintained; it can neither be concealed nor destroyed in oral interpretation without destroying the verse itself.

"Beside the subject matter of poetry, there is its style, its form."
From *The Beginnings of Poetry.* Francis B. Gummere. By permission of The Macmillan Company, Publishers.

"We may overlook in poetry, in any art, lack of depth, of intellectuality; lack of form we cannot overlook, for form is the artist's metier."
From *Channels of English Literature*, p. 287, W. M. Dixon, J. M. Dent and Sons, Publishers.

Special Pauses to be Observed in Reading Verse

The *general* pauses which are common to prose and verse have been considered in Chapter VIII. *Special* pauses that are used in verse are mentioned here.

Compensating Pause

When the writer of verse omits a syllable or more than one, from a metrical foot, the reader must compensate for this by pausing in his reading just long enough to have spoken

the missing syllable or syllables. In other words, the reader
must pause long enough to measure the proper interval of
time, thereby maintaining the proper rhythm.

> "Bury ‖ the Great Duke
> With an empire's lamentation,
> Let us bury the Great Duke
> To the noise of the mourning of a mighty nation."
> From *On the Death of the Duke of Wellington*. Tennyson.

Queen Katherine.

>   "yet like
> A queen, and daughter to a king, inter me—
> I can ‖ no more."
> From *King Henry VIII*. Shakespeare.

Gloucester.

> "And all the clouds that lour'd
>   upon our house
> In the deep bosom of the ocean ‖ buried."
> From *King Richard III*. Shakespeare.

THE CAESURA

In classical verse and in much other verse as well, there
is a "principal pause," the caesura, which often occurs about
the middle of the line, but it *may* occur almost anywhere
within the line following either a stressed or an unstressed
syllable. The caesura is *usually* but not always, a sense or
logical pause. *There may be more than one caesura within a
line*, depending upon the sense. As a general rule caesuras
are not indicated by punctuation marks.

The length of a caesura must be determined by the reader's
sense of rhythm and his sense of proportion and of poetic and
dramatic values.

Failure to observe caesuras is one of the things that helps
to turn verse reading into prose reading, which is an unforgivable crime against the author, and it is one of the principal
things that obscures the meaning and mood of the line, which
is an unforgivable crime against both the author and the
audience.

Examples of Caesuras

In the following quotations the caesuras are indicated by double bars.

"Dimly and dark the mesas ‖ broke on the starry sky.
A pall covered every color ‖ of their gorgeous glory at noon."
From *A Horse Thief*. William Rose Benét.
In *The New Poetry*, Editors, Monroe and Henderson,
By permission of The Macmillan Company, Publishers.

"Till on a day ‖ roving through the field, I chanced
A godly tree ‖ far distant to behold,
Loaden with fruit ‖ of fairest colors mixed."
Lines 575-577—Book IX *Paradise Lost*, Milton.

"I'd be glad to step ashore there ‖ glad to take a pick ‖ and go
To the lone blazed coco-palm tree ‖ in that place no others
      know,
And lift the gold and silver ‖ that has mouldered there for
      years
By the loud surf of Los Muertos ‖ which is beating in my
      ears."
From *Spanish Waters*.
In *The Poems and Plays of John Masefield*. By permission of
The Macmillan Company, Publishers.

The Rhyme Words

When there are rhyme words in lyrical poetry they are stronger and more prominent than other words. This necessitates discriminating care in speaking them to avoid turning the rhyme into a jingle. Nicety in placing the stress and in grouping the words, and careful consideration of pauses and intonation are technical means by which the rhyme words may be made to perform their function without becoming too conspicuous or too prominent.

The Ends of the Lines

Lines are said to be *end-stopt*, or *run-on*, depending on whether the thought *stops* at the end of the line or whether it *runs on* from one line to another.

> "This is the way," laughed the great god Pan,
> (Laughed as he sat by the river),
> "The only way since gods began
> To make sweet music, they could succeed."
> From *A Musical Instrument*. Mrs. Browning.

The third line is a *run-on* line, the other three are *end-stopt* lines.

END-STOPT LINES

In reading *end-stopt* lines one will need to guard against too much of a sing-song rhythm. There is danger of *exaggerating* the poetic form. Great care in *stressing* the rhyme words, and in the intonation given them, will help to keep the thought and the rhythm properly balanced. The right rise and fall of the intonation and the length of the glide will be determined by the sense and vigor of the line and by the general rhythm of the verse. The length or brevity of the glide must fit into the time intervals of the rhythm.

> "Oh, to have a little house!
> To own the hearth and stool and all!
> The heaped-up sods upon the fire,
> The pile of turf against the wall!"
> From *An Old Woman of the Roads*. Padraic Colum.

> "Sweet day, so cool, so calm, so bright,
> The bridal of the earth and sky,
> The dew shall weep thy fall to-night;
> For thou must die."
> From *Virtue*. George Herbert.

RUN-ON LINES

In reading *run-on* lines there is danger of *destroying the poetic form*, thereby turning the verse into prose. The length and position of the logical and the breath pauses and the caesuras should be carefully determined so that they will fit into and *maintain* the poetic rhythm.

Logical pauses and *breath* pauses do *not* come at the *ends* of run-on lines. It is here that a *special rhythmic pause* must be used and timed with infinite nicety. If the reader makes *no* pause at all at the end of a run-on line he is in danger of destroying the poetic form and turning the verse into a prose form; if a *full* pause is made he retains the poetic form but is in grave danger of breaking the continuity of the thought. It is difficult to explain what the reader *should* do in such a case, but he should hold the note, as it were, at the end of the line *just long enough to maintain the rhythm and the poetic form but not long enough to interrupt or break the sense.* He should in reality hesitate or mark time for a portion of a second. This is not much but it is sufficient to hold inviolate the beauty and symmetry of the poetic form without breaking or interrupting the thought.

> "Like a poet hidden
>   In the light of thought,
> Singing hymns unbidden,
>   'Till the world is wrought
> To sympathy with hopes and fears it heeded not."
> From *To a Skylark*. Shelley.

> "My master and the neighbours all
>   Make game of me and Sally,
> And, but for her, I'd better be
>   A slave and row a galley"
> From *Sally in Our Alley*. H. Carey.

> "With cold and rain and slow decay
> On woman and on tree till they

> Droop to the earth again, and be
> A withered woman, a withered tree."

> From *A Woman Is a Branchy Tree*.
> In *Collected Poems*, by James Stephens.
> By permission of The Macmillan Company, Publishers.

Special Points to be Remembered in Reading Lyrical Poetry

1. Maintain the rhythm and the poetic form of the verse without making it "sing-song."

2. Keep the sense of the verse clear without turning it into prose and thereby destroying its poetic form.

3. Make the rhyme words strong enough to give them their proper value and significance but not strong enough to make them conspicuous or to turn the rhyme into a jingle.

Extracts and Selections for Practice

Read the following extracts observing the three cautions just mentioned.

"I remember, I remember
The house where I was born,
The little window where the sun
Came peeping in at morn;"
From *I Remember, I Remember*. Thomas Hood.

"She was a phantom of delight
When first she gleamed upon my sight;
A lovely apparition, sent
To be a moment's ornament.
Her eyes as stars of twilight fair;
Like twilight's, too, her dusky hair,
But all things else about her drawn
From May-time and the cheerful dawn—
A dancing shape, an image gay.
To haunt, to startle and waylay."
From *She Was a Phantom of Delight*. Wordsworth.

"And the very leaves seemed to sing on the trees:
The castle alone in the landscape lay
Like an outpost of winter, dull and gray;
'Twas the proudest hall in the North Countree,

And never its gates might opened be,
Save to lord or lady of high degree."
From *The Vision of Sir Launfal.* James Russell Lowell.

Upon Westminster Bridge
September 3rd, 1802

Earth hath not anything to show more fair:
Dull would he be of soul who could pass by
A sight so touching in its majesty:
This City now doth, like a garment, wear
The beauty of the morning; silent, bare,
Ships, towers, domes, theatres, and temples lie
Open unto the fields, and to the sky;
All bright and glittering in the smokeless air.

Never did sun more beautifully steep
In his first splendour, valley, rock, or hill;
Ne'er saw I, never felt, a calm so deep!
The river glideth at his own sweet will:
Dear God! the very houses seem asleep;
And all that mighty heart is lying still!
                            William Wordsworth.

Silver

Slowly, silently, now the moon
Walks the night in her silver shoon:
This way and that, she peers, and sees
Silver fruit upon silver trees;
One by one the casements catch
Her beams beneath the silvery thatch;
Couched in his kennel, like a log,
With paws of silver sleeps the dog;
From their shadowy cote the white breasts peep
Of doves in a silver-feathered sleep:
A harvest mouse goes scampering by
With silver claws and silver eye;
And moveless fish in the water gleam,
By silver reeds in a silver stream.

In *Peacock Pie*, by Walter de la Mare.
Coypright, Henry Holt and Company, Publishers.

CLASSIFICATION OF LYRICAL POETRY FOR THE ORAL READER

Lyrical poetry may be classified for the oral reader *according to its external form*, into:—

1. Ballads
2. Songs or true lyrics
3. Odes
4. Sonnets

Each of these classes is considered in a separate chapter which follows.

Lyrical poetry may also be classified *according to the nature of the prevailing emotion* into:

1. Lyrics of nature
2. Lyrics of patriotism
3. Lyrics of love
4. Lyrics of devotion
5. Lyrics of grief

These classes are considered in Chapter XIX, *Songs or Pure Lyrics*.

CHAPTER XVIII

THE BALLAD

"A ballad is a simple spirited poem in short stanzas; originally a popular song in which some popular story is graphically narrated." *Murray's English Dictionary*.

"Dances . . . were the original stuff upon which dramatic, lyric and epic impulses wove a pattern that is traced in later narrative ballads mainly as incremental repetition."
Francis B. Gummere.

THE word "ballad" means a song that may be accompanied by a dance. The ballad has been called the "little epic" because originally it always recounted some heroic deed in a very vigorous and spirited manner. It must also have a definite rhythm which is an essential part of its structure. Professor Gummere says: (*The Popular Ballad*), "*the refrain is an organic part of the ballad . . . it must have a tune*." Since the ballad *tells a story* to *a tune* it combines the epic and lyric forms. It is, as a rule, more or less *objective;* it tells its story simply though vigorously, or it suggests a story, and points no moral.

As a form of literature the ballad has gone through a long process of evolution and development making most modern ballads differ greatly from old ballads.

Old ballads were simply folk songs; they grew into being on the *lips* of a *tribe or race of people:* they were communal, and were handed down from generation to generation *by word of mouth* in the form of songs or tales which recounted heroic deeds.

Modern ballads are literary ballads written by *one* person. They *resemble* old ballads to a certain degree in both subject matter and form, often recounting heroic deeds in a spirited manner and in vigorous rhythmic form. They *differ* from old ballads in the fact that they are written with great care and

189

nicety, and with full consideration of well formulated laws that aid and guide the poet in writing verse. The *rhythm* of *old* ballads was *instinctive, unstudied, natural;* the rhythm of *modern* ballads is *based upon* the instinctive and natural, but it has been selected, polished and refined by the artist who produces it. It is a *cultivated* form of the original ballad, as a hot-house rose is a cultivated form of the natural, wild rose. Old ballads *grew* into being, naturally; modern ballads were *evolved,* artistically, by selective methods. As a general rule, modern ballads will interest and entertain a modern audience much more than old ballads will. They are the expression of thoughts and emotions much more nearly like our own. As a people, we have outgrown, or at least grown away from, the old and primitive ballads for use as popular entertainment. We like something nearer to our own experiences.

Modern ballads are universally popular as a means of entertainment. They please almost all types of audiences, they are not above the heads of the most humble minded, nor beneath the dignity of the most sophisticated.

It is practically impossible to draw a hard and fast line between some ballads and some pure lyrics but it is not necessary for the reader to do so. The nature of the *subject matter* must determine his procedure in all cases.

The Purpose of the Ballad

The purpose of the ballad is to *tell a story*—or at least to *suggest* a story—in a manner that produces a clearly marked and spirited rhythm.

Classification of Ballads for Oral Interpretation

Narrative Ballads, which tell a story of a heroic deed.

Lyrical Ballads,   which tell or suggest a story and express personal emotion.

Dramatic Ballads, which tell a story and in which characters speak.

THE SPEAKER AND THE LISTENER IN THE BALLAD

In *narrative* ballads the reader takes the place of the author and tells the story directly to the audience.

In *lyrical* ballads, the reader may speak:
a—for the author,
  Sea Fever, Masefield;
b—for a character,
  Mandalay, Kipling;
  The Low-Backed Car, Samuel Lover.

In *dramatic* ballads, the reader speaks for the author directly to the audience in the *narrative* portion and he speaks for the *characters* in the *dialogue* or the monologue portions.

IMPERSONATION IN BALLADS

When characters are introduced in ballads it is for the purpose of making the narrative more vivid and dramatic and to help unravel the theme of the story through the speech and action of the characters. Ballads are not character studies, consequently, there should not be real impersonation of characters when ballads are read aloud. The reader should, however, reveal the mind and heart and spirit of the character by his own facial expression, general tone of voice and general bodily attitude; he should show the reaction of the characters to what is said and done in the story, but this is not impersonation. The fundamental purpose of a ballad would be lost if its characters were impersonated.

THE RHYTHM OF BALLADS

The story of ballads is told in a spirited rhythmic manner. *The telling of the story must produce the rhythm;* the more enthusiastic and vigorous the thought, the more care should be given to the telling of the story clearly and distinctly; at the same time the form of the verse must be kept inviolate.

In many modern ballads the rhythm has a special significance; it may suggest:

"the sound of arms and the tramp of feet
and the measured tread of the grenadiers."

"the crack of whips like shots in battle,"

or some one "riding, riding, riding."

It may be the rhythm of water lapping against a boat,

"The clucking sucking of the sea about the rusty hulls,"

Whatever the rhythm may be it must be made to serve the purpose of the story, thus making the story more vivid, more captivating and alluring. The reader will have to be on the alert continually to see that *both* the *story* and the *rhythm* have their just share of attention in order to maintain the balance and unity of the poem.

The rhythm of ballads almost invariably *seems* to be rapid. By using proper stresses and grouping of syllables, by carefully planning and timing the pauses, and by being particularly careful of the articulation and intonation, one may read as fast as the fastest ballad requires and yet read clearly and well.

NARRATIVE BALLADS

In narrative ballads the events of the story are related simply, impersonally and enthusiastically; there is little or no description or dialogue.

THE SAGA OF THE SILVER BIRD*

The young lad in the cockpit is limbed like Viking men;
His eyes are blue as heaven: his hair the silk of corn.
He might be curious Icarus, his frail wings found again;
He might be Viking Eric, peering beyond the morn.

But fingers on the joystick are numb with pain and cold,
And blue eyes are so weary and young limbs grown so faint,
The young heart's dreadful question is steadily retold—
There is no voice to answer, save the loud wind's complaint.

*This ballad commemorates the flight of Colonel Charles A. Lindbergh from New York to Paris in May, 1928.

The sleet spears at his window are white and hissing death;
The Silver Bird is tortured; the pale ice smites and clings;
The Ocean Hounds are raging; the North Wind bears their
    breath;
The slaver from their dewlaps befouls the silver wings.

Blacker and ever blacker the storm torn hours drop down;
Thicker and ever thicker fly the swift spears of hate.
The distant shore is very far, not seen, nor heard, nor known.
And still the lonely question comes, "Which is the road to
    Fate?"

But can this Spirit falter when such fires in it burn?
Can wind or hail or water teach it the feel of fear?
Shall he who climbed the morning now cravenly return?
Nay rather with the Silver Bird find deep a glorious bier!

Nay rather face all awful things that the night may hold,
Nay rather sleep beneath the fangs of the yelling Hounds!
Go out astride the neck of Death like the men of Old,
Knowing that even gods must yield when mortals scorn their
    bounds!

Frightened little Silver Bird, look you overhead,
Where across the angry heavens comes a flash of fire.
Down below, the gaping jaws slaver white and red—
What is this that comes so fast to balk their furious ire?

In the cockpit gentle hands have pulled the joystick back;
In this place was room for none but the Boy who started,
Yet there is One here beside, guiding the attack,
One who knows the ways of storm, great and valiant hearted:

He who leaped with laughter down, breast high in the flood,
Wading with his mighty sword swung above the wave,
Bearing to the Saracens Christ's own precious Blood—
Shall he leave his spirit's son to a bitter grave?

Now the old gods fail and fly, and the Hounds are flying;
Now Premetheus shakes his chains and shouts against new
    day;
Now around the Silver Bird the morning winds are crying
Now the Boy has raised his head and found the early gray!

He who sped the Silver Bird through her time of danger
Smiles upon the stirring lad very slow and sweet,

And his voice like swinging bells high above a Manger—
"Grace of God be with ye, Lad, till again we meet."

Turns the joyous Silver Bird like a daring rover,
Here are now the Irish hills, there the line of Gaul
Soon the ardor and the toil will be past and over
And a light immortal shine where she deigns to fall.

Now alone her young lad sits, neither spent nor broken;
Like a lover and his lass now he brings her in,
Star-dust on her silver head for a living token,
And a dream that will not fade for the hearts of men!

Alice Rogers Hager.

In Braithwaite's *Anthology of Magazine Verse*—1928.
Harold Vinal, Ltd., Publisher.
Reprinted by special permission of the author.

THE SKATER OF GHOST LAKE

Ghost Lake's a dark lake, a deep lake and cold:
Ice black as ebony, frostily scrolled;
Far in its shadows a faint sound whirrs;
Steep stand the sentineled deep, dark firs.

A brisk sound, a swift sound, a ring-tinkle-ring;
Flit-flit—a shadow, with a stoop and a swing,
Flies from a shadow through the crackling cold.
Ghost Lake's a deep lake, a dark lake and old!

Leaning and leaning, with a stride and a stride,
Hands locked behind him, scarf blowing wide,
Jeremy Randall skates, skates late,
Star for a candle, moon for a mate.

Black is the clear glass now that he glides,
Crisp is the whisper of long lean strides,
Swift is his swaying—but pricked ears hark.
None comes to Ghost Lake late after dark!

Cecily only—yes, it is she!
Stealing to Ghost Lake, tree after tree,
Kneeling in snow by the still lake side,
Rising with feet winged, gleaming, to glide.

Dust of the ice swirls. Here is his hand.
Brilliant his eyes burn. Now, as was planned,

Arm across arm twined, laced to his side,
Out on the dark lake lightly they glide.

Dance of the dim moon, a rhythmical reel,
A swaying, a swift tune—skurr of the steel;
Moon for a candle, maid for a mate.
Jeremy Randall skates, skates late.

Black as if lacquered the wide lake lies;
Breath is a frost-fume, eyes seek eyes;
Souls are a sword edge tasting the cold
Ghost Lake's a deep lake, a dark lake and old!

Far in the shadows hear faintly begin
Like a string pluck-plucked of a violin,
Muffled in mist on the lake's far bound,
Swifter and swifter, a low singing sound!

Far in the shadows and faint on the verge
Of blue cloudy moonlight, see it emerge,
Flit-flit—a phantom, with a stoop and a swing . . .
Ah, it's a night bird, burdened of wing!

Pressed close to Jeremy, laced to his side,
Cecily Culver, dizzy you glide.
Jeremy Randall sweepingly veers
Out on the dark ice far from the piers.

"Jeremy!" "Sweetheart?" "What do you fear?"
"Nothing, my darling,—nothing is here!"
"Jeremy?" "Sweetheart?" "What do you flee?"
"Something—I know not; something I see!"

Swayed to a swift stride, brisker of pace,
Leaning and leaning, they race and they race;
Ever that whirring, that crisp sound thin
Like a string pluck-plucked of a violin;

Ever that swifter and low singing sound
Sweeping behind them, winding them round;
Gasp of their breath now that chill flakes fret;
Ice black as ebony—blacker—like jet!

Ice shooting fangs forth—sudden—like spears;
Crackling of lightning—a roar in their ears!
Shadowy, a phantom swerves off from its prey . . .
No, it's a night bird flit-flits away!

Low-winging moth-owl, home to your sleep!
Ghost Lake's a still lake, a cold lake and deep,
Faint in its shadows a far sound whirrs,
Black stand the ranks of its sentinel firs.

In *Golden Fleece*, by William Rose Benét,
Used by permission of the Publishers,
Dodd, Mead and Company, Inc.

LYRICAL BALLADS

In lyrical ballads the expression of *emotion* predominates over the narrative, making them more or less like a song. Some are used as songs. They have certain personal and emotional qualities which are characteristic of the true lyric.

THE THREE FISHERS

Three fishers went sailing away to the West,
Away to the west as the sun went down;
Each thought of the woman who loved him the best,
And the children stood watching them out of the town;
For men must work, and women must weep,
And there's little to earn, and many to keep,
Though the harbor bar be moaning.

Three wives sat up in the light house tower,
And they trimmed the lamps as the sun went down;
They looked at the squall and they looked at the shower,
And the night-wrack came rolling up ragged and brown.
But men must work, and women must weep,
Though storms be sudden and waters deep,
And the harbor bar be moaning.

Three corpses lay out on the shining sands
In the morning gleam as the tide went down,
And the women are weeping and wringing their hands
For those who will never come home to the town;
For men must work, and women must weep,
And the sooner it's over, the sooner to sleep;
And good-by to the bar and its moaning.

Charles Kingsley.

Lines from *Spanish Waters*, by John Masefield.

Spanish waters, Spanish waters, you are ringing in my ears,
Like a slow sweet piece of music from the grey forgotten years,
Telling tales, and beating tunes, and bringing weary thoughts
    to me
Of the sandy beach at Muertos, where I would that I could be.

There's a surf breaks on Los Muertos, and it never stops to
    roar,
And it's there we went to anchor and it's there we went
    ashore.
Where the blue lagoon is silent amid snags of rotting trees,
Dropping like the clothes of corpses cast up by the seas.

We anchored at Los Muertos when the dipping sun was red
We left her half-a-mile to sea, to west of Nigger Head;
And before the mist was on the Cay, before the day was done,
We were all ashore at Muertos with the gold that we had won.

We bore it through the marshes in a half-score battered chests,
Sinking, in the sucking quagmires, to the sunburn on our
    breasts,
. . . .

The moon came white and ghostly as we laid the treasure
    down,
There was gear there'd make a beggarman as rich as Lima
    Town.
. . . .

We smoothed the place with mattocks, and we took and
    blazed the tree,
Which marks yon where the gear is hid that none will ever see,
And we laid aboard the ship again, and south away we steers,
Through the loud surf of Los Muertos which is beating in
    my ears.

I'm the last alive that knows it. All the rest have gone their
    ways
Killed, or died, or come to anchor in the old Mulatas Cays.
. . . .

And I see in dreams awhiles, the beach, the sun's disc dipping
    red,
And the tall ship under top sails, swaying in past Nigger
    Head.

I'd be glad to step ashore there. Glad to take a pick and go
To the lone blazed coco-palm tree in the place no others
    know,
And lift the gold and silver that has mouldered there for
    years—
By the loud surf of Los Muertos which is beating in my ears.

In *Poems and Plays of John Masefield*. By permission of
    The Macmillan Company, Publishers.

DRAMATIC BALLADS

In dramatic ballads characters and dialogue are introduced in connection with the story, but they are there to help
the development of the story, not as character studies.

"Then spake Sir Richard Grenville: 'I know you are no
    coward;
You fly them for a moment to fight with them again.
But I've ninety men and more that are lying sick ashore.
I should count myself the coward if I left them; my Lord
    Howard,
To these Inquisition dogs and the devildoms of Spain.' "
From *The Revenge*, Tennyson.

DRAMATIC BALLAD
THE RETURN OF MORGAN AND FINGAL

And there we were together again—
Together again, we three:
Morgan, Fingal, fiddle and all,
They had come for the night with me.

The spirit of joy was in Morgan's wrist
There were songs in Fingal's throat;
And secure outside, for the spray to drench,
Was a tossed and empty boat.

And there were pipes, and there was punch,
And somewhere was twelve years;
So it came, in the manner of things unsought,
That a quick knock vexed our ears.

The wind hovered and shrieked and snarled,
And I heard Fingal swear;

Then I opened the door—but I found no more
Than a chalk-skinned woman there.

I looked, and at last, "What is it?" I said—
"What is it that we can do?"
But never a word could I get from her
But "You—you three—it is you!"

Now the sense of crazy speech like that!
Was more than a man could make;
So I said "But we—we are what, we three?"
And I saw the creature shake.

"Be quick!" she cried, "for I left her dead—
And I was afraid to come;
But you, you three—God made it be—
Will ferry the dead girl home.

"Be quick! be quick!—but listen to that!
Who is it that makes it? hark!"
But I heard no more than a knocking splash
And a wind that shook the dark.

"It is only the wind that blows," I said,
"And the boat that rocks outside."
And I watched her there, and I pitied her there—
"Be quick be quick!" she cried.

She cried so loud that her voice went in
To find where my two friends were;
So Morgan came and Fingal came,
And out we went with her.

'Twas a lonely way for a man to take
And a fearsome way for three;
And over the water, and all day long,
They had come for the night with me.

But the girl was dead, as the woman had said,
And the best we could see to do
Was to lay her aboard. The north wind roared,
And into the night we flew.

Four of us living and one for a ghost,
Furrowing crest and swell,
Through the surge and the dark, for that faint far spark,
We ploughed with Azrael.

Three of us ruffled and one gone mad,
Crashing to south we went;
And three of these were too spattered to care
What this late sailing meant.

So down we steered and along we tore
Through the flash of the midnight foam:
Silent enough to be ghosts on guard
We ferried the dead girl home.

We ferried her down to the voiceless wharf,
And we carried her up to the light;
And we left the two to the father there,
Who counted the coals that night.

Then back we steered through the foam again,
But our thoughts were fast and few;
And all we did was to crowd the surge
And to measure the life we knew;—

Till at last we came where a dancing gleam
Skipped out to us, we three—
And the dark wet mooring pointed home
Like a finger from the sea.

Then out we pushed the teetering skiff
And in we drew to the stairs;
And up we went, each man content
With a life that fed no cares.

Fingers were cold and feet were cold,
And the tide was cold and rough;
But the light was warm and the room was warm,
And the world was good enough.

And there were the pipes, and there was the punch,
More shrewd than Satan's tears;
Fingal has fashioned it all by himself,
With a craft that comes of years.

And there we were together again again—
Together again, we three:
Morgan, Fingal, fiddle and all,
They were there for the night with me.

In *Collected Poems* by E. A. Robinson. By permission of
    The Macmillan Company, Publishers.

BRIEF LIST OF BALLADS SUITABLE FOR ORAL INTERPRETATION

Benét, Stephen Vincent   The Ballad of William Sycamore.
                              The Retort Discourteous.
                              The Mountain Whippoorwill.
    Ballads and Poems.
    Doubleday, Doran and Company, Garden City, New York,
1931.

Benét, William Rose   Master of the Flying Castle.
                              Tallefer.
                                  (Must be abridged, greatly).
                              The Horse Thief.
    Golden Fleece.
    Dodd, Mead and Company, New York, 1935.

Buchanan, Robert   The Ballad of Judas Iscariot.
    The Reciter's Treasury of Verse. Ernest Pertwee.
    George Routledge and Sons, Ltd., London, 1930.

Campbell, Thomas   The Battle of the Baltic.
    Palgrave's *Golden Treasury.*
    E. P. Dutton and Company, New York.

Coleridge, Samuel Taylor   Love.

Deane, Anthony C.   The Battle of the Billycock.
    Modern British Poetry, Editor, Louis Untermeyer.
    Harcourt, Brace and Company, New York, 1920.

Dobson, Austin   The Ballad of Beau Brocade.
                              The Ballad to Queen Elizabeth.
    Complete Poetical Works.
    Humphrey Milford, Oxford University Press, London, 1923.

Gilkey, John Augustus   The Heroes of the Yukon.
    Poems for Oral Interpretation, Shurter and Watkins.
    Noble and Noble, New York.

Kipling, Rudyard   Ballad of East and West.
                              Chant—Pagan.
                                  (Must be abridged, greatly).

Gunga Din.
Mandalay.
The Story of Ung.
Rudyard Kipling's Verse. Inclusive Edition.
Doubleday, Page and Company, Garden City, New York, 1922.

Knibbs, H. H.   Roll A Rock Down.
Modern American Poetry.

Lanier, Sidney   The Revenge of Hamish.
Poems of Sidney Lanier.
Charles Scribner's Sons, New York.

Le Galliene, Richard   A Ballad of London.
Modern British Poetry. Edited by Louis Untermeyer.
Harcourt, Brace and Company, New York.

Lindsay, Vachel   The Congo.
The Congo and Other Poems.
The Macmillan Company, New York, 1932.

Masefield, John   Salt Water Ballads.
                                 The New Bedford Whaler.

Morris, William   Winter Weather.
Types of Poetry, Zeitlin and Rinaker.
The Macmillan Company, New York, 1935.

Noyes, Alfred   Forty Singing Seamen.
                                 The Admiral's Ghost.
                                 The Highwayman.
                                 The River of Stars.
                                 The Two Painters.
Collected Poems.
Frederick A. Stokes Company, New York, 1913.

Rossetti, Daniel Gabriel   The Blessed Damozel.

Scott, Sir Walter   Allen-a-Dale.
                                 Brignall Banks.

Swinburne, Algernon Charles, A Jacobite's Farewell.

Southey, Robert   Mary, the Maid of the Inn.

Tennyson, Alfred   The Revenge.

Watson, Rosamund Marriott, Ballad of Pentyre Town.
  Ballads and Ballad Poems.
  E. P. Dutton and Company, New York, 1929.

Waller, J. F.   Magdalena, or The Spanish Duel.
                            (Must be abridged).
  In *Cumnock's Choice Readings.*
  A. C. McClurg and Company, Chicago, 1892.

CHAPTER XIX

THE SONG OR TRUE LYRIC

"The lyric has the function of revealing in terms of pure art, the secrets of the inner life, its hopes, its fantastic joys, its sorrows, its delirium. . . ." *Encyclopaedia Britannica.*

The lyric does not tell a story although it may hint at one. It deals with *any subject that permits of emotion.* Its rhythm is produced by the careful choice of sounds and words and the arrangement of words into definite patterns. A lyric may or may not have rhyme.

The Purpose of the True Lyric or Song

It is very difficult to state the purpose of a true lyric but one may enumerate some of its dominant characteristics. It expresses *personal* emotion in rhythmic form. It is *subjective* and *direct*, the sincere expression of the author's *innermost* feelings. It is short because the emotion is too *deep* and too *intense* to be sustained. It is *a sudden cry from the heart* which bursts forth like a flame and then subsides. Because it springs from the heart of the author in genuine sincerity and truth it usually goes straight to the heart of the hearer and finds understanding and sympathy there.

The Speaker and the Listener

As a general rule the reader should speak the lines of a lyric directly to the *audience* as if they were his own words, expressing his own innermost thoughts. In some lyrics, however, the author has addressed the lines to some particular person who is supposed to be present. In some such cases the reader may imagine this person present and speak the lines directly to him as an imaginary listener instead of speaking them directly to the audience. The reader will have to depend upon his own judgment and good taste for decision in these cases.

To Celia by Ben Johnson, may be spoken to an imaginary listener.

> "Drink to me only with thine eyes,
> And I will pledge with mine;
> Or leave a kiss but in the cup
> And I'll not ask for wine.
> The thirst that from the soul doth rise
> Doth ask a drink divine;
> But might I of Jove's nectar sup
> I would not change for thine."

To Althea From Prison by Richard Lovelace, is addressed to a particular person in the title but it should *not* be spoken directly to her as an imaginary listener.

> "When Love with unconfined wings
> Hovers within my gates,
> And my divine Althea brings
> To whisper at the grates;
> When I lie tangled in her hair
> And fetter'd to her eye,
> The Gods that wanton in the air
> Know no such liberty."

IMPERSONATION IN LYRICS

There should be no real impersonation in a true lyric The reader should give his whole mind and heart and soul, his whole being, to the interpretation of the lines, supplying all the sincerity and intensity of feeling that they demand, but this is not impersonation.

There are many lyrical monologues and lyrical ballads that are very close to the true lyric which may be perplexing to the reader at first. In such cases the *purpose* of the individual selection will have to be the reader's guide. The true lyric is an expression of the *personal* emotion of the *author* and this emotion is *deep* and *intense*.

> "How sweetly bloom'd the gay green birk,
> How rich the hawthorn's blossom,
> As underneath their fragrant shade
> I clasp'd her to my bosom!

The golden hours on angel wings
Flew o'er me and my dearie;
For dear to me as light and life
Was my sweet Highland Mary."
From *Highland Mary*. Burns.

THE RHYTHM OF TRUE LYRICS

The true lyric is a song. Rhythm is one of its *essential*
qualities. Without rhythm there can be no true lyric. The
rhythm may be tuned to the rhythm of the sea, the flight of
gulls, the sigh of the winds, or to anything else that man's
imagination may depict in rhythmic language.

Assuming that the reader properly understands and ap-
preciates the subject matter of lyrics, *adequate oral interpretation of them is largely dependent upon his mastery of the
sounds of his language and on a finely developed voice.* One
who has a thin, harsh voice, a voice that is husky or nasal, a
voice with monotony of pitch and intonation, or with lack of
general fullness, richness, or flexibility, should not attempt
the oral interpretation of a lyric because he is doomed to
certain failure before he has begun. Distinct and pleasing
speech, fine vocal equipment and the ability to use it well,
are indispensable to full and *adequate* oral interpretation of
lyrics. If one has no serious vocal or speech defects these
accomplishments may be acquired by faithful, intelligent
study and practice no matter how poor either speech or voice
or both may be when the training begins.

RHYTHM AND MEANING IN LYRICS

There is only a small step "from the sublime to the ridiculous" in reading lyrics aloud. There must be enough rhythm
to maintain the full beauty of the poetic form and enough
intensity of feeling to give full expression to the author's
mood and purpose, but constant care and discriminating taste
are necessary to avoid overdoing either rhythm or feeling
thereby causing the expression to lose sense and proportion.

The rhythm and emotion may be as pronounced as the most

extreme expression demands providing they are never allowed to overbalance the sense: while on the other hand, the sense should never be allowed to overbalance the rhythm and emotion. Each should be given its own value, adequately and fully—no more and no less.

The sense is what holds the expression up; it supplies the skeleton, the framework which supports the emotion. If the framework is weak or out of proportion to the weight it bears, the whole structure will be awry or will entirely collapse. The reader should give all the rhythm to the lines and all the emotion to the expression that the sense demands and will support with certainty, but not a bit more. When he knows that the sense is keeping one foot firmly fixed upon solid earth he may safely soar as high and as far as the rhythm and emotion need to go without danger of losing the proper balance of the expression or getting into the regions of bad taste.

LYRICAL POETRY CLASSIFIED ACCORDING TO THE NATURE OF THE PREVAILING EMOTION

1. Nature lyrics
2. Patriotic lyrics
3. Love lyrics
4. Sacred or devotional lyrics
5. Grief lyrics

LYRICS OF NATURE

Lyrics of nature were probably among the earliest lyrics. The emotion they express is, as a rule, the least intense and the most impersonal of any of the true lyrics. Consequently, they may be longer than the other types. Their beauty, however, does not lie in the *description* of the beauties of nature, but in the power of such beauties to *stimulate the imagination* and *awaken emotional responses*. This should be very clearly borne in mind by the reader. If a nature lyric is interpreted as if it were mere description, its beauty and whole purpose and significance will probably be lost. Nature lyrics more frequently express joy, enthusiasm and appreciation than sorrow or regret.

"And this is the dreamed-of wonder!
    This—at last—is the sea!
Billows of liquid thunder—
    Vocal immensity!
But where is the thrill of glory
    Born of a great surprise?
This is the old, old story;
    These are the ancient skies . . .

But out in my mother country,
    Ever since I was born,
This is the song my brother Winds
    Sang in the fields of corn.
And there, in the purple midnights
    Sullen and still with heat,
This is the selfsame drone that ran
    Over the heading wheat."

From *On First Seeing the Ocean.* John G. Neihardt,
In *Collected Poems.*
By permission of The Macmillan Company, Publishers.

EXTRACTS FROM LYRICS OF NATURE
From, *Song of the Chattahoochee.*

"Out of the hills of Habersham,
 Down the valleys of Hall
I hurry amain to reach the plain,
Run the rapid and leap and fall,
 Split at the rock and together again,
Accept my bed, or narrow or wide,
And flee from folly on every side
With a lover's pain to attain the plain,
Far from the hills of Habersham,
Far from the valleys of Hall.

And all down the hills of Habersham,
All through the Valleys of Hall,
The rushes cried *Abide, abide,*

The wilful waterweeds held me thrall,
The laving laurel turned my tide,
The ferns and the foundling grass said *stay*,
The dewberry dipped to work delay,
And the little reed sighed *Abide, abide.*
Here in the hills of Habersham,
Here in the valleys of Hall";
. . . .

Sidney Lanier.

From, *Aspect of The Pines.*

. . . .

"Tall, sombre, grim they stand with dusky gleams
Brightening to gold within the woodland's core,
Beneath the gracious noon tide's tranquil beams,—
When the weird winds of morning sigh no more.

A stillness, strange, divine ineffable,
Broods round and o'er them in the wind's surcease,
And on each tinted copse and shimmering dell
Rests the mute rapture of deep hearted peace".

. . . .

Paul Hamilton Hayne.

Used by special permission of the Publishers, Lothrop, **Lee**
and Shepard Company.

From, The Voice of the Grass.

"Here I come creeping, creeping everywhere:
You cannot see me coming,
Nor hear my low sweet humming:
For in the starry night,
And the glad morning light,
I am quietly creeping everywhere".

Sarah Roberts.

EXAMPLES OF LYRICS OF NATURE

THE COYOTE

Trailing the last gleam after,
In the valleys emptied of light,
Ripples a whimsical laughter
Under the wings of the night,

Mocking the faded west, airily,
Meeting the little bats merrily,
Over the mesas it shrills
To the red moon on the hills.

Mournfully rising and waning,
Far through the moon-silvered land
Wails a weird voice of complaining
Over the thorns and the sand.
Out of the blue silences eerily,
On to the black mountains wearily,
Till the dim desert is crossed,
Wanders the cry, and is lost.

Here by the fire's ruddy streamers,
Tired with our hopes and our fears,
We inarticulate dreamers
Hark to the song of our years.
Up to the brooding divinity
Far in that sparkling infinity
Cry our despair and delight,
Voice of the Western night!

From *Grass-Grown Trails* by Badger Clark.
Copyright. Chapman and Grimes, Publishers.

AH! SUN-FLOWER

Ah, Sun-flower! weary of time,
Who countest the steps of the sun;
Seeking after that sweet golden clime,
Where the traveller's journey is done;

Where the Youth pined away with desire,
And the pale virgin shrouded in snow,
Arise from their graves and aspire
Where my Sun-flower wishes to go.

In *Poems and Prophecies*, by William Blake.
Everyman's Library, E. P. Dutton and Company, Publishers.

THE SEA

The sea, the sea, the open sea,
The blue, the fresh, the ever free;
Without a mark, without a bound,
It runneth the earth's wide regions round;

It plays with the clouds, it mocks the skies,
Or like a cradled creature lies.
I'm on the sea, I'm on the sea,
I am where I would ever be,
With the blue above and the blue below
And silence wheresoe'er I go.
If a storm should come and awake the deep,
What matter? I shall ride and sleep.

I love, oh, how I love to ride
On the fierce, foaming, bursting tide,
Where every mad wave drowns the moon,
And whistles aloft its tempest tune,
And tells how goeth the world below,
And why the southwest wind doth blow!
I never was on the dull, tame shore
But I loved the great sea more and more,
And backward flew to her billowy breast,
Like a bird that seeketh her mother's nest,—
And a mother she was and is to me,
For I was born on the open sea.

The waves were white, and red the morn,
In the noisy hour when I was born;
The whale it whistled, the porpoise rolled,
And the dolphins bared their backs of gold;
And never was heard such an outcry wild,
As welcomed to life the ocean child.
I have lived since then in calm and strife,
Full fifty summers a rover's life,
With wealth to spend, and a power to range,
But never have sought nor sighed for change:
And death, whenever he comes to me,
Shall come on the wide, unbounded sea.

In *English Songs and Other Poems.* Bryan Waller Procter.
(Barry Cornwall).
Tichnor and Fields, Publishers.

*FIELDS AT EVENING

They wear their evening light as women wear
Their pale, proud beauty for a lover's sake,
Too quiet-hearted evermore to care
For moving worlds and musics that they make.
And they are hushed as lonely women are,

*Reprinted by special permission of the author.

So lost in dreams they have no thought to mark
How the wide heavens blossom, star by star,
And the slow dusk is deepening to the dark.

The moon comes like a lover from the hill,
Leaning across the twilight and the trees,
And finds them grave and beautiful and still,
And wearing always, on such nights as these,
A glimmer less than any ghostly light,
As women wear their beauty in the night.

In *Harvest*, by David Morton.
G. P. Putnam's Sons, Publishers, 1924.

*THE REVEALER

So great a thing as dawn comes quietly,
With all that morning light may have to say
Of the return of flower and field and tree
And mountains that had been awhile away.
Time and its dream that has been dark and dumb,
Deepens to brooding for a pregnant hour
That blossoms slowly . . . slowly . . . and they come:
The stately tree, the mountain, and the flower.

So much that had been buried from the world,
Lost in the grave, untroubled mood of time
Wherein all hidden shapes lie sleepily curled,
Is found again, returning in a rhyme,
Where brooding deepens to the gradual birth
Of lights and forms and colours of the earth.

In *Earth's Processional*, by David Morton.
G. P. Putnam's Sons, Publishers, 1932.

BRIEF LIST OF NATURE LYRICS

The Daffodils	Wordsworth
To a Skylark	Shelley
To a Waterfowl	Bryant
The Song of the Chattahoochie	Lanier
To a Mountain Daisy	Burns
The North Wind	Dinah Maria Milock Craik
The Linnet	Walter de la Mare

*Reprinted by special permission of the author.

To a Captive Crane	Hamlin Garland
The Harvest Moon	Henry Kirke White
Sea Lure	Cale Young Rice
Peewee	Alfred Kreymborg
Reluctance	Robert Frost
Autumn Song	E. C. Stedman
Northern California Night	William Rose Benét
Hymn to the Night	Henry W. Longfellow
Solitary Night	David Morton
Mendicant	,, ,,
Experience	,, ,,
Spring Sky	,, ,,
Unfailing Lights	,, ,,
Old Magic	,, ,,
Precedent	,, ,,

PATRIOTIC LYRICS

Patriotic lyrics are more impersonal than lyrics of love, grief or devotion. They *may* have a marked degree of intensity, but as a class, they are less intense than the other three types; they are more likely to express enthusiastic joy than sorrow. Enthusiasm is an essential element in their oral interpretation.

National hymns are among the best known of the patriotic lyrics. Each country has one that is pre-eminent and others of varying degrees of popularity. National hymns are not always of high literary value. Patriotic lyrics should be used as readings on special occasions rather than as a general form of entertainment.

EXTRACTS FROM PATRIOTIC LYRICS

From, *The Flag Goes By.*

"Hats off!
Along the street there comes
A blare of bugles, a ruffle of drums,
A flash of color beneath the sky;
Hats off!
The flag is passing by!"

Henry Holcomb Bennett.

From, *A Soldier Fallen in the Philippines*
   "A flag for the soldier's bier
   Who dies that his land may live;
   O, banners, banners here
   That he doubt not nor misgive!
   That he heed not from the tomb
   The evil days draw near
   When the nation robed in gloom,
   With its faithless past shall strive.
Let him never dream that his bullet's scream went wide of its
   Island mark,
Home to the heart of his native land where she stumbled
   and sinned in the dark.

                    William Vaughn Moody.

Used by special permission of the Publishers, Houghton,
   Mifflin Company.

EXAMPLES OF PATRIOTIC LYRICS

A TOAST TO THE FLAG

Here's to the Red of it—
   There's not a thread of it,
   No, nor a shred of it
   In all the spread of it
      From foot to head,
   But heroes bled for it,
   Faced steel and lead for it,
   Precious blood shed for it,
      Bathing it Red.

Here's to the White of it—
   Thrilled by the sight of it,
   Who knows the right of it,
   But feels the might of it
      Through day and night?
   Womanhood's care of it
   Made manhood dare for it,
   Purity's prayer for it
      Keeps it so White.

Here's to the Blue of it—
   Beauteous view of it,
   Heavenly hue of it,

Star-spangled dew of it,
    Constant and true.
States stand supreme for it,
Diadems gleam for it,
Liberty's beam for it
    Brightens the Blue.

Here's to the whole of it—
    Stars, stripes and pole of it.
Body and soul of it;
On to the goal of it,
    Carry it through.
Home or abroad for it,
Unsheath the sword for it,
Fight in accord for it,
    RED, WHITE AND BLUE!
                    John Jay Daly.

In *Poems of To-day*, Edited by Alice Cecilia Cooper.
Ginn and Company, Publishers, 1924.

The Soldier

If I should die, think only this of me:
That there's some corner of a foreign field
That is forever England. There shall be
In that rich earth a richer dust concealed;
A dust whom England bore, shaped, made aware,
Gave, once, her flowers to love, her ways to roam,
A body of England's breathing English air,
Washed by the rivers, blest by suns of home.

And think, this heart, all evil shed away,
A pulse in the eternal mind, no less
Gives somewhere back the mighty thoughts by
    England given;
Her sights and sounds; dreams happy as her day;
And laughter, learnt of friends; and gentleness,
In hearts at peace, under an English heaven.

In *The Collected Poems of Rupert Brooke*.
Used by permission of the Publishers.
Dodd, Mead and Company, Inc.

THE CONQUERED BANNER

(Written in memory of the defeat of the Confederate States
of America, 1865.)

Furl that Banner, for 'tis weary;
Round its staff 'tis drooping dreary;
Furl it, fold it, it is best.

. . . .

Furl it! for the hands that grasped it,
And the hearts that fondly clasped it,
Cold and dead are lying low;
And that Banner—it is trailing!
While around it sounds the wailing
Of its people in their woe.

For though conquered, they adore it!—
Love the cold dead hands that bore it!
Weep for those who fell before it!
Pardon those who trailed and tore it!
But, oh! wildly they deplore it,
Now who furl and fold it so.

Furl that Banner! True, 'tis gory,
Yet 'tis wreathed around with glory
And 'twill live in song and story,
Though its folds are in the dust;
For its fame on brightest pages,
Penned by poets and by sages,
Shall go sounding down the ages—
Furl its folds though now we must.

Furl that Banner, softly, slowly!
Treat it gently—it is holy—
For it droops above the dead.
Touch it not—unfold it never,
Let it droop there, furled forever,
For its people's hopes are dead!

In *Poems: Patriotic, Religious, Miscellaneous*, by Abram
J. Ryan.
P. J. Kenedy and Sons, Publishers.

THE VOICE OF FRANCIS DRAKE FROM NOMBRE DE DIOS BAY
1914
Oh England, mother England, the blue waves cover me
Where rainbow fires are flashing on crests of silver foam,

And strange flowers fling their cloying sweets over a tropic sea
   And tall palms sway on coral reefs a thousand leagues
      from home.

    Oh England, England, England
      I set your empire's bound
    When, my shadowy sails acrowding,
    Through the star-strewn billows plunging,
      I sailed the world around.

Oh England, mother England, I faced the might of Spain—
   In their shrouds of writhing sea-mist the huge black galleons
      hung;
But the God of storms fought for us and we beat them back
      again
And the sceptre of the waters from the lordly Phillip wrung.

    Oh England, England, England,
      Hold fast the gift I won,
    When, the wild gray waters ploughing,
    To an unknown splendor hasting,
      I outstripped the setting sun.

Oh England, mother England, the foe is at your door,
   And I cannot lie asleeping in this sun-drenched foreign
      grave.
I hear your navies thunder and the North Sea billows roar,
   Shattering the twilight silence where the deep-sea grasses
      wave.

    Oh England, England, England,
      I see your white cliffs stand
    With the gray fogs round them wreathing,
    Though three hundred years I'm sleeping
      In this painted sunset land.

Oh England, mother England, I rise to meet your foe,
   And my Devon lads come thronging from a thousand
      English graves.
And we launch our ghostly galleon in the stormy sunset glow,
   Clear we send our challenge ringing o'er the wild exultant
      waves.

    Oh England, England, England,
    We break death's leaden thrall;
    From flower-sweet turf awakening,

Or from ocean caverns rising,
We are answering your call;

For the scales of fate are wavering as the cannon thunders
roar,
And the lightnings flash and quiver where the battle
billows swell,
While the waves of living valor break on death's eternal shore
And men's souls, undaunted, grapple with the unchained
powers of hell;

So England, England, England,
As of old my place must be
With the sons of Britain, battling
Through the jaws of hell and crashing
Down to death and victory.
Ethelean Tyson Gaw.
Reprinted by permission of *The Lyric West* and of the author.

BRIEF LIST OF PATRIOTIC LYRICS

American	My Country 'Tis of Thee
	Star Spangled Banner
	Three Cheers for the Red White and Blue
	Dixie Land
English	God Save The King
	Rule Britannia
Canadian	Oh Canada
	The Maple Leaf Forever
French	Les Marseillaise
Scottish	The Campbells are Coming
	Scotts Wha Hae Wi Wallace Bled
Irish	The Wearing of the Green

The Battle Hymn of the Republic by Julia Ward Howe
and the *Charge of the Light Brigade* by Tennyson are called
patriotic lyrics by some authorities.

LOVE LYRICS

By far the greatest *number* of lyrics belong to this class.
They express man's love for his fellow men. They *cover the*

whole range of emotion, joy, sorrow, disappointment, hope, despair, etc; they are intensely personal, intimate and human. They should be interpreted with the intensity that befits each one, but with great simplicity and with the most genuine sincerity.

EXTRACTS FROM LYRICS OF LOVE

From, *She Walks in Beauty.*

"She walks in beauty, like the night
Of cloudless climes and starry skies;
And all that's best of dark and light
Meet in her aspect and her eyes:
Thus mellowed to that tender light
Which heaven to gaudy day denies."

Lord Byron.

From, *Love.*

"There's a place up Pelham brook,
Such·a shy and shady nook,
That I think you'd scarcely know
Why I can remember so,
How the bonfire on the hill
Startled the brown whippoorwill,
While we sang a happy song,
'Life is short, but love is long'."

Willard Wattles.

From, *The Indian Serenade.*

"I arise from dreams of thee
In the first sweet sleep, of night,
When the winds are breathing low
And the stars are shining bright;
I arise from dreams of thee,
And a spirit in my feet
Hath led me—who knows how?
To thy chamber window Sweet!"

From, *Maud.*

"Queen rose of the rosebud garden of girls,
Come hither, the dances are done,
In gloss of satin and glimmer of pearls,
Queen lily and rose in one;

.   .   .   .

She is coming, my own, my sweet;
Were it ever so airy a tread,
My heart would hear her and beat,
Were it earth in an earthy bed;
My dust would hear her and beat,
Had I lain for a century dead,
Would start and tremble under her feet
And blossom in purple and red."
Tennyson.

EXAMPLES OF LYRICS OF LOVE
MOTHER

She loved redbirds and bright mornings,
Honeysuckle and sweet spring rose,
Children's laughter and pansy faces,
All brave things that the sunlight knows;
She was frail at the last like lilies
But her smile was sunshine across the snows.

Music she loved and friendly greetings,
Kind words spoken and ill forgot;
She never faltered at any grievance
Though her heart was hurt and her eyes were hot . . .
There was nothing honest and wise and merry
And brave and tender that she was not.

Long ago in a lonely garden
Where dim leaves of the olive stir
The young Christ knelt; but had he never
Died for his truth and been laid in myrrh
I should have heard of the heart's high courage
And God's great mercy—because of her.
Willard Wattles.

In *Anthology of Magazine Verse*, Braithwaite, 1926
Copyright. The *New Outlook*.

THIS OUT OF ALL

This out of all life's giving
Has been the surpassing grace—
That your arms, O love, have held me,
And your eyes have loved my face.
This down the way of darkness

Shall light my path like flame—
That your heart has called me often
And your lips have loved my name.

In *The Slender Singing Tree* by Adelaide Love.
Used by permission of the Publishers, Dodd, Mead and
Company, Inc.

The Lover Tells of the Rose in His Heart

All things uncomely and broken, all things worn out and old,
The cry of a child by the roadway, the creak of a lumbering
    cart,
The heavy steps of the ploughman, splashing the wintry
    mould,
Are wronging your image that blossoms a rose in the deeps
    of my heart.
The wrong of unshapely things is a wrong too great to be
    told:
I hunger to build them anew and sit on a green knoll apart,
With the earth and the sky and the water, remade like a
    casket of gold,
For my dreams of your image that blossoms a rose in the
    deeps of my heart.

In *Collected Poems* by William Butler Yeats.
By permission of The Macmillan Company, Publishers.

O World, Be Nobler

O World, be nobler, for her sake!
    If she but knew thee what thou art,
What wrongs were borne, what deeds are done
In thee, beneath thy daily sun,
Know'st thou not that her tender heart
For pain and very shame would break?
O World, be nobler, for her sake!

In *Collected Poems*, by Lawrence Binyon.
By permission of The Macmillan Company, Publishers.

To Helen

Helen, thy beauty is to me
Like those Nicéan barks of yore,
That gently, o'er a perfumed sea,
The weary, wayworn wanderer bore
To his own native shore.

On desperate seas long wont to roam,
Thy hyacinth hair, thy classic face,
Thy Naiad airs, have brought me home
To the glory that was Greece
And the grandeur that was Rome.

'Lo! in yon brilliant window-niche
How statue-like I see thee stand,
The agate lamp within thy hand!
Ah, Psyche, from the regions which
Are Holy Land!

Edgar Allan Poe.

To a Friend

I ask but one thing of you, only one,
    That always you will be my dream of you!
That never shall I wake to find untrue
All this I have believed and rested on,
Forever vanished, like a vision gone
    Out into the night. Alas, how few
There are who strike in us a chord we knew
Existed, but so seldom heard its tone
    We tremble at the half-forgotten sound.
The world is full of rude awakenings
    And heaven-born castles shattered to the ground,
Yet still our human longing vainly clings
    To a belief in beauty through all wrongs.
    Oh, stay your hand, and leave my heart its songs!

Amy Lowell.

Brief List of Love Lyrics

Come Into the Garden Maude	Tennyson
The Flight of Love	Shelley
She Was a Phantom of Delight	Wordsworth
When We Two Parted	Byron
Dulce Ridentum	Stephen Vincent Benét
To The End	C. G. Rossetti
Love Poems	Emily Dickinson
The Heart on the Sleeve	Richard Le Galliene
The Door Ajar	,, ,, ,,
An Irish Face	George W. Russell ("AE")

I Will Not Let Thee Go	Robert Bridges
The Rain It Streams on Stone and Hillock	A. E. Houseman
The Cap and Bells	William Butler Yeats
Praise	Seumas O'Sullivan

SACRED OR DEVOTIONAL LYRICS

Sacred or devotional lyrics are the most *spiritual and exalted* of lyrics since they arise out of the love of God. Because they are addressed to the Supreme Being the emotion is less intimate and more lofty than that in lyrics of love and lyrics of grief; as a class they are more intense than lyrics of nature and lyrics of patriotism.

They should be interpreted with great dignity and sincerity but they should not be made ponderous or unduly solemn; the reader should express loftiness and nobility of thought but *he should not "preach."*

Hymns used in churches are sacred lyrics. Perhaps the greatest of all lyrics are to be found among the sacred lyrics of the Bible, which express deep emotion of the loftiest, most spiritual type.

EXAMPLES OF SACRED OR DEVOTIONAL LYRICS
THE NINETY-FIRST PSALM

1. He that dwelleth in the secret place of the most High shall abide under the shadow of the Almighty.

2. I will say of the Lord, He is my refuge and my fortress: my God; in Him will I trust.

3. Surely He shall deliver thee from the snare of the fowler, and from the noisome pestilence.

4. He shall cover thee with His feathers, and under His wings shalt thou trust; His truth shall be thy shield and buckler.

5. Thou shalt not be afraid for the terror by night; nor for the arrow that flieth by day;

10. There shall no evil befall thee,
    neither shall any plague come nigh thy dwelling.

11. For He shall give His angels charge over thee,
    to keep thee in all thy ways.

THE SIXTY-SEVENTH PSALM

God be merciful unto us, and
bless us: and cause his face
to shine upon us: . . .

That thy way may be known
upon earth, thy saving
health among all nations.

Let the people praise thee,
O God; let all the people
praise thee.

O let the nations be glad
and sing for joy:
for thou shall judge
the people righteously,
and govern the nations
upon earth. . . .

Let the people praise thee.
O God: let all the people
praise thee.

Then shall the earth yield
her increase; and God, even
our own God, shall bless us.

God shall bless us;
and all the ends of
the earth shall fear him.

*CHRISTMAS IN BETHLEHEM.

Shadows creep
Where Shepherds keep
    A watch upon His rest.

---

* This poem is written in the *trizad* form, which was devised and
named by Dr. Frederick Herbert Adler, of Western Reserve University.
The poem is used here with his kind permission and also with that of
the author.

Flickering low,
The torches glow
   Above His humble nest.

Still He lies
With sleepy eyes
   Upon His mother's breast.
                  Elizabeth S. Noble.

Brief List of Sacred or Devotional Lyrics

The Psalms—from the	Bible
Hymn	Theodore Parker
The Reign of Christ on Earth	James Montgomery
Jesus Shall Reign	Isaac Watts
An Eastern Hymn	Thomas Blackburn
Easter	George Herbert
My God I Love Thee	St. Francis Xavier
Jesus, Lover of My Soul	Charles Wesley
Recessional	Rudyard Kipling
Rock of Ages	Augustus Montague Toplady
Prayer	Louis Untermeyer
The Voice from Galilee	Horatius Bonar
Just for Today	Sybil F. Partridge
A Hymn to God the Father	John Donne
The World	Henry Vaughan
O God, Our Help in Ages Past	Isaac Watts
Hymn	Joseph Addison
Walking with God	William Cowper

Lyrics of Grief

Lyrics of grief might be included with lyrics of love since man grieves for the loss of those he loves or for the misfortunes that befall them. As a class, lyrics of grief are *intense* and *personal*. Sometimes the feeling is so deep that it is almost overpowering; Mrs. Browning's *Mother and Poet*, is an example of this. Perhaps there is no time when the oral reader will have to tread more carefully than when he is reading a lyric of grief. He should carefully avoid either of two extremes, that of *overdoing* them and that of *underrating* their intense sincerity. In either case they can be made almost unbearable to the hearer. Genuine simplicity and honesty, true sympathy and appreciation, which scorn affectation or show of any kind must guide the reader.

Perhaps there is no form of literature that requires a more perfect balance between *expression and suppression* than do lyrics of grief. In the reading of lyrics of grief, and lyrics of love, there should be about one-fourth expression and three-fourths suppression. Over-indulgence in the expression of emotion is very likely to offend an audience or to cause them to shut their hearts completely against all emotional response, and it shows extremely poor judgment or bad taste on the part of the reader. Care should be taken to distinguish between lyrics that express genuine sorrow of a noble nature and those that are only sentimental. Lyrics of grief are often reflective.

EXAMPLES OF LYRICS OF GRIEF
THE WAIL OF THE CORNISH MOTHER

They say 'tis a sin to sorrow,
That what God doth is best;
But 'tis only a month tomorrow
I buried it from my breast.

I thought it would call me Mother,
The very first words it said;
O, I never can love another
Like the blessed babe that's dead.

Well! God is its own dear Father;
It was carried to church and bless'd;
And our Saviour's arms will gather
Such children to their rest.

I will make my best endeavor
That my sins may be forgiven;
I will serve God more than ever;
To meet my child in heaven.

I will check this foolish sorrow,
For what God doth is best—
But O, 'tis a month tomorrow
I buried it from my breast!

R. S. Hawker.

Palgrave's *Golden Treasury.*
E. P. Dutton and Company, Publishers.

BREAK, BREAK, BREAK

Break, break, break,
On thy cold gray stones, O sea!
And I would that my tongue could utter
The thoughts that arise in me.

O well for the fisherman's boy,
That he shouts with his sister at play!
O well for the sailor lad,
That he sings in his boat on the bay!

And the stately ships go on
To their haven under the hill;
But O for the touch of a vanished hand,
And the sound of a voice that is still!

Break, break, break
At the foot of thy crags, O sea!
But the tender grace of a day that is dead
Will never come back to me.

Alfred Tennyson.

ALONE BY THE HEARTH

Here, in my snug little fire-lit chamber,
    Sit I alone:
And, as I gaze in the coals, I remember
    Days long agone.
Saddening it is when the night has descended,
    Thus to sit here,
Pensively musing on episodes ended
    Many a year.

Still in my vision a golden-haired glory
    Flits to and fro;
She whom I loved—but 'tis just the old story:
    Dead, long ago.

'Tis but a wraith of love; yet I linger
    (Thus passion errs),
Foolishly kissing the ring on my finger—
    Once it was hers.

Nothing has changed since her spirit departed,
    Here, in this room
Save I, who, weary, and half broken-hearted,
    Sit in the gloom.
Loud 'gainst the window the winter wind dashes,
    Dreary and cold;
Over the floor the red fire-light flashes
    Just as of old.

Just as of old—but the embers are scattered,
    Whose ruddy blaze
Flashed o'er the floor where the fairy feet pattered
    In other days!
Then, her dear voice, like a silver chime ringing,
    Melted away;
Often these walls have re-echoed her singing,
    Now hushed for aye!

Years have rolled by; I am wiser and older—
    Wiser, but yet
Not till my heart and its feelings grow colder,
    Can I forget.
So in my snug little fire-lit chamber,
    Sit I alone;
And, as I gaze in the coals, I remember
    Days long agone!

In *Drift: A Sea-Shore Idyl and Other Poems*. George Arnold.
Tichnor and Fields, Publishers.

TELLING THE BEES

Here is the place; right over the hill
Runs the path I took;
You can see the gap in the old wall still,
And the stepping-stones in the shallow brook.
There is the house, with the gate, red-barred,
And the poplars tall;
And the barn's brown length, and the cattle yard,
And the white horns tossing above the wall.

There are the beehives ranged in the sun;
And down by the brink of the brook
Are her flowers, weed o'errun,
Pansy and daffodil, rose and pink.
A year has gone as the tortoise goes.
Heavy and slow;
And the same rose blows, and the same sun glows,
And the same brook sings of a year ago.

I mind me how with a lover's care
From my Sunday coat
I brushed off the burrs, and smoothed my hair,
And cooled at the brookside my brow and throat.
Since we parted, a month has passed
To love, a year;
Down through the beeches I looked at last
On the little red gate and the well-sweep near.

I can see it all now—the slantwise rain
Of light through the leaves,
The sundown's blaze on her window-pane,
The bloom of her roses under the eaves,
The house and the trees,
The barn's brown gable, the vine by the door,
Nothing had changed—but the hives of bees.

Before them, under the garden wall,
Forward and back,
Went drearily singing the chore-girl small,
Draping each hive with a shred of black.
Trembling I listened: The summer sun
Had the chill of snow;
For I knew she was telling the bees of one
Gone on a journey we all must go!

Then I said to myself, "My Mary weeps
For the dead today:
Haply her blind old grandsire sleeps
The fret and pain of his age away."

But her dog whined low; on the doorway sill
With his cane to his chin,
The old grandsire sat; and the chore-girl still
Sung to the bees stealing out and in.
And the song she was singing ever since
In my ear sounds on:

"Stay at home, pretty bees, fly not hence!
Mistress Mary is dead and gone!"
                                    John Greenleaf Whittier.

BRIEF LIST OF LYRICS OF GRIEF

The Changeling	James Russell Lowell
She Came and Went	,, ,, ,,
The First Snowfall	,, ,, ,,
She Dwelt Among the Untrodden Ways	William Wordsworth
The Irish Emigrant's Lament	Lady Dufferin
The Phantom	Bayard Taylor
The Afternote of the Hour	C. Tennyson-Turner
On the Death of Joseph Rodman Drake	Fitz-Greene Halleck
Rugby Chapel	Matthew Arnold
On the Receipt of My Mother's Picture	William Cowper
When Lilacs Last in the Dooryard Bloomed	Walt Whitman.

MEMORIAL VERSE, DIRGES AND ELEGIES

Memorial verse, dirges and elegies belong in a general class with lyrics of grief. The emotion is often much less intense than in the short lyrics of grief, and because of this they may be and often are of considerable length.

EXAMPLE OF MEMORIAL VERSE
IN MEMORIAM

'Tis right for her to sleep between
Some of those old Cathedral walls,
And right too that her grave is green
With all the dew and rain that falls.

'Tis well the organ's solemn sighs
Should soar and sink around her rest,
And almost in her ear should rise
The prayers of those she loved the best.

'Tis also well this air is stirr'd
By Nature's voices loud and low,

By thunder and the chirping bird,
And grasses whispering as they grow.

For all her spirit's earthly course
Was as a lesson and a sign
How to o'errule the hard divorce
That parts things natural and divine.

Undaunted by the clouds of fear,
Undazzled by a happy day,
She made a Heaven about her here,
And took how much! with her away.
                    R. M. (Milnes), Lord Houghton.
Palgrave's *Golden Treasury*.

BRIEF LIST OF EXAMPLES OF MEMORIAL VERSE

The Burial of Sir John Moore	Charles Wolfe
Adonais	Shelley
Captain, My Captain	Walt Whitman
In Memoriam	Tennyson

EXAMPLE OF A DIRGE
A DIRGE

Naiad, hid beneath the bank
    By the willowy river side,
Where Narcissus gently sank,
    Where unmarried Echo died,
Unto thy serene repose
Waft the stricken Anteros.

Where the tranquil swan is borne,
    Imaged in a watery glass,
Where the sprays of fresh pink thorn
    Stoop to catch the boats that pass,
Where the earliest orchis grows,
Bury thou fair Anteros.

Glide we by, with prow and oar:
    Ripple shadows off the wave,
And reflected on the shore
    Haply play about his grave.
Folds of summer-light enclose
All that once was Anteros.

On a flickering wave we gaze,
    Not upon his answering eyes:
Flower and bird we scarce can praise,
    Having lost his sweet replies:
Cold and mute the river flows
With our tears for Anteros.
                    W. Johnson-Cory.

Palgrave's *Golden Treasury.*

Brief List of Examples of the Dirge

Bridal Song and Dirge	Thomas Lovell Beddoes
Dirge	Charles Gamage Eastman
Dirge for a Young Girl	James Thomas Fields
Sea Dirge	Shakespeare
The Dirge of Imogen	Shakespeare
Dirge of Love	Shakespeare
A Dirge	Tennyson

The Elegy

"The words elegy and elegiac must be used with caution . . .
'elegiac' refers more to the metre than to the subject. In
English we understand it generally to mean solemn or
plaintive poetry . . . in general terms an elegy is a song of
grief whether acute or mild."

From *Handbook of Poetics,* by Francis B. Gummere, pp. 49-50.
Ginn and Company, Publishers.

Gray's *Elegy in a Country Churchyard* is probably the
best known elegy in the English language. The following is
one of the best loved stanzas.

      "Full many a gem of purest ray serene
      The dark unfathom'd caves of ocean bear:
      Full many a flower is born to blush unseen,
      And waste its sweetness on the desert air."

EXAMPLE OF A BRIEF ELEGY

ELEGY

Oh snatch'd away in beauty's bloom!
On thee shall press no ponderous tomb:
But on thy turf shall roses rear
Their leaves, the earliest of the year,
And the wild cypress wave in tender gloom:

And oft by yon blue gushing stream
Shall Sorrow lean her drooping head,
And feed deep thought with many a dream,
And lingering pause and lightly tread;
Fond wretch! as if her step disturb'd the dead!

Away! we know that tears are vain,
That Death nor heeds nor hears distress:
Will this unteach us to complain?
Or make one mourner weep the less?
And thou, who tell'st me to forget,
Thy looks are wan, thine eyes are wet.

Lord Byron.

CHAPTER XX

THE SONNET

A sonnet is "a piece of verse (properly expressive of one main idea) consisting of fourteen decasyllabic* lines, with rimes arranged according to one of two certain definite schemes." *Murray's English Dictionary.*

T HE sonnet is *comparatively* modern and is highly literary or 'artificial.' It is produced by painstaking care and is closely bound by rules and conventions. It *must* have fourteen lines, no more, no less; there must be five stressed syllables in each line; each line must end in a rhyme word. It is formal, dignified and restrained.

The Purpose of the Sonnet

The purpose of the sonnet is to express one idea and one emotion in a certain fixed arrangement of fourteen lines.

Types of Sonnets

There are two types of sonnets.
 1. The Italian or Petrarchian.
 2. The English or Shakesperian.

These two types differ in the arrangement of the rhyme. The *Italian* rhyme arrangement has always been, and continues to be, used more than the English. It is divided into two parts which are separated by a distinct pause. The *first* part is the *octave* composed of the *first eight* lines; the *last* part is the *sestet* composed of the last six lines.

The arrangement of the *rhyme* is as follows:
Octave. First   line a
             Second   ” b

_____

*Having ten syllables.

	Third	"	b
	Fourth	"	a
	Fifth	"	a
	Sixth	"	b
	Seventh	"	b
	Eighth	"	a
Sestet.	Ninth	"	c or c
	Tenth	"	d " d
	Eleventh	"	e " c
	Twelfth	"	c " d
	Thirteenth	"	d " c
	Fourteenth	"	e " d

In the *English* rhyme scheme which is made up of three *quatrains* and a *couplet*, the arrangement of the rhyme is as follows:

First Quatrain:

First	line	a
Second	"	b
Third	"	a
Fourth	"	b

Second Quatrain:

Fifth	"	c
Sixth	"	d
Seventh	"	c
Eighth	"	d

Third Quatrain:

Ninth	line	e
Tenth	"	f
Eleventh	"	e
Twelfth	"	f

Couplet:

| Thirteenth | " | g |
| Fourteenth | " | g |

The Speaker and the Listener

The reader must speak for the author directly to the audience.

Impersonation in Sonnets

There is no impersonation in sonnets, but there must be understanding of, and deep sympathy with, persons and personalities, and these must be revealed properly by means of voice, speech, facial expression and bearing.

Rhythm in Sonnets

The rhythm is determined very definitely by the number of stresses in each line and by the formal and fixed rhyme arrangement.

Oral Interpretation of Sonnets

In the *interpretation* of a sonnet the reader should bear in mind that it expresses but one idea or one emotion, and that it is carefully and formally built up to a definite climax near the end. The meaning should be brought out very clearly: the emotion should be made to *underlie* the thought with great fullness and power, throbbing in its intensity, *ready* to break through the thought at any time, but rarely, if ever actually doing so.

The sonnet can never be used as a *popular* form of entertainment. It is too highly cultivated, too reserved and too formal for such use. It is, as a class, difficult to read, but, like the literary epic and the ode, it well repays one for the study it takes to master it. Like these two forms it belongs, as a general rule, only in the repertoire of the trained artist, but it holds an important and distinctive place there. Generally speaking, it should be used only for certain audiences on certain occasions. Modern sonnets, as a class, are more suited to use for the entertainment of the average audience than are the more classical examples. Perhaps they are closer to our own experiences because they deal with things we know, and use a language that we understand.

Examples of Sonnets

I Never See The Red Rose Crown The Year

I never see the red rose crown the year,
Nor feel the young grass underneath my tread,
Without the thought, "This living beauty here
Is earth's remembrance of a beauty dead:
Surely where all this glory is displayed
Love has been quick like fire to high ends,
Here, in this grass, an altar has been made
For some white joy, some sacrifice of friends;
Here, where I stand, some leap of human brains
Has touched immortal things and left its trace,
The earth is happy here, the gleam remains;
Beauty is here, the spirit of the place,
    I touch the faith which nothing can destroy,
    The earth, the living church of ancient joy.

In *Poems and Plays of John Masefield*, p. 413.
By permission of the Macmillan Company, Publishers.

Why He Was There

Much as he left it when he went from us
Here was the room again where he had been
So long that something of him should be seen,
Or felt—and so it was. Incredulous,
I turned about, loath to be greeted thus,
And there he was in his old chair, serene
As ever, and as laconic and as lean
As when he lived, and as cadaverous.

Calm as he was of old when we were young,
He sat there gazing at the pallid flame
Before him. "And how far will this go on?"
I thought. He felt the failure of my tongue,
And smiled: "I was not here until you came;
And I shall not be here when you are gone."

In *Sonnets*, by Edwin Arlington Robinson.
By permission of The Macmillan Company, Publishers.

A Bit of Mull

Today my little girl, behind a door,
Pulled out a sack which held old cloth and rags—
That dreams and memories may be found in bags,

When lost awhile, I never knew before.
A heap of scraps (silk, gingham, muslin, wool)
To me became the pages of a book
That told a story.—Then just one she took
And said: "O father, see how beautiful!"

A bit of mull! . . . (We sat beside a lake,
In April time, my love and I. The trees
Bent low and turned the shaded blue to gray.
We watched the sun and sky and waters make
The afterglow there weave a living frieze) . . .
"That mull? Your mother wore it yesterday!"

In *Leaven for Loaves*, by Frederick Herbert Adler.
Harold Vinal, New York, Publisher, 1927.

Reprinted by special permission of the author.

STONE WALLS OF NEW ENGLAND

O walls of stone, built carefully and straight,
You lie beneath the sunshine and the night,
The men who built you knew not they were great,
Nor ever dreamed you would reveal their might;
But every day they labored hard and long
To make their fields yield harvest to their hand,
Your stones, which would have vanquished men less
    strong,
Became submissive at their stern command.
They made of you the guardian of their homes,
Evoked a blessing from reluctant earth,
They built their souls forever in gray stones,
And left a heritage of manly worth.
No land of stones can labor's hand deny,
Gray guardian walls in silent witness lie.

                    Catherine Cate Coblentz.

Reprinted by special permission of the author.

TO MY FATHER
(Sir Herbert Beerbohm Tree)

I cannot think that you have gone away,
You loved the earth—and life lit up your eyes,
And flickered in your smile that would surmise
Death as a song, a poem, or a play.

You were reborn afresh with every day,
And baffled fortune in some new disguise.
Ah! can it perish when the body dies,
Such youth, such love, such passion to be gay?
We shall not see you come to us and leave
A conqueror—nor catch on fairy wing
Some slender fancy—nor new wonders weave
Upon the loom of your imagining.
The world is wearier, grown dark to grieve
Her child that was a pilgrim and a king.

In *Poems by Iris Tree.*
Used by permission of the Publishers, Dodd, Mead and
Company, Inc.

SONNET

They brought me tidings; and I did not hear
More than a fragment of the words they said.
Their further speech died dull upon my ear;
For my rapt spirit otherwhere had fled—
Fled unto you in other times and places.
Old memories winged about me in glad flight.
I saw your lips of longing and delight,—
Your grave glad eyes beyond their chattering faces.
I saw a world where you have been to me
More than the sun, more than the waking wind.
I saw a brightness that they could not see.
And yet I seemed as smitten deaf and blind.
I heard but fragments of the words they said.
Life wanes. The sunlight darkens. You are dead.

In *Collected Poems*, by Arthur Davison Ficke.
Copyright. Doubleday, Doran Company, Inc.

MARY

And when I seek the chamber where she dwelt,
Near one loved chair a well-worn spot I see,
Worn by the shifting of a feeble knee
While the poor head bow'd lowly—it would melt
The worldling's heart with instant sympathy:
The match-box and the manual, lying there,
Those sad sweet signs of wakefulness and prayer,
Are darling tokens of the Past to me:
The little rasping sound of taper lit
At midnight, which aroused her slumbering bird:

The motion of her languid frame that stirr'd
For ease in some new posture—tho' a word
Perchance, of sudden anguish, follow'd it;
All this how often had I seen and heard!

Palgrave's *Golden Treasury.* C. Tennyson-Turner.
E. P. Dutton and Company, Publishers.

WHEN THERE IS MUSIC

Whenever there is music, it is you
Who come between me and the sound of strings:
The cloudy portals part to let you through,
Troubled and strange with long rememberings.
Your nearness gathers ghostwise down the room,
And through the pleading violins they play,
There drifts the dim and delicate perfume
That once was you, come dreamily astray.

Behind what thin and shadowy doors you wait
That such frail things as these should set you free!
When all my need like armies at a gate,
Would storm in vain to bring you back to me;
When in this hush of strings you draw more near
Than any sound of music that I hear.

David Morton.

From *The Century Magazine.*
Used by permission of D. Appleton-Century Company, Inc.

*NOS IMMORTALES

Perhaps we go with wind and cloud and sun,
Into the free companionship of air;
Perhaps with sunsets when the day is done,
All's one to me—I do not greatly care;
So long as there are brown hills—and a tree
Like a mad prophet in a land of dearth—
And I can lie and hear eternally

The vast monotonous breathing of the earth.
I have known hours, slow and golden-glowing,
Lovely with laughter and suffused with light,
O Lord, in such a time appoint my going,

---

*Copyright, 1918, 1920, 1923, 1925, 1929, 1930, 1931, by Stephen
Vincent Benét.

When the hands clench, and the cold face grows white,
And the spark dies within the feeble brain,
Spilling its star-dust back to dust again.

In *Ballads and Poems*, published by Farrar and Rinehart, Inc.

GUESTS*

Browsing among old books long laid away
    In dusty corners and with none to care.
Nearly forgotten in our noisy day,—
    All suddenly there thronged about me there,
Fine ladies and such gentlemen of fashion,
    And such a stir of curtseying they made!
With quaint and stately speech and hinted passion
    Of tea-cup tints and delicate brocade.

And once— I swear—there drifted to my face,
    Across a century's disdainful span,
A wisp of perfume from a bit of lace,
    And once, the fainting rustle of a fan . . .
And only when I laughed my rude surprise,
    They floated off with grave and startled eyes.
                                        David Morton.

VISITOR*

The long, blue evening brings the golden moon,
From out the reaches of old, nameless lands,
To minds in need of beauty for a boon,
And hearts in need of healing at her hands.
Wearing as any queen her shadowy gown,

She comes in quiet to the grateful street,
A grave and thoughtful presence through the town,—
And peace is with the passing of her feet.

Into the grieved and fretful hearts of men,
The long-robed evening strays, a wanderer,
And there is rest and quietness again,
And the cool scented loveliness of her,—
Come, lately now, from old and weary lands,
Bearing the boon in beautiful, still hands.

In *Harvest*, by David Morton.
G. P. Putnam's Sons, Publishers.

---

*Reprinted by special permission of the author.

BRIEF LIST OF SONNETS THAT MAY BE USED AS READINGS

Autumn	Edwin Curran
Old Ships	David Morton
Symbols	,, ,,
To the Victor	William Ellery Leonard

The above are to be found in *Modern American Poetry* edited by Louis Untermeyer. Harcourt, Brace and Co., New York.

Shall I compare Thee to a Summer Day	Shakespeare
The World is too Much With Us	Wordsworth
On His Being Arrived at the Age of Twenty Three	Milton
Sonnets from the Portugese	Elizabeth Barrett Browning
The Might of One Fair Face	Michael Angelo
The Wayfarers	Rupert Brooke
Treasure	Hortense Flexner
April Moment	Arthur Davison Ficke
On Growing Old	John Masefield
Rupert Brooke	W. W. Gibson
To L. H. B.	Katherine Mansfield
Sonnet to a Plow-Woman of Norway	Margaret Tod Ritter
Driving Home the Cows	Kate Putnam Osgood
Vision	William Dean Howells

Many of the sonnets of David Morton in his books, *Earth's Processional*, *Harvest*, and *Nocturns and Autumnals*, make delightful readings.

CHAPTER XXI

THE ODE

The ode is "a rimed (rarely unrimed) lyric, often in the form of an address; generally dignified or exalted in subject, feeling and style, but sometimes (in earlier use) simple and familiar (though less so than a song)." *Murray's English Dictionary.*

The ode is "any strain of enthusiastic and exalted lyrical verse directed to a fixed purpose and dealing progressively with one dignified theme." Edmund Gosse.

THE ode is *consciously written*, and is *decidedly literary;* it does not spring freely and naturally from the lips of men as national epics and ballads do, nor from the inmost hearts of men as lyrics do. It is *formal and artistic*, having been *carefully planned* and *carefully executed*. It is *one of the most elaborate forms* of literature. It expresses exalted, sustained feeling and highly imaginative thought. It is usually of considerable length, and the style is dignified throughout. It does not tell a story although it may have some narrative, incidentally. It deals with a *theme* which is of serious nature.

PURPOSE OF THE ODE

The *purpose* of the ode may be said to be *elaborate exposition of a theme on a serious and exalted subject*, revealing the high thoughts and noble emotions of the author.

The interpreter will be obliged to state to himself in his own words just what the theme of an ode is, before he is ready to study it for the purpose of oral presentation.

TPYES OF ODES

There are three types of odes:

   1. The Horatian Ode—

      Example: *An Horatian Ode upon Cromwell's Return from Ireland*—Andrew Marvel.

2. The Pindaric Ode—
   Example: *The Progress of Poesy*—Thomas Gray.

3. The English Ode—
   Example: *On a Grecian Urn*—John Keats.

THE SPEAKER AND THE LISTENER

The interpreter speaks for the author directly to the audience.

THE RHYTHM OF ODES

Watts-Dunton says "the ear of the reader should catch a great metrical scheme . . . the varying form must embody and express the varying emotions of the singer."

By the time the student of oral interpretation comes to the study of the ode he should have learned how to catch the rhythm of a selection. He will be obliged to give an ode very serious study, such as a literary epic calls for, in order to read the lines with the proper rhythm but in a manner befitting the dignity and loftiness of the theme of the poem. The rhythm is not at all likely to leap at him from the page as it will often do from ballads and true lyrics. He will probably have to work hard to get it and to get it right, and still harder to reveal it properly.

ORAL INTERPRETATION OF THE ODE

The basic principles that should be observed in the oral interpretation of the ode are the same for all types. Each individual ode must be studied by the reader to enable him to *apply* the principles in a way that will bring out its significance and beauty to the best advantage.

In the oral interpretation of an ode the high dignity and noble quality of the thought and emotion, and the formal rhythm of the verse should be fully maintained. Its beauty should also be well brought out but it should be made as human and as intimate as possible. Then and then only will it touch the experience of most listeners. The reader should bring its loftiness and dignity to the listeners and share it with them, not speak it above their heads, or hold it up for display.

> ". . . the ode is a mono-drama, the actor in which is the poet himself; . . ., if the actor in the mono-drama is not affected by the sentiments he expresses, the ode must be cold and lifeless."
>
> Watts-Dunton.

The ode *will never be a popular* form of literature for oral interpretation because *it has not enough story* to be really entertaining; its *feeling is not personal or extreme enough* to grip the hearts of the masses; and *its tone is too serious* for their daily fare. The rhythm does not sweep one's attention on and on regardless of the thought as it does in some ballads and true lyrics, and there is *no dramatic action* to bring it close home to the mass of listeners. It can be read only on special occasions, but when one of these special,—and always important—occasions comes, nothing will be suitable and adequate but an ode. Then, the person who has studied this form well in order "to be ready when the chance would come" may walk proudly up the ladder to high success leaving the great mass of merely *good* interpreters far behind. Only a trained artist can interpret an ode fully, but when properly done the effect is genuinely magnificent, inspiring and noble.

Brief Extract from an Ode

"The praise of Bacchus then the sweet musician sung,
Of Bacchus ever fair and ever young:
The jolly god in triumph comes;
Sound the trumpets, beat the drums!
Flush'd with a purple grace
He shows his honest face:
Now give the hautboys breath; he comes, he comes!
Bacchus, ever fair and ever young,
Drinking joys did first ordain;
Bacchus' blessings are a treasure,
Drinking is the soldier's pleasure:
Rich the treasure,

Sweet the pleasure,
Sweet is pleasure after pain."
Alexander's Feast, or, The Power of Music. Dryden.

From, ODE ON THE DEATH OF THE DUKE OF WELLINGTON
(Abridged).

Bury the Great Duke
   With an empire's lamentation!
Let us bury the Great Duke
   To the noise of the mourning of a mighty nation.
Mourning when their leaders fall,
Warriors carry the warrior's pall,
And sorrow darkens hamlet and hall.

Where shall we lay the man whom we deplore?
Here, in streaming London's central roar,
Let the sound of those he wrought for,
And the feet of those he fought for,
Echo round his bones for evermore.

Lead out the pageant: sad and slow,
As fits a universal woe,
Let the long procession go,
And let the sorrowing crowd about it grow
And let the mournful martial music blow:
The last great Englishman is low!

Mourn, for to us he seems the last,
Remembering all his greatness in the past,
No more in soldier-fashion will he greet
With lifted hand the gazer in the street.
. . . .

. . . .

Great in council and great in war,
   Foremost captain of his time,
Rich in saving common sense,
And, as the greatest only are,
   In his simplicity sublime.

O good gray head which all men knew,
O voice from which their omens all men drew,

O iron nerve to true occasion true,
O fall'n at length that tower of strength
Which stood four-square to all the winds that blew!
Such was he whom we deplore.
The long self-sacrifice of life is o'er:
The great world-victor's victor will be seen no more.

. . . .

Peace! his triumph will be sung
By some yet unmoulded tongue,
Far on in summers that we shall not see.
   Peace! it is a day of pain
For one about whose patriarchal knee
Late the little children clung:
    O peace! it is a day of pain
    For one upon whose hand and heart and brain
Once the weight and fate of Europe hung:
    Ours the pain, be his the gain!

. . . .

We revere, and while we hear
The tides of Music's golden sea
Setting toward eternity,
Uplifted high in heart and hope are we,
Until we doubt not that for one so true
There must be other nobler work to do
Than when he fought at Waterloo,
And victor he must ever be.

For though the Giant Ages heave the hill
And break the shore, and evermore,
Make and break, and work their will;
   Though world on world in myriad myriads roll
Round us, each with different powers,
And other forms of life than ours,
   What know we greater than the soul?

On God and Godlike men we build our trust.
Hush! the "Dead March" wails in the people's ears:
The dark crowd moves, and there are sobs and tears:
The black earth yawns; the mortal disappears:
   Ashes to ashes, dust to dust.

He is gone who seemed so great—
   Gone; but nothing can bereave him

Of the force he made his own
    Being here, and we believe him
Something far advanced in state,
And that he wears a truer crown
    Than any wreath that man can weave him,
But speak no more of his renown;
Lay your earthly fancies down;
        And in the vast cathedral leave him.
        God accept him, Christ receive him!
                                Alfred Tennyson.

BRIEF LIST OF ODES

Alexander's Feast	Dryden
Commemoration Ode	Lowell
Intimations of Immortality	Wordsworth
Ode for Music on St. Cecilia's Day	Pope
Ode to Duty	Wordsworth
On a Grecian Urn	Keats
On Mrs. Arabella Hunt Singing	Congreve
On the Morning of Christ's Nativity	Milton
Song for St. Cecilia's Day	Dryden
The Departing Year	Coleridge
The First of April	Warton
To a Nightingale	Keats
To a Skylark	Shelley
To Victor Hugo in Exile	Swinburne
West Wind	Shelley

CHAPTER XXII

EPIC POETRY

The epic: "pertaining to or constituting an epos or heroic poem; narrating at length and in metrical form as a poetic whole with subordination of parts a series of heroic achievements of events under supernatural guidance." *Century Dictionary.*

THE epic deals with *deeds of the past.* The poet relates happenings, introduces characters and speaks alternately for himself and for the characters he presents, thus introducing *dialogue.* As a rule, the characters are natural, though important, human beings, and talk and act in a natural way regardless of the fact that a supernatural element usually pervades the poem as a whole. There is no preaching in an epic, it points no moral; it simply relates things as they happened or are supposed to have happened.

An epic has a "multiplicity of plots," containing many *episodes.* An episode is an *incident* or *short story* related to some *part* of the epic but not related to it *as a whole.*

Purpose of The Epic

The *purpose* of the epic is to recount in the form of a vigorous and heroic story, the happenings—true or imaginary—of a tribe or race of people covering a long period of time.

Types of Epics

There are two general types of epic poetry:

1. National or popular epics.

2. Literary or grand epics.

National or Popular Epics

The national or popular epic *is the work of many people* but it is usually given its final form by one or two people who

251

assemble the parts into one harmonious whole. It deals with the history and legends of a race of people through a long period of time. It narrates events that happened, or are supposed to have happened, centering them about a dominant heroic figure, real or imaginary. All the hoeric deeds of the race during centuries of development may be attributed to this one hero during a single life time. The hero represents the ideals of the race.

EXAMPLES OF NATIONAL OR POPULAR EPICS

The Greek *Iliad and Odyssey*
Anglo-Saxon *Beowulf*
German *Nibelungenlied*
Persian *Shah-Nameh*
Spanish *Poems of Cyd*
Finnish *Kalevala*
Sanskrit *Mahabharata*
French *The Song of Roland*

EXTRACTS FROM FRENCH NATIONAL EPIC

L XXX VII

"O Roland, sound on your ivory horn,
To the ear of Karl shall the blast be borne:
He will bid his legions backward bend,
And all his barons their aid will lend."
    "Now God forbid it, for very shame,
That for me my kindred were stained with blame,
Or that gentle France to such vileness fell:
This good sword that hath served me well,
My Durindana such strokes shall deal,
That with blood encrimsoned shall be the steel.
By their evil star are the fellows led;
They shall be numbered among the dead."

The Song of Roland. Translator, John O'Hagan.
The Harvard Classics, Vol. 10. P. F. Collier & Son Company, Publishers.

Literary or Grand Epics

The literary or grand epic *is the work of one man* who is a scholar and an artist.

For purposes of oral entertainment it is wise to distinguish the *classical* literary epic from the *modern*. The *classical* epic justifies the title "grand"; it deals in a grand manner with strange people in strange and extraordinary situations. The *modern* literary epic deals with human beings like ourselves; both in the subject matter and in its treatment it resembles the national or popular epic, but the supernatural element is usually lacking.

Extract from Literary or Grand Epic

"The tempter all impassioned thus began:

. . . .

'Queen of the universe! do not believe
Those rigid threats of death; ye shall not die:
How should ye? by the fruit? it gives you life
To knowledge . . . look on me,
Me who have touched and tasted, yet . . . live,
And life more perfect have attained than fate
Meant me, by vent'ring higher than my lot.
Shall that be shut to man, which to the beast
Is open?

From *Paradise Lost*, Book IX. Milton.

Brief List of Literary Epics

Classical.	The Aeneid	Virgil
	Paradise Lost	Milton
	Paradise Regained	"
	The Inferno	Dante
Modern.	Hiawatha	Henry W. Longellow
	Drake	Alfred Noyes
	John Brown's Body,	Stephen Vincent Benét

The Speaker and The Listener

The same rule of interpretation concerning speaker and listener applies to the epic as that which applies to any *story* where characters and dialogue are introduced. The reader speaks *for the author to the audience* in the narrative, and *for one character to another* in the dialogue. The transitions from narrator to character and from one character to another and back again to narrator, must be made with the most extreme simplicity and skill so that they are absolutely non-existant as far as the audience is concerned.

Impersonation in Epics

The characters should be *suggested* as in stories, not impersonated. Characters in *national* epics and in *modern literary* epics are very much *like* ourselves in nature and they speak and act very much as we do. In *classical literary* epics the characters are unusual and exceptional, often very *unlike* ourselves. The reader will be obliged to take his cue from the author's descriptions and explanations and suggest the characters accordingly. It will be necessary for him to suggest the mental and emotional states of the characters—and the general bodily poise or attitudes that suggest these emotional states.

"Wonder and admiration are the emotions proper to heroic poetry." W. M. Dixon.

The Rhythm of Epics

The rhythm of popular epics and of modern literary epics is, as a rule, more spirited than that of classical literary epics. In classical literary epics the general movement is more slow and stately, suggesting grandeur and magnificence. Epic rhythm is uniform, flowing smoothly and evenly, delightfully and alluringly. If one could not understand the words of the story the music of the sounds and rhythm would lead one on and on unto the end. The *rhythm of the metre* and the *rhythm of the sense* should be made to synchronize so perfectly that they are blended together and become one.

Extracts from Epics Make Good Readings

Short extracts from *national* epics and from *modern literary* epics make very pleasing and popular readings. They tell a straight-forward and heroic story about people in nature like ourselves, introducing a pronounced dramatic element in characters and dialogue. The story is told in melodious language arranged in rhythmic form, thereby including all the elements of entertainment that please the greatest number of human beings on the greatest number of occasions.

Classical literary epics do not supply *popular* readings but they give great pleasure to audiences whose literary education is so far advanced that they understand and appreciate their superior qualities.

> "The power to appreciate work of high artistic quality is only a little more common than the power to produce it . . . Great art usually makes its way slowly."
> *Channels of English Literature,* p. 285. W. M. Dixon, J. M. Dent and Sons, Publishers.

As a rule, extracts from classical literary epics should be short; they should depict action or express deep emotion and include as much narrative and drama as possible. The descriptive portions, noble and magnificent though they be, seldom make good readings for public entertainment.

Oral Interpretation of Epics.

The reader should use *variety* of pitch of voice, of rate of utterance, of volume of tone and of degree of stress, to avoid any possibility of *monotony* in his reading. The grandeur of the poem and its nobleness of expression are its great assets, but they give the reader his greatest problems. He should reveal the grandeur without making the reading heavy, and should reveal the nobleness without making it "too good." The expression should be made as human as possible without losing its majestic quality. A proper and finely adjusted balance between sense and rhythm, between thought and feeling, between reality and unreality, between formality and informality should be maintained. Only an experienced and efficient reader should attempt the oral interpretation of extracts from classical literary epics, but he will be richly rewarded for his study and his effort when he has mastered them. He should always remember he is treading the highest peaks of literary interpretation and that "the very height bids him tread carefully lest he fall into the depths below."

EXTRACT FROM BEOWULF
(Abridged).

Lo, praise of the prowess of people-kings
of spear-armed Danes, in days long sped.
Hrothgar, the King of the Danes
bid his henchmen a hall uprear,
a master mead-house mightier far
than ever was seen by the sons of earth.
　　It fell, as he ordered,
in rapid achievement that ready it stood there,
of halls the noblest; Heorot, he named it.
So lived the clansmen in cheer and revel.

With envy and anger an evil spirit
heard each day the din and revel
high in the hall.
Grendel this monster grim was called;
fiend of hell in moorland living.

Went he forth to find at fall of night
that haughty house,
Found within it the atheling band
asleep after feasting and fearless of sorrow.
Grim and greedy, he grasped betimes,
thirty of the thanes, and thence he rushed
laden with slaughter, his lair to seek.

Then at the dawning, as day was breaking
the might of Grendel to men was known;
then after wassail was wail uplifted,
loud moan in the morn.
With night returning, anew began

ruthless murder. Ceaselessly Grendel
harassed Hrothgar.

Twelve years' tide the trouble he bore.
The evil one ambushed old and young.
Such heaping of horrors the hater of men,
wrought unceasing! O'er Heorot he lorded,
and ne'er could the prince have joy in his hall.

Now Beowulf bode in the burg of the Scyldings;
heard in his home of Grendel's doings.
He was the mightiest man of valor
in that same day of this our life.
And now the bold one comrades chose;
the keenest of warriors e'er he could find
and led them on to the land's confines.
Time had now flown; afloat was the ship;
on board they climbed, warriors ready;
Then moved o'er the waters by might of wind
that bark like a bird with breast of foam,
till in season due, their haven was found,
their journey ended.

Quickly the clansmen climbed ashore
anchored their sea-wood. God they thanked
for passing in peace o'er the paths of the sea.

They bent them to march till the hall they saw
where Hrothgar lived,
and the gleam of it lighted o'er lands afar.
Corselets glistened as they strode along
in mail of battle, and marched to the hall.
The wall along, they set their bucklers;
their weapons stacked.

      A warrior proud
asked of the heroes their home and kin,
Him the sturdy-in-war bespake with words,
"Hygelac's, we; I am Beowulf named.
I am seeking to say this mission of mine
to thy master-lord, if he deign at all
grace that we meet him."

Then hied the troop where the herald led them,
under Heorot's roof: Beowulf spake,
"Thou Hrothgar, hail! Hygelac's I,

kinsman and follower. These Grendel-deeds
I heard in my home-land heralded clear,
So, from thee, a boon I seek,—
that I alone with my liegemen here,
this hardy band, may Heorot purge!
And Grendel now be mine to quell
in single battle.

More I hear, that the monster dire,
of weapons recks not; hence shall I scorn
brand or buckler to bear in the fight,
but with gripe alone
must I front the fiend and fight for life,
foe against foe.

Hrothgar spake, "Friend my Beowulf,
to succor and save, thou hast sought us here.
No wish shall fail thee
if thou bidest the battle with blood-won life."

"Never to any man erst I trusted,
this noble Dane-Hall, till now to thee,
Have now and hold this house unpeered;
remember thy glory; thy might declare;
watch for the foe!"
Then Hrothgar went with his hero-train
forth from the hall.

Beowulf Geat, ere the bed he sought
Cast off then his corselet of iron,
helmet from head; to his henchman gave
choicest of weapons.
Reclined then the chieftan, while all about him
seamen hardy on hall-beds sank.

Then from the mooreland, by misty crags
with God's wrath laden, Grendel came.
The wine-palace there he gladly discerned.
To the house the monster walked apace,
The portal opened when his fists had struck it,
and baleful he burst in blatant rage,
the house's mouth. All hastily, then,
the fiend trod on; there streamed from his eyes
fearful flashes like flames to see.
He spied in hall the hero-band,

clustered asleep. Then laughed his heart;
for the monster was minded, ere morn should dawn,
savage, to sever the soul of each,
life from body. Eagerly watched
Hygelac's kinsman his cursed foe.

Then the monster was minded to pause,
for the hardy hero with hand he grasped,
for the hero reclining,—who clutched it boldly.
Soon then saw the shepherd-of-evils
that never he met in this middle world
another wight with heavier hand-gripe;
at heart he feared!
Fain would he flee, his fastness seek.
Then the hardy Hygelac-thane, up he bounded,
grasped firm his foe, whose fingers cracked.
The monster knew his finger's power
in the gripe of the grim one.

Din filled the room; the house resounded.
Wonder it was, in the strain of their struggle
the fair house fell not, where the grim foes wrestled.
Again uprose din redoubled,
God's foe sounding his grisly song.

He was safe by his spells from sword of battle,
from edge of iron. Yet soon he found
that the frame of his body failed him now.
A mighty wound
showed on his shoulder, and sinews cracked,
and the bone-frame burst. To Beowulf now
the glory was given, and Grendel thence
death-sick his den in the dark moor sought:
he knew too well
that here was the last of life, an end
of his days on earth,—To all the Danes
by that bloody battle the boon has come.

. . . The morning sun
was climbing higher. Clansmen hastened
to the high-built hall. The king himself
measured the path to the mead-house fair,
stood by the steps, the steep roof saw,
garnished with gold, and Grendel's hand.

Hrothgar spake:—
"For the sight I see to the Sovran Ruler
be speedy thanks! God still works
wonder on wonder, the Warden-of-Glory.
This hero now, a work has done
that not all of us erst could ever do
by wile and wisdom. Now, Beowulf, thee,
of heroes best, I shall heartily love
as mine own, my son; thou shalt never lack
wealth of the world that I wield as mine!
Thy fame shall endure through all the ages.

Beowulf spake:—"Most willingly
we have fought this fight,
and fearlessly dared force of the foe.
He left behind him his hand in pledge,
None the longer liveth he, loathsome fiend."

To Beowulf gave the bairn of Healfdene
a gold-wove banner, guerdon of triumph,
broidered battle-flag, breastplate and helmet;
and a splendid sword was seen of many
borne to the brave one.

Home then rode the hoary clansmen
back from the mere. Then Beowulf's glory
eager they echoed, and all averred
that from sea to sea, or south or north,
there was no other in earth's domain,
under vault of heaven, more valient found,
of warriors none more worthy to rule."

From *The Oldest English Epic;* Beowulf.
Translated in the original metres by Francis B. Gummere.
By permission of The Macmillan Company, Publishers.

"If the poet may take his colors from that nature by
which he is surrounded, if he may depict the men with whom
he lives, "Kalevala" possesses merits not dissimilar from
those of the Iliad, and will claim its place as the fifth national epic of the world, side by side with the Ionian songs,
with the Mahabharata, the Shahnameh, and the Nibelunge"
Max Müller in *The Science of Language,* First Series.
Published by Scribner, Armstrong & Co. New York, 1874.

No. 1. Extract from the Finnish Epic—Kalevala

"When my loving mother left me,
Young was I, and low of stature;
Like the cuckoo of the forest,
Like the lark I learned to twitter,
Learned to sing my simple measures,
Guided by a second mother,
Stern and cold without affection;
Drove me helpless from my chamber
To the wind side of her dwelling,
Where the chilling winds in mercy
Carried off the unprotected.
As a lark I learned to wander
Wander as a lonely song-bird
Quietly o'er hill and heather;
Learned the songs of winds and waters,
Learned the music of the ocean
And the echoes of the woodlands.
    Many men that live to murmur
Many women live to censure,
Blame my tongue for speaking wisdom
Call my ancient songs unworthy.
Be not thus my worthy people
Blame me not for singing badly.
Unpretending as a minstrel
I have never had the teaching,
Never learned the tongues of strangers
Never claimed to know much wisdom
Others have had language-masters,
Nature was my only teacher,
Woods and waters my instructors.
Homeless, friendless, lone and needy
Save in childhood with my mother
When beneath her painted rafters,
Where she twirled the flying spindle,
By the work bench of my brother
By the window of my sister
In the cabin of my father
In my early days of childhood."

From *The Epilogue of Kalevala.*
Translated by John Martin Crawford.
Copyright. Used by permission of D. Appleton-Century
    Company, Inc.

No. 2. Extract from Kalevala, Rune L
(Abridged)

Mariatta

Mariatta, child of beauty,
Grew to maidenhood in Northland,
In the cabin of her father,
In the chambers of her mother,
Golden ringlets, silver girdles
Glittering upon her bosom;

Mariatta, child of beauty
Lived a virgin with her mother,
As a maiden highly honored,
Lived in innocence and beauty.
Daily drove her flocks to pasture
Walking with the gentle lambkins.
Skipping through a grove of lindens,
Looked about, intently listened,
It was but the mountain-berry
Calling to the lonely maiden:
"Come, O Virgin, come and pluck me,
Come and take me to thy bosom—
Take me, tinsel breasted virgin.
Hundreds pass my way unmindful
Children come in countless numbers,
None of these has come to gather,
Come to pluck this ruddy berry."

Mariatta, child of beauty,
Listened to its gentle pleading,
Ran to pick the berry, calling,
Saw it smiling near the meadow,
When it rose as if by magic,
Darted upward to her bosom,
On her lips it perched a moment,
Hastened to her tongue expectant;
Then it hastened on its journey,
Settled in the maiden's bosom.
Mariatta, child of beauty
Thus became a bride impregnate,
Wedded to the mountain berry;

Thus the watchful mother wonders:
"What has happened to our Mary,

To our virgin, Mariatta?"
On the floor a babe was playing,
And the young child thus made answer:
"This has happened to our Mary
She has lingered by the meadows,
Played too long among the lambkins,
Tasted of the mountain-berry."

Long the virgin watched and waited,
Anxiously the days she counted,
Finally she asked her mother,
"Faithful mother fond and tender,
Make for me a place befitting."
This the answer of the mother:
"Woe to thee, thou Hisi-Maiden,
Since thou art a bride unworthy,
Wedded only to dishonor!"
As the mother was relentless
Asked the maiden of her father,
"Oh my father, full of pity,
Build for me a place befitting."
This the answer of the father,
"Go thou child of sin and sorrow,
To the Great Bear's rocky chamber,
To the stone cave of the growler,
There to lessen all thy troubles,
There to cast thy heavy burdens!"

Thereupon the virgin-mother
Wandered hither, wandered thither.
Seeking for a worthy birth-place
For her unborn son and hero;
Finally these words she uttered:
"Piltti, thou my youngest maiden,
Trustiest of all my servants,
Seek a place within the village,
For the troubled Mariatta."
Thereupon the servant, Piltti,
Hastened like the rapid river,
To the dwelling of Ruotus.

At his table in his cabin
Sat Ruotus, eating, drinking,
With his elbows on the table
Spake the wizard in amazement:

"Why hast thou a maid of evil,
Come to see me in my cavern,
What the message thou are bringing?"
Thereupon the servant, Piltti,
Gave this answer to the wizard:
"Seek I for a worthy birth-place;
For an unborn child and hero;"
Spake the wife of old Ruotus,
Evil minded, cruel-hearted:
"Occupied are all our chambers,
All our bath-rooms near the reed-brook;
In the mount of fire are couches,
Is a stable in the forest,
For the flaming horse of Hisi;
In the stable is a manger,
Fitting birth-place for the hero
Worthy couch for Mariatta!"
Mariatta, virgin-mother
Fell to bitter tears and murmurs,
Spake these words in depths of sorrow:

"I, alas! must go an outcast,
Wander as a wretched hireling,
Like a servant in dishonor,
To the stable in the forest,
Make my bed within a manger,
Near the flaming steed of Hisi!"
    Quick the helpless virgin-mother,
Spake these words in supplication:
"Come, I pray thee, my Creator,
Only friend in time of trouble,
Come to me and bring protection
To thy child the virgin-mother.
Come, thou only hope and refuge
To the maiden, Mariatta."

When the virgin, Mariatta
Had arrived within the stable,
She addressed the steed as follows:
"Breathe, O sympathizing fire-horse,
Let thy pleasant warmth surround me,
Let this pure and helpless maiden
Find a refuge in thy manger!"
Thereupon the horse, in pity,

Gave her warmth and needed comforts
Gave his aid to the afflicted,
   To the virgin, Mariatta.

There the babe was born and cradled
Cradled in a woodland manger,
There the mother rocks her infant,
In his swaddling clothes she wraps him,
Carefully the babe she nurtures,
Well she guards her much beloved,
Guards her golden child of beauty,
Her beloved gem of silver,
There the infant grew in beauty
Gathered strength and light and wisdom,
No one knew what name to give him;
When the mother named him, Flower,
Others named him, Son-of-Sorrow.

When the virgin, Mariatta
Sought the priesthood to baptize him,
Came an old man, Wirokannas,
Of the wilderness the ruler,
Touched the child with holy water,
Gave the wonder-babe his blessing,
Gave him rights of royal heirship,
Free to live and grow a hero,
To become a mighty ruler,
King and Master of Karyala.

From *The Kalevala*, Vol. II.
Translated by John Martin Crawford.
Copyright. Used by permission of D. Appleton Company,
  Inc.

EXTRACT FROM A MODERN LITERARY EPIC

(Abridged and written with one breath group to a line).

     One long year,
     two years had passed
     since Drake set sail
     from grey old Plymouth Sound.
     But now,
     on a dreadful summer morn
     there came, home to the Thames,

a bruised and battered ship,
all that was left,
so said her crew,
of Drake's ill fated fleet.
John Wynter, her commander,
told the tale,
bearing to England
and to England's Queen
the tale that Drake was dead.

The imperial wrath of Spain
now surged all round this little isle
with one harsh roar,
"The Golden Hynde
ye swore had foundered,
Drake, ye swore was drowned;
what answer
what account
what recompense
now can ye yield our might invincible?"

And then,
quietly,
one grey morn,
one grey October morn of mist and rain,
when all the window-panes in Plymouth
dripped with listless drizzle,
a little weed-clogged ship,
grey as a ghost,
glided into the Sound
and anchored:
Scarce a soul to see her come,
and not an eye,
to read the faded scroll
around her battered prow—
the *Golden Hynde.*

Then,
thro' the dumb grey misty listless port,
a rumor,
like the colors of the dawn,
streamed o'er the shining quays,
up the wet streets,
in at the tavern doors,
flashed from the panes
and turned them into diamonds,

fired the pools in every muddy lane
with Spanish gold,
flushed in a thousand faces,
Drake
is come!

Down every crowding alley
the urchins leaped
tossing their caps,
the *Golden Hynde* is come!
Fisherman, citizen, prentice,
dame and maid,
fishwife, minister and apothecary,
down the seething streets,
panting, tumbling, jostling,
helter skelter
to the water-side they rushed,
and some
knee-deep beyond it,
all one wild welcome
to Francis Drake.
Wild kerchiefs fluttering,
thunderous hurrahs
rolling from quay to quay,
a thousand arms outstretched
to that grey ghostly little ship,
at whose masthead—
the British flag
still flew;
Then, over all,
in one tumultuous tide of pealing joy,
the Plymouth bells outclashed
a nation's welcome home
to Francis Drake.

From *Drake*. Alfred Noyes.
In *Collected Poems*, Volume I.
Frederick A. Stokes Company, Publishers.
Copyright, 1906.

EXTRACT FROM CLASSICAL LITERARY EPIC
(Abridged and written with one principal breath group on a line)
Soon as the force of that fallacious fruit had left them,
up they rose as from unrest,

and found their eyes opened,
their minds darkened:
innocence,
that as a veil
had shadowed them from knowing ill,
was gone.
Long they sate, as strucken mute,
destitute of all their virtue.

Adam, at length,
gave utterance to these words:
    "O Eve,
    in evil hour
    thou didst give ear to that false worm,
    false, in our promised rising;
    our eyes
    opened we find indeed,
    and find we know both good and evil,
    good, lost,
    and evil, got.
    Would thou hadst harkened to my words,
    and stayed with me, as I besought thee
    we had then remained still happy
    not, as now,
    despoiled of all our good,
    shamed,
    naked,
    miserable."

To whom,
soon moved with touch of blame,
thus Eve:
    "Adam!
    what words severe have passed thy lips?
    Hadst thou been there
    thou couldst not have discerned fraud
    in the serpent
    speaking as he spake;
    no ground of enmity between us known
    why he should mean me ill,
    or seek to harm.
    Was I to have never parted from thy side?"

Adam replied:
    "Eve,

I also erred.
I thought no evil durst attempt thee;
but I rue the error now,
which is become my crime.
How shall I, henceforth,
behold the face of God
or angel?
O, might I here in solitude livè savage
in some glade obscured.
Cover me, ye pines!
Ye cedars,
with innumerable boughs,
hide me,
where I may never see them more."

Together they weep.
Tears rained at their eyes.
But within began to rise
high winds of passion.
Mistrust,
suspicion,
discord,
shook their inward state of mind,
calm once
and full of peace,
now tost
and turbulent.

From *Paradise Lost*. Book IX. Milton.

CHAPTER XXIII

NARRATIVE POETRY AND METRICAL ROMANCE

NARRATIVE poetry and metrical romance are forms of poetry which offer to the exploring dramatic reader and teacher of oral reading vast fields of enchanting riches which have scarcely been touched except in a very few places.

But no matter how great or near great such poetry may be, only certain details may be selected for the purpose of oral presentation, and the selection must be made with the wisest and most discriminating care, and with a keen and far-seeing understanding of the modern mind and the things that will interest it.

If students are to know our literature they must first become interested in individual examples of it. Lines from narrative poetry—and from many other forms of literature as well—can be so chosen and combined as to make a unit that *will interest* them, and this will help to awaken a desire to know the whole from which the part was taken. When the desire to know literature has been awakened, the biggest part of the problem has been solved.

The first thing to be done in considering a long narrative poem or a romantic narrative for use as a reading, is to read the *entire* poem, carefully, to discover the portions of the theme that will best serve the purpose of the reader. Having decided upon the incidents or episodes to be used, *pick out the lines that will tell the story directly and in definite sequence,* and weave them together into a unit. With careful study one can invariably find lines that make the necessary connections. Although the descriptions in such poems may be superb and may have received the highest praise from the wisest critics, most of them must be *omitted for the sake of the continuity of the story.* Only enough description may be retained to give the proper and adequate setting and to create the necessary atmosphere. *All that halts or retards the progress of the story must be left out.*

NARRATIVE POETRY

Narrative: An account or narration; a history, tale, story, recital (of facts, etc.). *The Oxford English Dictionary.*

There is no hard and fast division to be made between narrative poetry and metrical romance or romantic narrative. As far as the oral interpretation is concerned they have *two very essential things* in common and these are: the *story*, and the *poetic form* in which the story is told. Each individual selection must be studied and interpreted according to the demands it makes. Certain general rules can be given, however, which should prove useful.

INTERPRETATION OF EXTRACTS FROM NARRATIVE POETRY

Narrative poetry, as the name signifies, is a story told in poetic form. It must be told directly to the listeners as any other story is told, except when characters speak, in which case the lines must be given as nearly as possible as the character speaking would naturally give them to the specified listener, at the time and in the place and situation depicted by the lines. The beauty and significance of the *poetic form must be given* their *full value*, but no more. *The rhythm of the sense and the rhythm of the verse must be made to coincide,* and each one must be given its rightful consideration and attention. The events of the story must be narrated in lively and definite sequence. If the events are indefinite and the sequence vague or halting, the reading will fail to interest the listeners, and failure to interest them means failure of the reading.

The careful choice of *sounds* and *words* which the author has made must be fully recognized and appreciated by the reader, and by means of the proper and adequate use of his speech and voice he must keep them *a part of the very fabric of the tale* and thereby enrich and enhance the telling of it. The beauty of sounds and words must be kept—as they **must** be in all literature—an integral part of the literature itself, inseparable from it, not something to be added or omitted by the reader. The reader must be wholly aware of them and then utter them in such a way as to make them serve, truly and fully, the purpose for which the author built them into the basic structure of the verse.

Lines from "Marmion" (Abridged).

Note: The following extract should give a general idea of what may be done in selecting lines from a long narrative poem to use as short readings. This particular selection, however, is *too* short to represent its full dramatic possibilities. The brevity is necessary here. With the addition of about as much again the selection can be made adequate. As it is, it should give the reader a glimpse of the courage and nobility of the brave men of another day, and some appreciation of the strength and beauty of the verse that Scott has given us.

> Day set on Norham's castled steep,
> And Tweed's fair river, broad and deep,
> The scouts had parted on their search,
>   The castle gates were barred;
> Above the gloomy portal arch,
> The warder kept his guard.
>
> A distant trampling sound he hears;
> He looks abroad, and soon appears,
> O'er Horncliff-hill, a plump of spears
>   Beneath a pennon gay.
> A horseman, darting from the crowd
> Spurs on his mettled courser proud,
>   Before the dark array.
> Beneath the sable palisade
> That closed the castle barricade,
> His bugle-horn he blew;
> The warder hastened from the wall
> For well the blast he knew.
>   "Now . . .
>   . . . quickly make the entrance free
>   And bid my heralds ready be,
>   And every minstrel sound his glee,

Lord Marmion waits below!"
Then to the castle's lower ward
   Sped forty yeomen tall,
The iron-studded gates unbarred,
Raised the portcullis ponderous guard,
   And let the drawbridge fall.

Along the bridge Lord Marmion rode,
Proudly his red-roan charger trode,
He was a stalwart knight and keen,
And had in many a battle been;
His eyebrow dark and eye of fire
Showed spirit proud and prompt to ire,
Yet lines of thought upon his cheek
Did deep design and counsel speak.
His thick mustache and curly hair,
Coal-black and grizzled here and there,
   But more through toil than age,
His square turned joints and strength of limb,
Showed him no carpet knight so trim,
But in close fights a champion grim,
   In camps a leader sage:
Well was he armed from head to heel
In mail and plate of Milan steel.
They marshalled him to the castle-hall.
And loudly flourished the trumpet-call.

The guards their morrice pikes advanced,
The trumpets flourished brave,
The cannon from the ramparts glanced,
And thundering welcome gave.

"Welcome to Norham, Marmion!
Stout heart and open hand!
Well dost thou brook thy gallant roan,
Thou flower of English land!"

Then stepped to meet the noble lord—
   Sir Hugh the Heron bold,
He led Lord Marmion to the dais,
Raised o'er the pavement high
And placed him in the upper place—
They feasted full and high:
"Now good Lord Marmion" Heron said
   "Of your fair courtesy,

I pray you bide some little space ·
  In this poor tower with me?"
"Nay
For to the Scottish court addressed
I journey at our king's behest—,
And pray you of your grace provide
For me and mine a trusty guide.
Were I in warlike wise to ride,
A better guard I would not lack
Than your stout forayers at my back—
But in forms of peace I go
A friendly messenger, to know
Why, through all Scotland, near and far,
Their king is mustering troops for war?"

With early dawn Lord Marmion rose:
And first the chapel doors unclose.
Lord Marmion's bugles blew to horse—
When came the stirrup-cup in course.
Between the baron and his host
No point of courtesy was lost.
High thanks were by Lord Marmion paid,
Till, filing from the gate, had passed
That noble train, their lord the last.
The livelong day Lord Marmion rode
The mountain path the Palmer showed,
At length up that wild dale they wind
Where Crichtoun Castle crowns the bank;
For there the Lion's care assigned
A lodging meet for Marmion's rank.
And here two days did Marmion rest,
With every right that honor claims,
Attended as the King's own guest;—
Such the command of Royal James.
Meanwhile the Lion's care assigns
A banquet rich and costly wines
    To Marmion and his train.

Old Holy-Rood rung merrily
That night with wassail, mirth and glee:
Through the mixed crowd of glee and game
The king to greet Lord Marmion came,
    While, reverent, all made room.
An easy task it was I trow,
King James's manly form to know.

He doffed to Marmion bending low
   His broidered cap and plume.

The king . . . .
   took . . . forth the parchment broad
Which Marmion's high commission showed:
   "Our borders sacked by many a raid,
   Our peaceful liege-men robbed" he said,
   "Unworthy were we here to reign
   Should these for vengeance cry in vain;
   Our full defiance, hate, and scorn,
   Our herald has to Henry borne.
   Lord Marmion, since these letters say
   That in the North you needs must stay
   While slightest hope of peace remain,
   Until my herald come again
   . . . rest you in Tantallon hold;
   Your host shall be the Douglas bold.
   Southward I march at break of day,
   And if within Tantallon strong
   The good Lord Marmion tarries long
   Perchance our meeting next may fall
   At Tamworth in his castle-hall."

The haughty Marmion felt the taunt,
And answered grave the royal vaunt:
   "Much honored were my humble home,
If in its walls King James should come;
   But Nottingham has archer's good,
   And Yorkshire men are stern of mood,
   Northumbrian prickers wild and rude.
   And many a banner will be torn,
   And many a knight to earth be borne,
   And many a sheaf of arrows spent
   Ere Scotland's king shall cross the Trent:"
   The monarch lightly turned away,
   And to his nobles loud did call
   "Lords, to the dance,—a hall! a hall!"

Shift we the scene.—The camp doth move;
Bold Douglas, to Tantallon fair
They journey in thy charge!
But scant three miles the band had rode,
When o'er a height they passed,
And, sudden, close before them showed
His towers Tantallon vast.

Broad, massive, high, and stretching far,
And held impregnable in war.
On a projecting rock they rose
And round three sides the ocean flows,
The fourth did battled walls enclose.
By narrow drawbridge, outworks strong,
Through studded gates, an entrance long,
To the main court they cross.

Here did they rest. . . .
. . . why should I declare
Or say they met reception fair?
Or why the tidings say,
Which varying to Tantallon came
By hurrying posts or fleeter fame,
With every varying day?
And first they heard King James had won,
That Norham castle strong was ta'en.
At this sore marvelled Marmion.
But whispered news there came,
And that brave Surrey many a band
Had gathered in the Southern land
And marched into Northumberland.

Marmion, like a charger in the stall,
That hears, without, the trumpet call,
   Began to chafe and swear:—
"A sorry thing to hide my head
In castle like a fearful maid,
When such a field is near.
Needs must I see this battle-day;
Death to my fame if such a fray
Were fought, and Marmion away!
Then Douglas, too, I wot not why,
Hath bated of his courtesy;
No longer in his halls I'll stay."
Then bade his band they should array
For march against the dawning day.

Not far advanced was morning day
   When Marmion did his troops array
   To Surrey's camp to ride;
He had safe-conduct for his band
Beneath the royal seal and hand.
   And Douglas gave a guide.

The train from out the castle drew,
But Marmion stopped to bid adieu:
"Though something I might plain," he said,
"Of cold respect to stranger guest,
Sent hither by your king's behest,
While in Tantallon's towers I stayed,
Part we in friendship from your land,
And, noble earl, receive my hand."

But Douglas round him drew his cloak,
Folded his arms, and thus he spoke:—
    "My manors, halls, and bowers shall still
Be open at my sovereign's will
To each one whom he lists, howe'er
Unmeet to be the owner's peer.
My castles are my king's alone,
From turret to foundation-stone—
The hand of Douglas is his own,
And never shall in friendly grasp
The hand of such as Marmion clasp."

Burned Marmion's swarthy cheek like fire
And shook his very frame for ire,
And—"This to me!" he said,
"An 'twere not for thy hoary beard,
Such hand as Marmion's had not spared
    To cleave the Douglas' head!
And first I tell thee haughty peer,
He who does England's message here,
Although the meanest in her state,
May well, proud Angus, be thy mate;
And, Douglas, more I tell thee here,
    Even in thy pitch of pride,
Here in thy hold, thy vassals near,
    I tell thee thou'rt defied!
And if thou saidst I am not peer
To any lord in Scotland here,
    Lowland or Highland, far or near,
    Lord Angus, thou hast lied!"

O'er the earl's cheek the flush of rage
O'er came the ashen hue of age:
Fierce he broke forth,—"And darest thou then
To beard the lion in his den
    The Douglas in his hall?

And hopest thou hence unscathed to go?—
   No, by saint Bride of Bothwell no!
Up, drawbridge, grooms—what, warder, ho!
   Let the portcullis fall."—

Lord Marmion turned,—well was his need,—
And dashed the rowels in his steed,
Like arrow through the archway sprung,
The ponderous gate behind him rung:
To pass there was such scanty room,
The bars descending razed his plume.

The steed along the drawbridge flies
Just as it trembled on the rise;
And when Lord Marmion reached his band,
He halts, and turns with clenched hand,
And shouts of loud defiance pours
And shook his gauntlet at the towers.
"Horse! horse!" the Douglas cried, "and chase!"
   But soon he reigned his fury's pace:
   "A royal messenger he came,
Though most unworthy of the name.
Old age ne'er cools the Douglas blood,
I thought to slay him where he stood.
   "Tis pity of him, too," he cried:
Bold can he speak and fairly ride,
I warrant him a warrier tried."
With this his mandate he recalls,
And slowly seeks his castle walls.
                Sir Walter Scott.

EXTRACT FROM SOHRAB AND RUSTUM (Abridged).

Introduction.

Rustum lived in Persia or "Iran" as it was then called, in the sixth century before Christ. He was the greatest Persian warrior of all time and one of the most noble, the most widely loved, and the most tender hearted of men.

Although he was an indomitable warrior, he hated warfare, and never went into battle without first praying for divine guidance. In his early manhood he loved and married the daughter of a king of an enemy country. Shortly after the marriage Rustum was obliged to return to the wars of his own country, leaving his beautiful bride with her father. Rustum instructed her that when their child should be born she should have the sign of his own seal pricked indelibly upon its arm, as an unmistakable proof of its parentage.

The child was a boy, but knowing that Rustum would take him from her and rear him as a soldier if he knew this, the mother sent word to Rustum that the child was a girl. Rustum was detained at the wars for the remainder of his life, and until the time of the events of this poem he did not know that his child was a boy.

The boy was named Sohrab. Everywhere about him he heard tales of his noble and illustrious father and he longed to know him with all the fire of his youth. While he was still very young he joined the Tartar army hoping that on some great day of days he would meet his father. His vivid imagination pictured what this meeting would be like, and the determination to find his father became the one and only object of his life.

For political reasons Sohrab was never told that Rustum was wholly unaware of the existence of his son.

"And the first grey of morning fill'd the east,
And the fog rose out of the Oxus stream.
But all the Tartar camp along the stream
Was hush'd, and still the men were plung'd in sleep;
Sohrab alone, he slept not; all night long
He had lain wakeful, tossing on his bed.
But when the grey dawn stole into his tent,
He rose, and clad himself, and left his tent,
And went abroad into the cold wet fog,
Through the dim camp, to Peran-Wisa's tent.
And Sohrab came there, and went in,
And found the old man sleeping on his bed.
And he rose quickly on one arm, and said:—
    "Who art thou? for it is not yet clear dawn.
Speak! is there news, or any night alarm?"
        But Sohrab came to the bedside, and said:—
"Thou know'st me, Peran-Wisa: it is I.

The sun is not yet risen, and the foe
Sleep, but I sleep not; all night long I lie
Tossing and wakeful; and I come to thee.
For so did King Afrasiab bid me seek
Thy counsel, and to heed thee as thy son,
And I will tell thee what my heart desires.

Thou know'st
I have serv'd Afrasiab well, and shown
At my boy's years, the courage of a man.
This too thou know'st, that while I still bear on
The conquering Tartar ensigns through the world
And beat the Persians back on every field,
I seek one man, one man, and one alone:
Rustum, my father; who I hop'd should greet,
Should one day greet, upon some well-fought field
His not unworthy, not inglorious son.
So I long hop'd, but him I never find.
Come then, hear now, and grant me what I ask!
Let the two armies rest to-day; but I
Will challenge forth the bravest Persian lords
To meet me, man to man; if I prevail,
Rustum will surely hear it: if I fall—
Old man, the dead need no one, claim no kin.
Dim is the rumor of a common fight
Where host meets host, and many names are sunk
But of a single combat fame speaks clear."

 He spoke; and Peran-Wisa took the hand
Of the young man in his, and sigh'd, and said:—
 "O Sohrab, an unquiet heart is thine!
Can'st thou not rest among the Tartar chiefs,
And share the battle's common chance with us
Who love thee, but must press for ever first,
In single fight, incurring single risk,
To find a father, thou has't never seen!
But, if this one desire indeed rules all,
To seek out Rustum, seek him not through fight!
Seek him in peace and carry to his arms,
O Sohrab, carry an unwounded son!
But far hence seek him, for he is not here.
Fain would I
  send thee hence, in peace
To seek thy father, not seek single fights

In vain. But who can keep the lion's cub
From ravening, and who govern Rustum's son?
Go: I will grant thee what thy heart desires."

　　　So said he and left
His bed whereon he lay; and clad himself and took
In his right hand a ruler's staff, no sword;
　　　　　　　　and call'd
His herald to his side, and went abroad.
　　　The sun by this had risen, and clear'd the fog—
From the broad Oxus and the glittering sands.
And from their tents the Tartar horsemen fil'd
Into the open plain;
And on the other side the Persians form'd:
The royal troops of Persia, horse and foot,
Marshall'd battalions bright in burnish'd steel.
But Peran-Wisa with his herald came,
Betwixt the silent hosts, and spake, and said:—
　　　"Ferood, and ye, Persians and Tartars, hear!
Let there be truce, between the hosts to-day,
But choose a champion from the Persian lords
To fight our champion Sohrab, man to man."
　　　When they heard what Peran-Wisa said,
A thrill through all the Tartar squadron ran
Of pride and hope for Sohrab, whom they lov'd.

But the pale Persians held their breath with fear,
And to Ferood his brother chiefs came up
To counsel; and then Gudurz said:—
　　　"Ferood, shame bids us take their challenge up,
Yet champion have we none to match this youth.
He has the wild stag's foot, the lion's heart.
But Rustum came last night; aloof he sits
And sullen, and has pitch'd his tents apart.
Him will I seek, and carry to his ear
The Tartar challenge, and this young man's name:
Haply he will forget his wrath, and fight.
Stand forth the while, and take their challenge up."
　　　So spake he; and Ferood stood forth and cried:—
"Old man, be it agreed as thou hast said!
Let Sohrab arm, and we will find a man."
　　　He spake: and Peran-Wisa turn'd, and strode
Back through the opening squadrons to his tent.
But through the anxious Persians Gudurz ran,

And cross'd the camp which lay behind, and reach'd,
Out on the sands beyond it, Rustum's tents.
Of scarlet cloth they were, and glittering gay,
Just pitch'd; the high pavilion in the midst
Was Rustum's, and his men lay camp'd around.
And Gudurz enter'd Rustum's tent, and found
Rustum; his morning meal was done, but still
The table stood before him, charg'd with food:
    And there he sate
Listless, and held a falcon on his wrist,
And play'd with it; but Gudurz came and stood
Before him; and he looked, and saw him stand,
And with a cry sprang up and dropp'd the bird,
And greeted Gudurz with both hands, and said:—
    "Welcome! these eyes could see no better sight.
What news? but sit down first, and eat and drink."

"Not now! a time will come to eat and drink,
But not to-day: to-day has other needs,
The armies are drawn out, and stand at gaze;
For from the Tartars is a challenge brought
To pick a champion from the Persian lords
To fight their champion, and thou know'st his name:
Sohrab men call him, but his birth is hid.
O Rustum, like thy might is this young man's!
He has the wild stag's foot, the lion's heart;
And he is young, and Iran's chiefs are old,
Or else too weak, and all eyes turn to thee.
Come down and help us, Rustum, or we lose!"
    But Rustum answered with a smile
"Go to! if Iran's chiefs are old, then I
Am older;
The young may rise at Sohrab's vaunts, not I.
For would that I myself had such a son,
And not that one slight helpless girl I have:
A son so fam'd so brave, to send to war,
And rest my age, and hear of Sohrab's fame,
And leave to death the hosts of thankless kings,
And with these slaughterous hands draw sword no more."

    He spoke, and smil'd; and Gudurz made reply:—
"What then, O Rustum, will men say to this,
When Sohrab dares our bravest forth, and seeks
Thee most of all, and thou, whom most he seeks,

Hidest thy face! Take heed lest men should say:
Like some old miser, Rustum hoards his·fame,
And shuns to peril it with younger men."
"O Gudurz, wherefore dost thou say such words?
Thou knowest better words than this to say.
What is one more, one less
Valiant or craven, young or old, to me?
Are not they mortal, am not I myself?
Come, thou shalt see how Rustum hoards his fame!
But I will fight unknown, and in plain arms;
Let not men say of Rustum, he was match'd
In single fight with any mortal man."

He spoke, and frown'd; and Gudurz turn'd and ran
Back quickly through the camp in fear and joy:
Fear at his wrath, but joy that Rustum came.
But Rustum strode to his tent-door, and call'd
His followers in, and bade them bring his arms,
And clad himself in steel; the arms he chose
Were plain, and on his shield was no device,
Only his helm was rich, inlaid with gold,
And, from the fluted spine atop, a plume
Of horsehair wav'd, a scarlet horsehair plume.
So arm'd he issued forth;
                                    and cross'd
The camp, and to the Persian host appear'd.
And all the Persians knew him, and with shouts
Hail'd; but the Tartars knew not who he was.

And Rustum to the Persian front advanc'd,
And Sohrab arm'd in Haman's tent, and came.
On each side were squares of men, with spears
Bristling, and in the midst, the open sand.

And Rustum came upon the sand, and cast
His eyes toward the Tartar tents, and saw
Sohrab come forth, and eyed him as he came
                                    eyed
The unknown adventurous youth, who from afar
Game seeking Rustum, and defying forth
All the most valiant chiefs: long he perus'd
His spirited air, and wonder'd who he was.
For very young he seem'd, tenderly rear'd;
Like some young cypress, tall, and dark, and straight,
And a deep pity enter'd Rustum's soul

As he beheld him coming; and he stood,
And beckon'd to him with his hand and said:—
  "O thou young man, the air of heaven is soft,
And warm, and pleasant; but the grave is cold!
Behold me: I am vast, and clad in iron,
And tried; and I have stood on many a field
Of blood, and I have fought with many a foe:
Never was that field lost, or that foe sav'd.
O Sohrab, wherefore wilt thou rush on death?
Be govern'd! quit the Tartar host, and come
To Iran, and be as my son to me,
And fight beneath my banner till I die!
There are no youths in Iran brave as thou."

     Sohrab heard his voice,
The mighty voice of Rustum, and he saw
His giant figure planted on the sand,
     and he saw his head,
Streak'd with its first grey hairs; hope fill'd his soul,
And he ran forward and embrac'd his knees,
And clasp'd his hand within his own, and said:—
  "Oh, by thy father's head! by thine own soul!
Art thou not Rustum? speak: art thou not he?"
  But Rustum eyed askance the kneeling youth,
And turn'd away, and spake to his own soul:—
  "Ah me, I muse what this young fox may mean."
And then he turn'd, and sternly spake aloud:—
"Rise! wherefore dost thou vainly question thus
Of Rustum? I am here, whom thou hast call'd
By challenge forth: make good thy vaunt, or yield!
Is it with Rustum only thou would'st fight?
Rash boy, men look on Rustum's face and flee!
For well I know, that did great Rustum stand
Before thy face this day, and were reveal'd,
There would be then no talk of fighting more.
But being what I am, I tell thee this:
Do thou record it in thine inmost soul:
Either thou shalt renounce thy vaunt and yield,
Or else thy bones shall strew this sand, till winds
Bleach them, or Oxus with his summer-floods,
     wash them all away."

     Sohrab answer'd, on his feet:—
"Art thou so fierce? Thou wilt not fright me so!

I am no girl, to be made pale by words.
Yet this thou hast said well, did Rustum stand
Here on this field, there were no fighting then.
But Rustum is far hence, and we stand here.
Begin! thou art more vast, more dread than I,
And thou art prov'd, I know, and I am young:
And though thou thinkest that thou knowest sure
Thy victory, yet thou can'st not surely know;
Only the event will teach us, in its hour.''

Rustum answer'd not, but hurl'd
His spear: down from the shoulder, down it came,
    like a plummet: Sohrab saw it come,
And sprang aside, quick as a flash; the spear
Hiss'd and went quivering down into the sand,
Which it sent flying wide; then Sohrab threw
In turn, and full struck, Rustum's shield
                              rang sharp, but turn'd the spear.
And Rustum seiz'd his club, which none but he
Could wield; an unlopp'd trunk it was, and huge,
                                        huge
The club which Rustum lifted now, and struck
One stroke; but again Sohrab sprang aside,
Lithe as the glancing snake, and the club came
Thundering to earth, and leapt from Rustum's hand.
And Rustum follow'd his own blow, and fell
To his knees, and with his fingers clutch'd the sand;
And now might Sohrab have unsheath'd his sword
And pierc'd the mighty Rustum while he lay
Dizzy, and on his knees, and chok'd with sand:
But he look'd on, and smil'd, nor bar'd his sword,
But courteously drew back, and spoke, and said:—
    "Thou strik'st too hard! that club of thine will float
Upon the summer-floods, and not my bones.
But rise, and be not wroth! not wroth am I;
No, when I see thee, wrath forsakes my soul.
Thou say'st, thou are not Rustum: be it so!
Who art thou then, that canst so touch my soul?
Boy as I am, I have seen battles too;
And heard their hollow roar of dying men;
But never was my heart thus touch'd before.
Are they from Heaven, these softenings of the heart?
O thou old warrior, let us yield to Heaven!
Come, plant we here in earth our angry spears,

And make a truce,
And pledge each other in red wine, like friends;
And thou shalt talk to me of Rustum's deeds.
There are enough foes in the Persian host,
Whom I may meet and strike, and feel no pang;
But oh, let there be peace 'twixt thee and me!"

  while he spake, Rustum had risen
And stood erect, trembling with rage; his club
He left to lie, but had regain'd his spear,
Whose fiery point now in his mail'd right-hand
Blaz'd bright and baleful,
        dust had soil'd
His stately crest, and dimm'd his glittering arms.
His breast heav'd, and twice his voice
Was chok'd with rage; at last these words broke way:—
 "Girl! nimble with thy feet, not with thy hands!
Curl'd minion, dancer, coiner of sweet words!
Fight: let me hear thy hateful voice no more.
Thou art not in Afraziab's gardens now
With Tartar girls,
But on the Oxus-sands, and in the dance
Of battle, and with me, who make no play
Of war: I fight it out, and hand to hand.
 All the pity I had is gone:
Because thou hast sham'd me, before both the hosts
With thy light skipping tricks, and thy girl's wiles."

  Sohrab, kindled at his taunts,
And he, too, drew his sword: at once
         their shields
Dash'd with a clang together, and a din
Rose
And you would say that sun and stars took part
In that unnatural conflict; for a cloud
Grew suddenly in heaven, and dark'd the sun
  and a wind rose
  and moaning swept the plain,
And in a sandy whirlwind wrapp'd the pair.

But in the gloom they fought,
      first Rustum struck the shield
Which Sohrab held stiff out: the steel-spik'd spear
Rent the tough plates, but fail'd to reach the skin,
And Rustum pluck'd it back with angry groan.

Then Sohrab with his sword smote Rustum's helm,
Nor clove its steel quite through; but all the crest
He shore away, and that proud horsehair plume,
Never till now defil'd, sank to the dust;
And Rustum bow'd his head;
But Sohrab rush'd on,
And struck again;
　　　　but this time all the blade, like glass
Sprang in a thousand shivers on Rustum's helm,
And in Sohrab's hand the hilt remain'd alone.
Then Rustum raised his head; his dreadful eyes
Glar'd, and he shook on high his menacing spear,
And shouted: *Rustum!*—Sohrab heard that shout
And shrank amaz'd; back he recoil'd one step,
And scann'd with blinking eyes the advancing form;
　　　　he stood bewilder'd; and he dropped
His covering shield: and Rustum's spear pierc'd his side.
He reel'd, and staggering back, sank to the ground;
　　　　then the gloom dispers'd, and the wind fell,
And the sun broke forth, and melted all
The cloud; and the two armies saw the pair:
Saw Rustum standing, safe upon his feet,
And Sohrab, wounded, on the bloody sand.

　　　　Then with a bitter smile, Rustum began:—
"Sohrab, thou thoughtest in thy mind to kill
A Persian lord this day, and strip his corpse,
And bear thy trophies to Afrasiab's tent,
Or else that the great Rustum would come down
Himself to fight, and that thy wiles would move
His heart to take a gift and let thee go.
Fool, thou art slain, and by an unknown man!"

And with a fearless mien, Sohrab replied:—
"Unknown thou art: yet thy fierce vaunt is vain.
Thou dost not slay me, proud and boastful man!
No: Rustum slays me, and this filial heart.
For were I match'd with ten such men as thee,
And I were that which till to-day I was,
They should be lying here, I standing there.
But that beloved name unnerv'd my arm:
That name, and something, I confess, in thee,
Which troubles all my heart, and made my shield
Fall; and thy spear transfix'd an unarm'd foe.

And now thou boastest, and insult'st my fate.
But hear thou this, fierce man, tremble to hear:
The mighty Rustum shall avenge my death,
My father, whom I seek through all the world!
He shall avenge my death, and punish thee."

"What prate is this of fathers and revenge?
The mighty Rustum never had a son."

"Ah yes, he had! and that lost son am I.
Surely the news will one day reach his ear,
And pierce him like a stab, and make him leap
To arms, and cry for vengeance upon thee.
Fierce man, bethink thee, for an only son
What will that grief, what will that vengeance be?
Yet him I pity not so much, but her,
My mother, who in Ader-baijan dwells
Her most I pity, who no more will see
Sohrab returning from the Tartar camp,"
        and he wept aloud
Thinking of her he left.

Rustum listen'd, plung'd in thought,
Nor did he yet believe it was his son
Who spoke, although he call'd back names he knew;
And so he deem'd that either Sohrab took,
By a false boast, the style of Rustum's son,
Or that men gave it him, to swell his fame.
And his soul set to grief,
                    tears gather'd in his eyes;
For he remember'd his own early youth,
And all its bounding rapture; and he saw
    Sohrab's mother, in her bloom,
  and all the pleasant life they led,
  in that long-distant summer-time:
    And he saw that youth,
Piteous and lovely, lying on the sand,
Like some rich hyacinth which by the scythe
Of an unskillful gardener has been cut.
    "O Sohrab, thou indeed art such a son
Whom Rustum, wert thou his, might well have lov'd.
Yet here thou errest, Sohrab, or else men
Have told thee false: thou art not Rustum's son,
For Rustum had no son:"

But Sohrab answered him in wrath; for now
The anguish of the deep-fix'd spear grew fierce,
But first he would convince his stubborn foe.
And, rising sternly on one arm, he said:—
  "Man, who art thou who dost deny my words?
Truth sits upon the lips of dying men;
And falsehood, while I liv'd, was far from mine.
I tell thee, prick'd upon this arm I bear
That seal which Rustum to my mother gave
That she might prick it on the babe she bore."
        all the blood left Rustum's cheeks,
And his knees totter'd.
        And in a hollow voice he spake and said:—
  "Sohrab, that were a proof which could not lie
If thou show this, then art thou Rustum's son."

Then, with weak hasty fingers, Sohrab loos'd
His belt, and near the shoulder bar'd his arm
And show'd a sign,
        pricked in faint vermillion points:
On Sohrab's arm, the sign of Rustum's seal.
And Sohrab scann'd it long with mournful eyes,
And then he touch'd it with his hand, and said:—
  "How say'st thou? Is that the proper sign
Of Rustum's son, or of some other man's?"
    But Rustum gaz'd, and gaz'd
    and then he utter'd one sharp cry:
"O boy—thy father!" and his voice chok'd there.
And then a dark cloud pass'd before his eyes
And his head swam, and he sank down to earth.

But Sohrab crawl'd to where he lay, and cast
His arms about his neck, and kiss'd his lips,
And with fond faltering fingers strok'd his cheeks.
    Rustum op'd his eyes,
And they stood wide with horror;
And his sobs chok'd him;
    Sohrab said:—
  "Father!!
Surely my heart cried out that it was thou,
When first I saw thee, and thy heart spoke too,
        but fate trod those promptings down,
        and hurl'd me on my father's spear.

                    I but meet to-day
The doom which at my birth was written down
In Heaven; and thou art Heaven's unconscious hand.
                              I find
My father, let me feel that I have found!
Come, sit beside me on this sand, and take
My head betwixt thy hands, and kiss my cheeks,
And wash them with thy tears, and say: 'My son!'
Quick, quick! for number'd are my sands of life,
And like the wind I go away."
          And his voice releas'd the heart
Of Rustum, and his tears broke forth: he cast
His arms round his son's neck, and wept aloud,
And kissed him. And awe fell on both the hosts,
When they saw Rustum's grief;

    Then with a grave mild voice, Sohrab said:—
          "my father!
    thou seest this great host of men
Which follow me; I pray thee, slay not these!
Let them all cross the Oxus back in peace.
But me thou must bear hence, not send with them.
And thou must lay me in that lovely earth,
And plant a far-seen pillar over all,
That so the passing horseman on the waste
May see my tomb a great way off, and cry:
Sohrab, the mighty Rustum's son lies there."

    "Fear not: as thou hast said, Sohrab, my son,
So shall it be: I will bear thee hence with me,
And carry thee away to Seistan,
          and mourn for thee.
And plant a far-seen pillar over all,
And men shall not forget thee in thy grave,
And I will spare thy host; yea, let them go:
What should I do with slaying any more?
Would that all that I have ever slain
Might be once more alive: my bitterest foes,
So thou mightest live too, Sohrab, my son, my son!"

    And Rustum gaz'd in Sohrab's face,
          and then Sohrab smil'd on him, and took
The spear, and drew it from his side, and eas'd
His wound's imperious anguish; but the blood
Came welling from the open gash, and life

Flowed with the stream;
                              his head droop'd low,
                       motionless, white, he lay,
                       then he ope'd his eyes
And fix'd them feebly on his father's face;
Unwillingly the spirit fled away,
And youth, and bloom, and this delightful world.

   So, on the bloody sand, Sohrab lay dead:
And the great Rustum drew his horseman's cloak
Down o'er his face, and sate by his dead son.
   And night came down over the solemn waste,
And the two gazing hosts, and that sole pair,
And darken'd all; and a cold fog, with night
Crept from the Oxus. Soon a hum arose
                       and fires
Began to twinkle through the fog, for now
Both armies mov'd to camp, and took their meal
The Persians took it on the open sands
       the Tartars by the river marge:
And Rustum and his son were left alone.

Matthew Arnold.

Houghton Mifflin Company, Publishers.

METRICAL ROMANCE

"Metrical Romance," "Romantic Narrative" and "Romantic Poetry" are names which are variously applied to a particular type of verse which grew out of the chivalry of the Middle Ages. It deals with kings and princesses, knights and ladies, castles and tournaments, heroic deeds and supernatural beings, giants and enchantresses, with the nobility and their courts. It is concerned with aristocrats and high society. Ordinary human beings who carry on the work of the world hold the place of serfs and scullions if they have any place at all. Happenings are quite as likely to be improbable or impossible as otherwise, but they are filled with "dash and danger," romance and courage. The poems are written in beautiful and elegant language that is highly suited to the superior social standing of the characters that come and go on the pages, and the lines have a smooth but spirited rhythm befitting the refinement, nobility, and vigorous daring in the behavior of these alluring men and women who are too perfect "for human nature's daily fare."

Although there is much that is impossible and unreal in the metrical romance, it nevertheless *contains a great abundance of material for the oral reader's use.* There are a great number of episodes in the poems which may be most profitably chosen for readings. The language is so elegant and beautiful, the rhythm so captivating, the incidents so dramatic, the emotion so deep and all-pervading that they cannot fail to please a great number and variety of people. They are gems we should know well so that we may fully enjoy their richness. They are especially pleasing to young people because *they make a vigorous appeal to the heroic imagination.*

Interpretation of a Metrical Romance

The metrical romance is essentially a *story* and must be interpreted as such. It contains a great deal of dialogue as a rule, and this demands that the different characters be *suggested* in general manner of speech and behavior, and they must be made to harmonize with the lines they speak. The mystic characters must be surrounded with an atmosphere of unreality. This may be done technically by making the intonations less definite than when normal human beings speak.

The normal characters should be made as normal as the lines suggest and the great virtues that they usually have should be made to seem a genuine part of their spiritual makeup rather than something put on from the outside.

The reader will find it necessary to use all his skill and ingenuity to go from the narrator's lines to those of the different characters inconspicuously, and without interrupting the story or dispelling its atmosphere in any way. He must

create the appropriate atmosphere in all cases; sometimes it
will be joyous, sometimes sad, sometimes it must be myster-
ious and unreal, sometimes it must be supercharged with
love, sometimes ominous and forboding, sometimes full of
serenity and peace. But be the atmosphere what it may the
situation is always dramatic and the language is always fine.

EXTRACTS FROM METRICAL ROMANCES (Abridged).

Note: The Giaour speaks to the Friar to unburden the sorrow
of his soul.

"I loved her, Friar! nay, adored—   Line 1029.
But these are words that all can use—
I proved it more in deed than word;
There's blood upon that dinted sword,
A stain its steel can never lose:
'Twas shed for her, who died for me.
. . . .

I loved her—Love will find its way
Through paths where wolves would fear to prey;
And if it dares enough, 'twere hard
If Passion met not some reward—
No matter how, or where, or why,
I did not vainly seek, nor sigh:
Yet sometimes, with remorse, in vain
I wish she had not loved again.
She died—I dare not tell thee how;
But look—'tis written on my brow!
. . . .

Still, ere thou dost condemn me, pause;
Not mine the act, though I the cause.
. . . .

If bursting heart, and maddening brain,
And daring deed, and vengeful steel,
And all that I have felt, and feel,
Betoken love—that love was mine.
. . . .

And reft of all, yet undismayed
But for the thought of Leila slain,

Give me the pleasure with the pain,
So would I live and love again.

. . . .

She was a form of Life and Light,
That, seen, became a part of sight;
And rose, where'er I turned my eye,
The Morning-star of Memory!"   Line 1130.

From *The Giaour*, by Lord Byron.
In *The Works of Lord Byron*. Vol. III.

How Sigurd Took to Him the Treasure of the Elf
Andvari (Abridged).

. . . Sigurd
. . . . leapeth aback of Greyfell, and rideth the desert bare,
And the hollow slot of Fafnir, that led to the Serpent's lair.
So far o'er the waste he wended, and when the night was come
He saw the earth-old dwelling, the dread Gold-wallower's home:
On the skirts of the Heath it was builded by a tumbled stony
    bent;
High went that house to the heavens, down 'neath the earth it
    went.
Of unwrought iron fashioned for the heart of a greedy King:
'Twas a mountain, blind without, and within was its plenishing,
. . . the Hoard of Andvari the ancient, and the sleeping Curse
    unseen,
The Gold of the Gods that spared not and the greedy that
    have been.

Through the door strode Sigurd the Volsung, and the grey moon
    and the sword
Fell on the tawny gold-heaps of the ancient hapless Hoard.
Gold gear of hosts unburied, and the coins of cities dead,
Great spoils of the ages of battle, lay there on the Serpent's bed:
There Sigurd seeth moreover Andvari's *Ring* of Gain
The hope of Loki's finger, the Ransom's utmost grain;
For it shone on the midmast gold-heap like the first star set in
    the sky
In the yellow space of even when moon-rise draweth anigh.
Then laughed the Son of Sigmund, and stooped to the golden
    land,
And gathered that first of the harvest and set it on his hand;

He toiled and loaded Greyfell, and the cloudy war-steed shone
And the gear of Sigurd rattled in the flood of the moonlight wan;

"Bind the red rings, O Sigurd! Let the gold shine free and clear!
For what hath the Son of the Volsungs the ancient Curse to
    fear?"

Now down to the west he wendeth, and goeth swift and light,
And the stars are beginning to wane, and the day is mingled
    with night.

How Sigurd Awoke Brynhild Upon Hindfell

By long roads rideth Sigurd, when low on a morning of day
From out of the tangled crag-walls, amidst the cloud-land
    grey
Comes up a mighty mountain, and it is as though there burns
A torch amidst of its cloud-wreath; so thither Sigurd turns,

. . . he rideth higher and higher, and the light grows great
    and strange,
And forth from the clouds it flickers, till at noon they gather
    and change.
Night falls, but yet rides Sigurd, and hath no thought of rest,
For he longs to climb that rock-world and behold the earth at
    its best;
So up and up he wendeth till the night is wearing thin;
And he rideth a rift of the mountain, and all is dark therein,
Till the stars are dimmed by dawning and the wakening world
    is cold;
Then afar in the upper rock-wall a breach doth he behold,
And a flood of light poured inward the doubtful dawning blinds:
So swift he rideth thither and the mouth of the breach he finds,
He sitteth awhile on Greyfell on the marvellous thing to gaze:
For lo, the side of Hindfell enwrapped by the fervent blaze,
And naught twixt earth and heaven save a world of flickering
    flame,
And a hurrying shifting tangle, where the dark rents went and
    came.

Sigurd
. . . crieth aloud to Greyfell, and rides at the wildfire's heart;
. . . the white wall wavers before him and the flame-flood
    rusheth apart,
But he rideth *through* its roaring, and a little farther on,
And all is calm about him, and he sees the scorched earth wan,

Then Sigurd looked before him and a Shield-burg there he saw,
A wall of the tiles of Odin wrought clear without a flaw.
And lo, to the gate he cometh, and the doors are open wide,
And no warder the way withstandeth, and no earls by the
  threshold abide,
And below in the very midmost is a Giant-fashioned mound,
Piled high as the rim of Shield-burg above the level ground;
And there, on that mound of the Giants, o'er the wilderness
  forlorn,
A pale grey image lieth, and gleameth in the morn.
And he set his face to the earth-mound, and beheld the image
  wan
And the dawn was growing about it, and, lo, the shape of a man!

Now he comes to the mound and climbs it, and will see if the
  man is dead;
Some King of the days forgotten laid there with crowned head,
Now over the body he standeth, and seeth it shapen fair,
And clad from head to foot-sole in pale grey-glittering gear,
In a hauberk wrought as straightly as though to the flesh it
  were grown:
But a great helm hideth the head and is girt with a glittering
  crown.

So thereby he stoopeth and kneeleth, for he deems it were good
  indeed
If the breath of life abide there and the speech to help at need,
Then he saith he will look on the face, if it bear him love or hate,
Or the bonds for his life's constraining, or the sundering doom
  of fate,
So he draweth the helm from the head, and, lo, the brow snow-
  white,
And the smoothe unfurrowed cheeks, and the wise lips breathing
  light;
And the face of a woman it is, and the fairest that ever was born,
Shone forth to the empty heavens and the desert world forlorn:
But he looketh, and loved her sore, and he longeth her spirit
  to move,
And awaken her heart to the world, that she may behold him
  and love.
And he toucheth her breast and her hands, and he loveth her
  passing sore;
And he saith: "Awake! I am Sigurd;" but she moveth never
  the more.

Then he looked on his bare bright blade, and he said: "Thou—
    what wilt thou do?
For indeed as I came by the war-garth thy voice of desire I
    knew."
So the eager edges he setteth to the Dwarf-wrought battle-coat
Where the hammered ring-knit collar constraineth the woman's
    throat;
Then he driveth the blue steel onward, and through the skirt,
    and out,
Till naught but the rippling linen is wrapping her about;
Then he deems her breath comes quicker and her breast begins
    to heave,
So he turns about the War-Flame and rends down either sleeve,
Till her arms lie white in her raiment, and a river of sun-bright
    hair
Flows free o'er bosom and shoulder and floods the desert bare.

Then a flush cometh over her visage and a sigh upheaveth her
    breast,
And her eyelids quiver and open, and she wakeneth into rest;
Wide-eyed on the dawning she gazeth, too glad to change or
    smile,
And but little moveth her body, nor speaketh she yet for a while;
But yet kneels Sigurd moveless her wakening speech to heed,
While soft the waves of daylight o'er the starless heavens speed;
Then she turned and gazed on Sigurd, and her eyes met the
        Volsung's eyes,
And mighty and measureless now did the tide of his love arise,
For their longing had met and mingled, and he knew of her
        heart that she loved,
As she spake unto nothing but him and her lips with the speech-
    flood moved:

"O, what is the thing so mighty that my weary sleep hath torn,
And rent the fallow bondage, and the wan woe over-worn?"

He said: "The hand of Sigurd and the Sword of Sigmund's son,
And the heart that the Volsungs fashioned this deed for thee
    have done."

But she said: "Where then is Odin that laid me here alow?
Long lasteth the grief of the world, and the man-folk's tangled
    woe!"

"He dwelleth above," said Sigurd, "but I on the earth abide,
And I came from the Glittering Heath the waves of thy fire to
    ride."

And they twain arose together, and with both her palms out-
     spread,
And bathed in the light returning, she cried aloud and said:

"All hail, O Day and thy Sons, and thy kin of the coloured things!
Hail, following Night, and thy Daughter that leadeth thy
     wavering wings!
Look down with unangry eyes on us to-day alive,
And give us the hearts victorious, and the gain for which we
     strive!"

Then Sigurd looketh upon her, and the words from his heart
     arise;
"Thou art the fairest of earth, and the wisest of the wise;
O who art thou that lovest, thou fairest of all things born?
And what meaneth thy sleep and thy slumber in the wilderness
     forlorn?"

She said: "I am she that loveth. I was born of the earthly folk,
But of old Allfather took me from the Kings and their wedding
     yoke.
And he called me the Victory-Wafter, and I went and came
     as he would,
And I chose the slain for his war-host, and the days were
     glorious and good;
But Allfather came against me and the God in his wrath uprose;
And he cried: "Thou hast thought in thy folly that the Gods
     have friends and foes,
Thou hast cast up the curse against me; it shall fall aback on
     thine head;
Go back to the sons of repentance, with the children of sorrow
     wed."

"Then somewhat smiled Allfather; and he spake: 'So let it be!
The doom thereof abideth; the doom of me and thee.
Yet long shall the time pass over ere thy waking day be born:
Fare forth, and forget and be weary 'neath the Sting of the
     Sleepful Thorn!

"So I came to the head of Hindfell and the ruddy shields and
     white,
And the wall of the wildfire wavering around the isle of night;
And there the Sleep-thorn pierced me, and the slumber on me
     fell,
And the night of nameless sorrows that hath no tale to tell.

Now I am she that loveth; and the day is nigh at hand
When I, who have ridden the sea-realm and the regions of the
    land,
And dwelt in the measureless mountains and the forge of stormy
    days,
Shall dwell in the house of my fathers and the land of the
    people's praise;

"Know thou most mighty of men, that the Norns shall order all'
And yet without thine helping shall no whit of their will befall;
Be wise! 'tis a marvel of words, and a mock for the fool and the
    blind;
But I saw it writ in the heavens, and its fashioning there did I
    find.

"Be wise and cherish thine hope in the freshness of the days,
And scatter its seed from thine hand in the field of the people's
    praise;
Then fair shall it fall in the furrow, and some of the earth shall
    speed,
And the sons of men shall marvel at the blossom of the deed.

Love thou the Gods—and withstand them, lest thy fame should
    fail in the end,
And thou be but their thrall and their bondsman, who wert
    born for their very friend.

"I have spoken the words, beloved, to thy matchless glory and
    worth;
But thy heart to my heart hath been speaking, though my
    tongue hath set it forth:"

Then words were weary and silent, but oft and o'er again
They craved ·and kissed rejoicing, and their hearts were full
    and fain.

Then spake the Son of Sigmund: "Fairest, and most of worth,
Hast thou seen the ways of man-folk and the regions of the
    earth?
Then speak yet more of wisdom; for most meet me seems it is
That my soul to thy soul be shapen, and that I should know
    thy bliss."
So she took his right hand meekly, nor any word would say,
Not e'en of love or praising, his longing to delay;
And they sat on the side of Hindfell, and their fain eyes looked
    and loved,
As she told of the hidden matters whereby the world is moved.

So they climb the burg of Hindfell, and hand in hand they fare,
Till all about and above them is naught but the sunlit air,
And there close they cling together rejoicing in their mirth;
For far away beneath them lie the kingdoms of the earth.

Then spake the Victory-Wafter; "O King of the Earthly Age.
As a God thou beholdest the treasure and the joy of thy heritage,
And I bid thee look on the land 'twixt the wood and the silver
    sea
In the bright of the swirling river, and the house that cherished
    me!

The little land of Lymdale by the swirling river's side,
Where Brynhild once was I called in the days ere my father died;
The little land of Lymdale 'twixt the woodland and the sea,
Where on thee mine eyes shall brighten and thine eyes shall
    beam on me."

"I shall seek thee there." said Sigurd, "when the day-spring is
    begun,
Ere we wend the world together in the season of the sun."

"I shall bide thee there," said Brynhild, "till the fulness of the
    days,
And the time for the glory appointed, and the springing-tide
    of praise."

From his hand then draweth Sigurd Andvari's Ancient Gold;
There is naught but the sky above them as the ring together
    they hold,
The shapen ancient token, that hath no change nor end,
No change, and no beginning, no flaw for God to mend:
Then Sigurd cries, "O Brynhild, now hearken while I swear,
That the sun shall die in the heavens and the day no more be fair,
If I seek not love in Lymdale and the house that fostered thee,
And the land where thou awakedst 'twixt the woodland and the
    sea!"

And she cried: "O Sigurd, Sigurd, now hearken while I swear
That the day shall die forever and the sun to blackness wear,
Ere I forget thee, Sigurd, as I lie 'twixt wood and sea
In the little land of Lymdale and the house that fostered me!"
Then he set the ring on her finger and once, if ne'er again,
They kissed and clung together, and their hearts were full and
    fain.

    From *Sigurd The Volsung.* William Morris.

BRIEF LIST OF NARRATIVE AND ROMANTIC POEMS

Childe Harold	Byron
Lara	"
Parisina	"
The Bride of Abydos	"
The Corsair	"
The Giaour	"
The Siege of Corinth	"
The Ancient Mariner	Coleridge
Christabel	"
The Lay of the Last Minstrel	Scott
The Lady of the Lake	"
Faerie Queen	Edmund Spenser
Idylls of the King	Tennyson

CHAPTER XXIV

SOCIETY VERSE, OR, VERS DE SOCIÉTÉ

Society Verse is a type of verse that is especially useful to the oral reader because it is essentially individual and entertaining.

It is usually *light* though often pretending to be serious, and sometimes it really is serious; it is always *well written and charming*. It is usually *quite short*, and it may treat of practically any subject, but it does so in a manner quite different from that found in other forms of literature. Very often its theme is love, but it is treated far less seriously than it is in true lyrics of love. Some examples may bring honest tears to the eyes of the reader but they are usually accompanied with smiles.

Society verse is almost invariably *written by cultured and experienced men and women* who have learned to look at life as a whole, and who choose to record in their verse the lighter aspects of it, but these are very often well supported and buttressed by a full and deep appreciation of life's more serious side. And somehow a bit of this appreciation and full understanding creeps in unbidden, or at least seemingly unbidden, and hovers around and between the lines, awakening the imagination of the reader and giving it wings that may carry it into enchanting places.

In speaking of society verse in *Forms of English Poetry*, published by the American Book Company, New York, Dr. C. F. Johnson says:

"It is written by men of a happy mood who enjoy to-day, are careless of tomorrow, and who do not regard yesterday as wasted because it is a day of pleasure past . . . . Its spirit is that of refined comedy, free from all exaggeration or burlesque, and restricted to a limited field of gay and graceful sentiment."

In the preface of *Lyra Elegantiarum* published by Ward, Lock and Company, London, New York and Melbourne, Frederick Locker-Lampson says:

"A reviewer in *The Times* newspaper has made the following noteworthy remarks on the subject of Social Verse. . . . "It is the poetry of men who belong to society, who have a keen sympathy with the lightsome tone and airy jesting of fashion; who are not disturbed by the flippances of small talk, but on the contrary can see the gracefulness of which it is capable, and who nevertheless, amid all this froth of society, feel that there are depths in our nature which even in the gaiety of the drawing-rooms cannot be forgotten. Theirs is the poetry of bitter-sweet, of sentiment that breaks into humour, and of solemn thought, which, lest it be too solemn, plunges into laughter;. . . . ."

Mr. Locker-Lampson also quotes the following from Pliny to Tuscus which expresses with astonishing accuracy the reactions of the general public of today to carefully selected examples of Society Verse.

"It is surprising how much the mind is entertained and enlivened by these little poetical compositions, as they turn upon subjects of gallantry, satire, tenderness, politeness, and everything, in short, that concerns life, and the affairs of the world."

. . . .

The Oral Interpretation of Society Verse

The essentials that must be remembered in reading all lyrical poetry must be remembered in reading society verse. In addition to these one must be able to *suggest*, with clever delicacy, the *sophistication* that characterizes much of this type of poetry. This can be done, in part at least, by extreme *care in the place and degree of stress*, lest the points be made too obvious; by skilful use of *intonations that suggest*, rather than reveal or explain; by the use of a *seemingly casual style of delivery* in general; and with the aid of a *very expressive* face— as well as tone—that seems to be aware of hosts of interesting angles of the theme under consideration that could be told if the reader chose to do so. A timely twinkle in the eye, or a delicately lifted brow at precisely the right moment will prove to be of genuine service in revealing the particular flavor of many examples of this interesting form. *An expressive voice* is a necessity. If any of these devices are obvious in the slightest degree they will defeat their purpose completely. The interpretation must *seem* to be casual, natural and spontaneous.

THE SPEAKER AND THE LISTENER

The reader speaks for the author directly to the audience in many of these poems, in others he speaks for a particular individual to a particular listener. "In Arcadia" (p. 307) a father speaks to his daughter. But when lines are spoken by a particular character it is almost invariably the mood and the incident that are interesting and significant. They are seldom character studies as in true monologues.

RHYTHM IN SOCIETY VERSE

The rhythm must be the rhythm of conversation which the author has fitted into the rhythm of the verse. The sense and meaning and mood, when properly given, create the rhythm. The reader must not seem to be aware of anything but the spontaneous expression of his thought but he must study this expression until he has the meaning and the poetic form absolutely unified and blended into one.

EXAMPLES OF SOCIETY VERSE

*A MARRIAGE Á LA MODE

Have you heard what they are saying
O'er the walnuts and the wine
Secrets eagerly betraying
About your affairs and mine?
Foes and friends receive attention

*Very extensive search has been made for the name of the copyright owner of this poem, but without success. If the poem is copyrighted will the owner please communicate with the author or publishers of this text so that proper recognition and acknowledgment may be made.

From each chatting beau and belle,
And they casually mention
That Marie has "married well."

"Married well!" Ah, that's expressive,
And from it we understand
That the bridegroom has excessive
Stores of ducats at command.
Is he good? He has his vices!
Has he brains? We scarce can tell.
Handsome? Hardly! It suffices
If Marie has married well.

Does she love him? Love's a passion,
Childish in this latter day.
She will dress in height of fashion
And her bills he'll promptly pay.

. . . .

Is she happy? That's a trifle;
Happiness is bought and sold;
And she readily can stifle
Love she used to know of old.
Well she knows his heart is broken;
As for hers—she cannot tell;
But her bridal vows are spoken
And Marie has married well.

In this game one should give heeding
To the stakes, not gentle arts,
And when diamonds are leading
Where's the use in playing hearts.
I congratulate her gladly—
But the wish I can't dispel
That other girls may marry badly,
If Marie has married well.

Henry B. Smith.

In *Society Verse by American Writers.*
Selected by Earnest de Lancey Pierson.
Benjamin and Bell. Publishers. New York.

THE MESSAGE OF THE ROSE

He

She gave me a rose at the ball to-night,
And I—I'm a fool, I suppose,

For my heart beat high with a vague delight
Had she given me more than a rose?

I thought that she had for a little while
Till I saw her, fairest of dancers,
Give another rose with the same sweet smile
To another man in the Lancers.

Well, roses are plenty, and smiles not rare—
It is really rather audacious
To grumble because my lady fair
Is to other men kind and gracious.

Yet who can govern his wayward dreams?
And my dream so precious and bright
Now foolish, broken, and worthless seems
As it fades with her rose to-night!

She

I gave him a rose at the ball to-night,
A deep red rose, with a fragrance dim,
And the warm blood rushed to my cheeks with fright
I could not, dared not, look at him.

For the depths of my soul he seemed to scan;
His earnest look I could not bear;
So I gave a rose to another man
Any one else—I did not care.

And yet, spite of all, he has read, I know,
My message—he could not have missed it;
For *his* rose I held to my bosom, so,
And then to my lips while I kissed it.
Bessie Chandler.

In Arcadia

Because I choose to keep my seat,
Nor join the giddy dancers' whirl,
I pray you, do not laugh, my girl,
Nor ask me why I find it sweet
In my old age to watch your glee,—
I, too, have been in Arcady.

And though full well I know I seem
Quite out of place in scenes like this,
You can't imagine how much bliss
It gives me just to sit and dream,
As you flit by me gracefully,
How I, too, dwelt in Arcady.

For, sweetheart, in your merry eyes
A vanished summer buds and blows,
And with the same bright cheeks of rose
I see your mother's image rise,
And, o'er a long and weary track,
My buried boyhood wanders back.

And as with tear-dimmed eyes I cast
On your sweet form my swimming glance,
I think your mother used to dance
Just as you do, in that dead past
Long years ago—yes, fifty-three—
When I, too, dwelt in Arcady.

And in the music's laughing notes
I seem to hear old voices ring
That have been hushed, ah, many a spring;
And round about me faintly floats
The echo of a melody
I used to hear in Arcady.

And yonder youth,—nay, do not blush,—
The boy's his father o'er again,
And hark ye, miss! I was not plain
When at his age—what! must I hush?
He's coming this way? Yes, I see,—
You two yet dwell in Arcady.

                    R. F. W. Duke, Jr.

From *The Century Magazine*. Coypright. Used by special
permission of D. Appleton-Century Company, Inc.

Encouragements to a Lover

Why so pale and wan, fond lover?
Prithee why so pale?
Will, when looking well can't move her,
Looking ill prevail?
Prithee why so pale?

Why so dull and mute, young sinner?
    Prithee why so mute?
Will, when speaking well can't win her,
Saying nothing do't?
    Prithee why so mute?

Quit, quit, for shame, this will not move,
    This cannot take her;
If of herself she will not love,
    Nothing can make her:
        The devil take her.
              Sir John Suckling.

In Palgrave's *Golden Treasury.*
E. P. Dutton and Company, Publishers.

Ad Ministram

Dear Lucy, you know what my wish is,—
    I hate all your Frenchified fuss;
Your silly entrees and made dishes
    Were never intended for us.
No footman in lace and in ruffles
Need dangle behind my arm chair;
And never mind seeking for truffles,
Although they be ever so rare.

But a plain leg of mutton, my Lucy,
    I prithee get ready at three:
Have it smoking, and tender and juicy,
    And what better meat can there be?
And when it has feasted the master,
    'Twill amply suffice for the maid;
Meanwhile I will smoke my canaster,
And tipple my ale in the shade.
           William Makepeace Thackeray.

*A Southern Girl

Her dimpled cheeks are pale;
She's a lily of the vale,
    Not a rose.

---

*Very extensive search has been made for the name of the copyright owner of this poem, but without success. If the poem is copyrighted will the owner please communicate with the author or publishers of this text so that proper recognition and acknowledgment may be made.

In a muslin or a lawn
She is fairer than the dawn
    To her beaux.

Her boots are slim and neat,—
She is vain about her feet,
    It is said
She amputates her r's,
But her eyes are like the stars
    Overhead.

On a balcony at night,
With a fleecy cloud of white
    Round her hair—
Her grace, ah, who could paint?
She would fascinate a saint,
    I declare.

'Tis a matter of regret,
She's a bit of a coquette,
    Whom I sing:
On her cruel path she goes
With a half a dozen beaux
    To her string.

But let all that pass by,
As her maiden moments fly,
    Dew-empearled;
When she marries, on my life,
She will make the dearest wife
    In the world.

                            Samuel Mintern Peck.

In *Society Verse by American Writers.*
Selected by Earnest de Lancey Pierson.
Benjamin and Bell. Publishers. New York.

ULYSSES RETURNS

I

Penelope Speaks

Ulysses has come back to me again!
I listen when he tells me of the sea,
But he has strange reserves . . . . and strangely he
Stares into the fire—. . . . I question him, and then

He tells me more of arms . . . . and men—
But there is something . . . . Heart what can it be
He sees there that he will not tell to me?
What swift withdrawal makes him alien?

Oh, there are many things that women know,
That no one tells them, no one needs to tell;
And that they know, their dearest never guess!
Because the woman heart is fashioned so.
I know that he has loved another well,
Still his remembering lips know her caress!

II
Circe Speaks

So swift to bloom, so soon to pass, Love's flower!
The sea that brought him, took him back again—
Ah, well, so is the world and so are men!
But he was happy with me here an hour,
Or almost happy, here within my bower.
He had his silences, his moments when
A strange abstraction took him. . . . . I knew then
That he remembered. . . . . slipped beyond my power!

I brought him strange bright blossoms that were grown
In emerald gardens, underneath the sea,
We rode white horses, far beyond the shore—
I would not let him sit and think alone!
One day he held me long and tenderly
I knew, I knew that he would come no more.

III
Ulysses Speaks

Was it I, was it I who dallied there
With a strange, sweet woman beside the sea?
Did she race the wind on the beach with me?
Was it I who kissed her and called her fair?
Was it I who fondled her soft gold hair—
While she wove and waited me patiently
The woman I love, my Penelope?
Was it I who lingered in Circe's snare?

Now my foot again in my hall is set,
And my keel is dry and my sails are furled:
Beside me, the face I could not forget,

That called me back across the world—
But there in the fire. . . . . those red lips wet,
And that soft, gold hair by the sea-mist curled!

IV
Penelope Sews

Oh, the hearts of men, they are rovers, all!
And men will go down to the sea in ships,
And they stop when they hear the sirens call,
And lean to the lure of those red, wet lips!

But never a Circe has snared one yet,
In a green, cool cavern beside the sea,
Who could make the heart of him quite forget
A patiently waiting Penelope!

Yet—there's never a roving one returns
But will sit him down in his easy chair,
While Penelope sews and the fire burns,
And into the depths of it stare. . . . . . and stare,
The fire burns and Penelope sews. . . . . .
He never tells—but Penelope knows!

Roselle Mercier Montgomery.

In *Ulysses Returns and Other Poems.*
Copyright: John S. Montgomery, New York.

Names of Books on Society Verse

American Familiar Verse. Edited by Brander Matthews. Longmans, Green and Company, New York, 1904.

A Vers de Société Anthology. Collected by Carolyn Wells. Charles Scribner's Sons, New York, 1907.

Lyra Elegantiarum by Frederick Locker-Lampson. Ward, Lock and Company. London, New York and Melbourne.

Society Verse by American Writers. Compiled by Earnest de Lancey Pierson. Benjamin and Bell, New York.

Vers de Société. Selected by Charles H. Jones. Henry Holt and Company, New York.

CHAPTER XXV

DRAMATIC LITERATURE

Monologues and Plays

An attempt to define the word "dramatic" would occupy a whole book, but its meaning is pretty generally understood without any definition.

Aristotle calls drama "imitated action"; it represents human beings thinking, talking, feeling and acting very much as they do in real life.

Dramatic literature has always been popular; in it man sees himself or his friends as they are, or as they aspire to be, or as they dream that they might be, reflected, as in a mirror, and it is always interesting and entertaining to him.

Brander Matthews has called the art of drama, "the art which most completely displays the life of man." *The Development of the Drama.* Charles Scribner's Sons, Publishers.

Classification of Dramatic Literature

Dramatic Literature may be classified in at least three different ways.

    I. According to its *outward form.*

    II. According to the *general number of characters.*

    III. According to the *general nature of its subject matter.*

I. Classification According to Outward Form

1. *Dramatic Prose:* this is considered under the headings of monologues and plays.

2. *Dramatic Poetry:* in *epic* and other narrative poetry the author speaks alternately for himself and for the characters he presents; in *lyric* poetry he speaks for himself entirely; in *dramatic* poetry (or prose) he does not speak for himself at all; he speaks only for the characters he presents.

"The Epic deals with the *past*, the Lyric with the *present*. Events are the epic basis; but they unroll themselves before our eyes. We have the epic *objectivity* . . . . in the lifelike course of events; we have lyric fire in the different *characters*. . . . . A drama, then, may be called *an epic whole made up of lyric parts*. . . . . The lyric element in the drama makes it more rapid, more tumultuous than the epic. . . ."
Handbook of Poetics. Francis B. Gummere.
Ginn and Company, Publishers.

II. ACCORDING TO THE GENERAL NUMBER OF CHARACTERS

1. A *monologue* has *one* character.
2. A *Dialogue* has *two* characters.
3. A *Play* has more than two characters.

III. ACCORDING TO THE GENERAL NATURE OF ITS SUBJECT MATTER

1. Comedy
2. Tragedy
3. Drama

Since the interpretation of both *prose* and *verse* has been considered in previous chapters, dramatic *literature* is considered in this chapter under the heads of *monologues* and *plays* whether they be written in verse or prose. The general nature of the subject matter—comedy, tragedy, or drama—determines the general spirit of the interpretation.

THE MONOLOGUE

The monologue is "a scene in which a person of the drama speaks by himself. Also, in modern use, a dramatic composition for a single performer; a kind of dramatic entertainment performed throughout by one person." *Murray's English Dictionary.*

In every monologue one person, only, does the talking, but all forms of literature in which one person does the talking are not monologues. One person does the talking in lyrics, orations, essays, soliloquies; but the monologue is essentially different from all of these forms because of its *general purpose*.

General Purpose of the Monologue

The general *purpose* of the monologue is to *reveal character*. This is done *indirectly*, by presenting the character's thoughts and emotions, his motives, his understanding of truth: not—necessarily—the truth as it really is, or as the author or as the interpreter sees it, but truth as the *character* sees it. If an incident or a story is introduced it must be presented through the mind and heart of the *character*, not through that of the author or of the interpreter.

> "A character. . . . . exists by its own idiosyncrasy, by its contrast with other natures, by its development of one side only, of our native capacities. . . . . . Not the character, but its effects and causes is the truly interesting thing. . . . . . ."
> *The Elements and Functions of Poetry*, George Santayana.
> In *Poetry and Religion*,
> Charles Scribner's Sons, Publishers, 1921

It is not the purpose of the monologue to teach, to persuade or to arouse others to action, although it *may* do so.

Robert Browning has written a greater number of monologues than any other writer. He was not, however, the originator of the form, as is commonly supposed, but he did develop it and brought it to a high point of artistic and dramatic excellence and individuality.

> "Browning . . . . used this form, which, though one cannot say he invented it, was made by him so thoroughly his own and handled in so characteristic a fashion that it must be regarded as one of his important contributions to the forms of English poetry. The men and women are of all kinds, all countries, all times."
> *A History of English Literature*,—p. 375. Neilson and Thorndyke.
> By permission of The Macmillan Company, Publishers.

"Browning . . . analyzes with marked keenness and subtlety the experiences of the soul. . . . In nearly all of his poems whether narrative lyric or dramatic, the chief interest centers about some 'incidents in the development of a soul.' The poetic form which he found best adapted to 'the development of a soul' was the dramatic monologue. Requiring but one speaker, this form permits all the force to be concentrated upon his emotions, character and growth. Browning is one of the greatest masters of the dramatic monologue. . . . .

Browning excels in the portrayal of unusual, intricate and difficult characters, that have complicated problems to face, weaknesses to overcome, or lofty ambitions to attain."

Halleck's *History of English Literature*, p.p. 454 and 456.
Copyright. American Book Company, Publishers, 1900.

The writer of the dramatic monologue "can exhibit a character with reference to all the phenomena in its little world and turn every experience to account. He can not only unveil the secret heart of his persons but thread his way through the mental labyrinth of motives and pretexts and calculations in the most composite and sophisticated; as, conversely, he can unclasp the clenched hand of a high resolve in the simple hero and saint, who are quite unaware of the spiritual mechanism that enables them to strike or to hold. He is able to ransack all the recesses and galleries of man's nature and penetrate to its most sacred or opprobrious shrines. This, the drama,. . . . . . cannot do in the same way to the same degree."

M. W. MacCallum.

From a lecture delivered at the British Academy Feb. 4, 1925; Humphrey Milford, Oxford University Press.

The dramatic monologue almost invariably represents some great crisis in the life of a character, or pictures a character in some critical and significant situation. It does not lead up to, or down from a climax; it simply gives the climax; although in this climax the past may be revealed or the future foreshadowed. It is as if a spotlight were suddenly turned on one in a supreme moment, revealing motives and actions in their full intensity, then, as suddenly turned off again.

THE SPEAKER AND THE LISTENER

There is no form of literature in which the speaker and the listener are of greater importance than in the monologue. Sometimes the speaker is named in the title, as in Browning's *Andrea Del Sarto, Fra Lippo Lippi, Rabbi Ben Ezra*. If the speaker and listener are not named by the author the reader must discover them from careful study of the lines if they are at all important. Mistakes in determining the identity of speaker or listener may cause serious misrepresentation of the author's purpose. In the monologue—as in other forms of literature—the author, not the reader, determines the nature of the characters which are to be represented. The *reader must discover the author's intentions and portray them* to the best of his ability. He should make his conception of the character harmonize in every possible way with that which the character says and does. There must be union of thought and personality.

There is always a more or less *definite* speaker in a monologue and almost always a more or less definite listener or listeners. Frequently, a third character enters into consideration in the person of some one who is *talked about* and sometimes he is very important.

The reader should reveal the thoughts and emotions of the characters indirectly, in their own words and deeds. It is not sufficient for him to reveal only what the *speaker* thinks and says and does, but he must also show the effect these have upon the imaginary *listener*, and he must show what the imaginary listener thinks and says and does. The speaker is often greatly influenced by the supposed speech or behavior of the imaginary listener and his train of thought or his line of action may be completely changed thereby, as is done in the following lines.

"But do not let us quarrel any more,
No, my Lucrezia; bear with me for once:
Sit down and all shall happen as you wish,
You turn your face, but does it bring your heart?

I'll work then for your friend's friend, never fear,
Treat his own subject after his own way,
Fix his own time, accept too his own price,
And shut the money into this small hand
When next it takes mine. Will it? tenderly?
Oh, I'll content him,—but to-morrow Love!' "
Andrea Del Sarto, Browning.

The speaker should speak to different listeners differently as is done in real life. We speak quite differently to children and adults, to servants and masters, to strangers and acquaintances, to friends and enemies, to cultivated and uncultivated persons; characters in monologues must do the same if they are truly portrayed.*

TIME, PLACE AND SITUATION IN MONOLOGUES

Time, place and situation are often of very great importance in monologues. The reader needs almost an unlimited amount of perception, discernment and understanding to determine them in all cases, but they reward him by giving an equally unlimited truth and variety to his work.

The action of a monologue always takes place in the *present* while the speaker is speaking. He may refer to the past, recount happenings of the past or refer to, or forecast the future, but he always speaks in the *present*. The time is not stationary. A definite living moment is revealed and the speaker expresses his thoughts and emotions as he experiences them in that moment.

We speak differently at different times of day and of life, in the very early morning and at noon, in the evening and at midnight, in the vigor and enthusiasm of youth and in the more quiet hours of age. Characters in monologues must do the same if they are to reflect life truly.

---

*In her charming monologue *The Children's Party*, Miss Ruth Draper applies this principle of interpretation most delightfully. She speaks to the dignified mothers, to the friendly mothers, to the babe-in-arms, and to the other children, each in his own tongue, as it were. The result fascinates and captivates all who are privileged to hear her.

Place and *situation* share importance with *time*. They set the atmosphere of a selection giving its keynote and color.

The title of a monologue—particularly those of Browning —often tells the place.

Down in the City	Browning
By the Fireside	Browning
In an Atalier	Thomas Bailey Aldrich

The first words of a monologue often show that the speaker has been placed in a new and significant situation. The lines quoted from *Andrea Del Sarto* are good examples of this.

Place and situation both affect *what* the speaker says and *how* he says it. He will speak differently in a church and on a busy street; he will speak differently in the same church on different occasions, at a wedding or a funeral; in his own home in the presence of strangers or of his own family. Almost any place or situation will color what one says or does; the more unusual or significant the place or situation the more pronounced the color will be. As a rule, place and situation are fairly clearly shown in the lines of a monologue.

ONE CLASSIFICATION OF MONOLOGUES

Monologues may be classified according to the *general nature of their subject matter.*

1. Narrative monologues.

2. Lyrical monologues.

3. Dramatic monologues.

NARRATIVE MONOLOGUES

In a *narrative* monologue the character of the person or persons *talked about* is sometimes of greater importance than that of the speaker or listener; it is revealed *indirectly* through the incidents of the narrative.

Incident in a French Camp	Browning
Saul	Browning

In *Incident in a French Camp,* the characters of the persons talked about—Napoleon and a boy who was one of his soldiers,—are of prime importance. The character of the speaker—probably an old soldier—and of the listener, are of practically no consequence. There should be no *impersonation* of Napoleon nor of the boy, but their spirits should be suggested clearly.

In *Saul,* the character of David, the speaker, and of Saul, who is the person talked about, are important but they are revealed through the narrative. There is no definite listener indicated; consequently, the audience should be made the listener.

Narrative monologues should be read in a *general* way as any narrative should be read except that the *character* is supposed to be telling the story instead of the author. When narrative monologues are written in verse, the reader should obey the principles that guide the reader of verse combined with the principles that guide the reader of monologues. When monologues are written in prose the principles of reading prose should be combined with the principles of reading monologues.

LYRICAL MONOLOGUES

Lyrical monologues are those in which a character—not the author—expresses deep emotion to a listener. They are usually quite devoid of action, and, as a rule, there should be little or no characterization. In such monologues the reader must be guided by the principle of reading lyrics combined with the principle of reading monologues.

Boot and Saddle	Browning
The Lost Leader	"
The Lost Mistress	"
A Woman's Last Word	"

A Serenade at the Villa   "
Memorabilia   "
John Anderson   Burns

JOHN ANDERSON

John Anderson, my jo, John,
When we were first acquent,
Your locks were like the raven,
Your bonnie brow was brent;
But now your brow is beld, John
Your locks are like the sna;
But blessings on your frosty pow,
John Anderson, my jo.

John Anderson, my jo, John
We clamb the hill thegither;
And monie a canty day, John,
We've had wi' ane anither;
Now we maun totter doun, John,
But hand in hand we'll go,
And sleep thegither at the foot,
John Anderson, my jo.*

Robert Burns.

DRAMATIC MONOLOGUES

Dramatic monologues have been discussed by different authorities under various heads. They may be summed up as follows:

1. That in which the character of the *speaker* is of prime importance, the listener is definite but of no particular importance.

   My Last Duchess,   Browning
   Garden Fancies,   "

2. That in which the character of the *listener* is as important as that of the speaker.

   Andrea Del Sarto,   Browning
   By the Fireside,   "
   In an Atelier,   Thomas Bailey Aldrich

---

*Jo means *darling* or *dear.*

3. That in which the person or persons *talked about*, are of greater importance than speaker or listener. In such cases the listener is often so unimportant as a character or so indefinite that the speaker speaks to the audience.

> *The Last Ride Together*, Browning
> *The Italian in England*,   ”
> *Incident in a French Camp*, ”

Some monologues are told in the heat of the occasion.

> *The Patriot*,   Browning
> *Evelyn Hope*,   ”

Some are told as a memory—

> *Count Gismond*,   ”
> *The Confessional*,   ”

Some *reflect* the past and forecast the future.

> *By the Fireside*,   Browning

IMPERSONATION IN MONOLOGUES

More impersonation is required in a monologue than is required in any other form of literature except the play. The whole personality and behavior of the speaker must be in perfect harmony with the thought and emotion he expresses. The reader will find it necessary to determine what *must* be done in order to justify the lines; such things will be *essential*, anything beyond this is *superfluous*. In some cases certain things must be *done*. For example, in the first stanza of *Evelyn Hope* it is imperative that the reader set the scene, as it were, by the glance of the eye or the turn of the head.

> "Beautiful Evelyn Hope is dead!
> Sit and watch by her side an hour,
> That is her book-shelf, this her bed;
> She plucked that piece of Geranium-flower,
> Beginning to die too, in the glass;
> Little has yet been changed, I think;
> The shutters are shut, no light may pass
> Save two long rays through the hinges chink."
>
> Browning.

The more an interpreter can *suggest* a character by thinking his thoughts and experiencing his emotions, and then *reveal* them in the tones of the voice, the expression of the face, and the general bodily attitude, and the less he does of additional things, the better.

THE RHYTHM OF MONOLOGUES

The rhythm of monologues is primarily the rhythm of conversation. It may be lyrical and rhymed conversation but nevertheless, conversation it must be. The speaker must *talk* to the listener. The talk may be inspired, noble, spiritual, beautiful; it may be happy, sad, trivial, serious; it may be as poetical and musical as human speech can be but it must be *talk*, the natural conversation of human beings.

Note. There is some difference of opinion concerning the proper procedure in the reading of monologues where the speaker is supposed to be seated, as in *By the Fireside* and *Count Gismond*. The decision with regard to this will have to be left to the taste and ability of the individual interpreter. Some of our leading scholars and readers of Browning do sit when they interpret such monologues and the effect is most pleasing, natural and sincere.

EXAMPLES OF MONOLOGUES
A TALE
(Abridged).

What a pretty tale you told me
    Once upon a time
—Said you found it somewhere (scold me!)
    Was it prose or was it rhyme,
    Greek or Latin? Greek, you said,
    While your shoulder propped my head.

Anyhow there's no forgetting
    This much if no more,
That a poet (pray, no petting!)
Yes, a bard, sir, famed of yore,
Went where such like used to go,
Singing for a prize, you know.

Well, he had to sing, not merely
    Sing but play the lyre;
Playing was important clearly
Quite as singing: I desire,
Sir, you keep the fact in mind
For a purpose that's behind.

There stood he, while deep attention
    Held the judges round,
  —Judges able, I should mention,
    To detect the slightest sound
    Sung or played amiss: such ears
    Had old judges, it appears!

None the less, he sang out boldly,
Played in time and tune,
Till the judges, weighing coldly
Each note's worth, seemed, late or soon,
Sure to smile "In vain one tries
Picking faults out: take the prize!"

When, a mischief! Were there seven
Strings the lyre possessed?
Oh, and afterwards eleven,
Thank you! Well, sir—who had guessed
Such ill luck in store?—it happed
One of those same seven strings snapped.

All was lost, then! No! a cricket
    (What "cicada"? Pooh).
Some mad thing that left its thicket
For mere love of music—flew
With its little heart on fire,
Lighted on the crippled lyre.

So that when (ah joy!) our singer
    For his truant string,
    Feels with disconcerted finger,
What does cricket else but fling
Fiery heart forth, sound the note
Wanted by the throbbing throat?

Ay, and, ever to the ending,
Cricket chirps at need,
Executes the hand's intending,—

Promptly, perfectly,—indeed
Saves the singer from defeat
With her chirrup low and sweet.

Robert Browning.

In an Atelier

I pray you, do not turn your head,
And let your hands lie folded, so.
It was a dress like this, wine-red,
That Dante liked so long ago,
You don't know Dante? Never mind,
He loved a lady wondrous fair—
His model? Something of the kind.
I wonder if she had your hair!

I wonder if she looked so meek,
And was not meek at all (my dear
I want that side light on your cheek).
He loved her, it is very clear,
And painted her, as I paint you,
But rather better, on the whole
(Depress your chin, yes, that will do):
He was a painter of the soul!

(And painted portraits, too, I think,
In the INFERNO—devilish good!
I'd make some certain critics blink
If I'd his method and his mood.)
Her name was (Fanny let your glance
Rest there, by that majolica tray)—
Was Beatrice; they met by chance—
They met by chance, the usual way.

(As you and I met, months ago,
Do you remember? How your feet
Went crinkle—crinkle on the snow
Along the bleak gas-lighted street!
An instant in the drug-store's glare
You stood as in a golden frame,
And then I swore it, then and there,
To hand your sweetness down to fame.)

They met and loved and never wed
(All this was long before our time),

And though they died, they are not dead—
Such endless youth gives mortal rhyme!
Still walks the earth, with haughty mien,
Great Dante, in his soul's distress;
And still the lovely Florentine
Goes lovely in her wine-red dress.

You do not understand at all?
He was a poet; on his page
He drew her; and, though kingdoms fall,
This lady lives from age to age:
A poet—that means painter, too,
For words are colors, rightly laid;
And they outlast our brightest hue,
For varnish cracks and crimsons fade.

The poets—they are lucky ones!
When *we* are thrust upon the shelves,
Our works turn into skeletons
Almost as quickly as ourselves;
For our poor canvas peels at length,
At length is prized—when all is bare:
"What grace!" the critics cry, "what strength!"
When neither strength nor grace is there.

Ah, Fanny, I am sick at heart,
It is so little one can do;
We talk our jargon—live for Art!
I'd much prefer to live for you.
How dull and lifeless colors are!
You smile, and all my picture lies:
I wish that I could crush a star
To make a pigment for your eyes.

Yes, child, I know I'm out of tune;
The light is bad; the sky is gray;
I paint no more this afternoon,
So lay your royal gear away.

.   .   .   .

I see! I've put you in a miff—
Sitting bolt-upright, wrist on wrist
How *should* you look? Why, dear, as if—
Somehow—as if you'd just been kissed.

In *The Poems of Thomas Bailey Aldrich*—p. 140.
Houghton Mifflin Company, Publishers.

The Woodcutter's Wife

Times she'll sit quiet by the hearth, and times
She'll ripple with a fit of twinkling rhymes
And rise and pirouette and flirt her hand,
Strut jackdaw-like, or stamp a curt command
Or, from behind my chair, suddenly blind me;
Then, when I turn, be vanished from behind me.

Times she'll be docile as the gentlest thing
That ever blinked in fur or folded wing,
And then, like lightning in the dead of night,
Fill with wild, crackling, intermitting light
My mind and soul and senses,—and next be
Aloof, askance as a dryad in a tree.

Then she'll be gone for days; when next I turn,
There, coaxing yellow butter from the churn,
Rubbing to silver every pan of tin,
Or conjuring color from the rooms within
Through innocent flowers, she'll hum about the house
Bright-eyed and secret as a velvet mouse.

.   .   .   .

But if I leave her seriously alone
She comes quite near, preëmpts some woodland stone,
Spreads out her kirtle like a shimmering dress
And fills my mind's remorseful emptiness
With marvelous jewels made of words and wit
Till all my being sings because of it,

Sings of the way her bronze hair waves about
And how her amber-lighted eyes peer out;
Sings of her sudden laughter floating wild,
Of all her antics of a fairy child,
Of her uplifted head and swift, demure
Silence and awe, than purity more pure.

So I must scratch my head and drop my ax,
While in her hands my will is twisted wax;
So, when she goes, deaf, dumb and blind I sit
Watching her empty arm-chair opposite,
Witched by evasive brightness in the brain
That grows full glory when she comes again.

In *Golden Fleece*, by William Rose Benét.
Used by permission of the Publishers, Dodd, Mead and
Company, Inc.

Monologues May Be Extracted From Plays

There are many plays which as a whole, have become too old-fashioned and out-moded for popular modern use, and yet they have many portions that are excellent. It is often possible to extract delightful monologues—or dialogues—from such plays. The following monologue taken from Oscar Wilde's *The Importance of Being Earnest* will serve as an example.*

Lady Bracknell, a very conventional, but very likable mid-Victorian mother, enters a room and finds her daughter Gwendolen, in the arms of Mr. Worthing. She is greatly shocked at the sight but far too well bred to show more than a vital surprise. As she enters, Gwendolen hurriedly steps to one side of the room and Mr. Worthing moves in the general direction of the other side, and Gwendolen announces that she is engaged to Mr. Worthing. As soon as Lady Bracknell can catch her well-bred breath after receiving this disquieting bit of news she begins a very wise dissertation on girls and matrimony, near the beginning of which she sits down—elegantly—in an elegant chair.

She always carries a small note-book and pencil in her "reticule," these she takes out and uses during her talk.

> Note: The lines have been arranged in general breath groups as they would be spoken. Some words have been changed from the written literary form to the contracted spoken form. For example: *it is* has been changed to *its*, and *I am* to *I'm*, when so doing gives the proper rhythm of conversation.

After Gwendolen announces that she is engaged to Mr. Worthing, Lady Bracknell speaks:

Pardon me,
you're not engaged to anyone.
When you do become engaged to someone,
I, or your father,

*Reprinted by special permission of Parker Garrett, London, solicitors for Oscar Wilde's estate.

should his health permit him,
will inform you of the fact.
An engagement
should come on a young girl as a surprise
pleasant or unpleasant
as the case may be.
It's hardly a matter
that she could be allowed to arrange for herself.
    (She turns around majestically in the general direction
    of Mr. Worthing.)
And now, Mr. Worthing
I have a few questions to put to you.
    (Smilingly, to Gwendolen)
While I'm making these inquiries,
you, Gwendolen,
will wait for me below in the carriage.
    (Gwendolen doesn't go. Sternly Lady Bracknell repeats:)
In the carriage, Gwendolen!
    (Gwendolen goes. Lady Bracknell watches her until she
    is out of sight, then turns her attention again to Mr.
    Worthing.)
You can take a seat Mr. Worthing.
I feel bound to tell you,
that you are not down on my list of eligible young men,
although I have the same list as the dear Duchess of Bolton
        has.
However
I'm quite ready to enter your name,
should your answers
be what a really affectionate mother requires.
Do you smoke?
    (She takes out her note-book and pencil and makes entries
    as Mr. Worthing answers her questions).
I'm glad to hear it.
A man should have an occupation of some kind.
There are far too many idle men in London, as it is.
How old are you?
Twenty-nine.
A very good age to be married at.
I've always been of opinion
that a man who desires to get married
should know everything or nothing.
Which do you know?

(writes) n-o-t-h-
I'm pleased to hear it.
I do not approve of anything
that tampers with natural ignorance.
Ignorance is like a delicate exotic fruit;
touch it
and the bloom is gone.
The whole theory of modern education
is radically unsound.
Fortunately,
in England, at any rate,
education produces no effect whatsoever,
If it did,
it would prove a serious danger to the upper classes.
What is your income?
eight-thousand—a year!
In investments, chiefly.
That's satisfactory.
What between the duties expected of one during one's life
time,
and the duties exacted from one after one's death,
land has ceased to be either a profit or a pleasure.
It gives one position,
and prevents one from keeping it up.
That's all that can be said about land.
You have a country house with some land attached to it!
You have a town house, I hope?
A girl with a simple, unspoiled nature,
like Gwendolen,
could hardly be expected to reside in the country.
Oh!
you own a house in Belgrave Square!
What number in Belgrave Square?
149! (shakes her head disapprovingly)
The unfashionable side!
I thought there was something.
However,
that could easily be altered.
Now to minor matters.
Are your parents living?
Dead!
Both dead!
That seems like carelessness.

Who was your father?
He was evidently a man of some wealth.
You don't actually know *who* you are!!
You were—you were—*found!!!*
by an old gentleman!
Where did he find you?
In—in—a hand-bag!
a black leather hand-bag!
with handles to it!
an ordinary hand-bag!!
In what locality
did the gentleman come across
this ordinary hand-bag?
The Victoria Station!
The cloak-room at the Victoria Station!!
Mr. Worthing,
I confess I feel somewhat bewildered.
To be born,
at anyrate bred,
in a hand-bag
whether it had handles or not,
seems to me to display a contempt for the ordinary decencies
of family life
that remind one of the worst excesses of the French
Revolution.
I presume you know what that unfortunate movement led to?
As for the particular locality
in which the hand-bag was found,
a cloak-room at a railway station
might serve to conceal a social indiscretion.
I would strongly advise you, Mr. Worthing,
to try and acquire some relations as soon as possible,
and to make a definite effort
to produce at any rate one parent,
of either sex,
before the season is quite over.
But you can hardly imagine
that I and Lord Bracknell
would dream of allowing our only daughter
to marry into a cloak-room,
and form an alliance with a parcel.
Good morning Mr. Worthing!
Good morning!

THE PLAY

The terms *play* and *drama* are used more or less synonomously. *The Concise Oxford Dictionary* says a play is a "dramatic piece, drama."

The term *play* is used here to mean *that form of literature which was written to be "performed by actors in a theater before an audience"* (Brander Matthews), as Shakespeare's plays were written.

The actors in such plays "make themselves up," dress, act and speak as much like the characters they represent as human knowledge and understanding, skill and practice, can devise. To-day this is supplemented by appropriate stage settings and lighting.

A play is given *for* the audience—not *to* them. The actors speak to each other—or to themselves as is done in soliloquies —and should *seem* to be entirely unaware of the presence of an audience.

The story or plot of a play unfolds *indirectly* as the action of the play proceeds. If there is a moral in the play it also must be revealed indirectly, the hearer seeming to discover it for himself without aid.

The subject matter of plays may deal with any phase of human existence or thought. Plays are interesting to the majority of people in the majority of places because they can be brought within the experience of all. Almost everyone likes to play at make-believe, to pretend he is someone he is not. People who have devoted their lives to far different things usually enjoy seeing others do the acting that they would, in their heart of hearts, have enjoyed doing themselves. People usually enjoy plays which deal with things they know best.

From the literary point of view plays range from the highest to the lowest.

Reading, Not Acting of Plays Considered

The province of this book is to consider the oral interpretation—by one person—of different forms of literature, therefore, the play will be considered from this view-point, not from the view-point of the actor who acts the part of one character only, in a play, although most demands are identical in the two arts.

The Oral Reading of Plays From a Book

In the usual method of reading plays aloud from a book, the reader should apply—in as large or as small measure as the nature of each play requires—the various principles of oral reading which have been given in preceding chapters. When a play is read in this way it may be treated very much as a dramatic story is treated or there may be some impersonation of characters.

The Art of the Impersonation by One Person of the Characters in an Entire Play

This particular form of oral interpretation of a play differs greatly from the ordinary method of reading it from a book and was used very extensively and successfully by the late Leland Powers of Boston. It was he who developed the detailed technique which makes it possible to teach the art to others. In writing of the work of Mr. Powers, Richard Burton says: "His whole idea is sound and based on principles of psychology and personality."

The presentation of an entire play, from memory, by one person, in which all of the characters are impersonated, is the most intricate and highly specialized—and undoubtedly the most difficult—*form of oral interpretation of literature.* The reader has *no special make up* or *lighting, no costuming* and *no stage settings* to help—or hinder—him. He simply and briefly explains, in the proper places, whatever is *essential* concerning costumes, stage settings and situations, thus setting the stage and costuming the characters in the *imaginations of the audience.* He impersonates the individual characters as they speak, in such a way that it keeps the whole play unfolding smoothly and with proper unity and balance, and at the same time he so *completely obliterates himself* behind the characters he impersonates, that it gives an audience the impression that the entire play is being enacted before them. If this is properly done an audience will see it all so clearly in their mind's eye that they will be able to discuss details of scenery, settings, costumes, etc., exactly as if these had been present in reality, instead of existing only in their imaginations.

By means of a highly developed technique the interpreter is able to awaken in the minds and imaginations of his audience the exact mental and emotional responses *he wishes them to have* and—what is infinitely more difficult—*keeps them from creating* unnecessary or irrelevant mental pictures. The impersonator does not use a book or "properties" of any kind, he does not dress to suit any particular character in the play. *He awakens and directs the imaginations of his hearers* so that they see and hear what he wants them to see and hear.

This form of oral interpretation of plays requires special training and should not be undertaken by those who lack such training.

THE PURPOSE OF THE PRESENTATION OF A PLAY BY ONE PERSON

The *purpose* of the presentation of a play by one person is to give the hearers as complete an understanding of the play as a whole, of its purpose and its characters, as if they had witnessed it in a theater played by an entire cast of good actors.

While the talking pictures have brought many plays to the doors of multitudes of people who have had little or no opportunity to see plays before these pictures came—thus, in a measure, lessening the need for the oral interpretation of plays by one person—nevertheless there are a great many plays of the highest literary value that are not to be heard or seen in the talking pictures or on the legitimate stage. Many of Shakespeare's plays have not been played on any public stage for decades, and when they are done the number of performances is usually limited and they are given in but few cities, sometimes in one city only. Only an infinitesimal number of the great dramas of the world's literature is presented to the public in *any* form. We are a play loving people and our interest in plays is growing by leaps and bounds as is proved by the rapid growth of little theaters and community theaters all over America. The well trained oral reader of plays can render an untold service to a wide and discriminating public by presenting good plays in recital.

Speaker and Listener

The interpreter speaks directly to the audience in his introductions, explanations and descriptions; the characters speak to each other in the dialogue.

The reader will be obliged to change from one character to another, and from character to narrator with extreme simplicity, economy and skill so that the audience is entirely unaware of such changes, at the same time each character must be so distinct a personality that he is recognized by the audience the instant he speaks or acts without the reader having to mention his name after he has once been established in the imagination of the audience. The reactions of the different characters should be clearly and truly revealed. The reader must think their individual thoughts and live their individual lives while he speaks their lines and plays their parts, even though the line be but a word, or the act be but one brief look.

Time, Place and Situation

It will be necessary to acquaint the audience with *essentials* concerning time, place and situation in order that they may follow the theme of the play without effort or confusion. In some plays the unfoldment of the plot will reveal all that is necessary concerning these things, in other plays it will be necessary for the reader to explain what they are as briefly and simply as possible, either in his own words or in the words of the author. In many modern plays, particularly those of Barrie and Shaw, the author's descriptions of the characters and places and their explanations of the situations are quite as delightful as the plays themselves. In such cases the authors' description should be used. They may be abbreviated if necessary.

IMPERSONATION IN PLAY-READING

A reader may impersonate the characters in a play as much as he wishes to, and is able to, as long as it *really contributes something of importance* to the purpose and significance of *the play as a whole*, and as long as the changes from character to character, and from character to narrator, and back again, can be made, unnoticed. The audience should never be aware of such changes—they should see and hear only the *play*. The play *must* be the thing.

The quality, tone, pitch, rate and range of the character's voice, his manner of speaking and his bodily poise and habits of action may be suggested by the reader *as long as they truly add something to the play* and are directed and controlled by unimpeachable good taste and judgment.

Before the impersonation of the different characters in a play is undertaken by the reader, it will be necessary for him to have mastered the details of the technique of oral interpretation, and the basic principles of characterization, in order that he may portray the characters truly, consistently and convincingly, *every time* he presents the play. If his interpretations are left to the inspiration of the moment the quality of his work will fluctuate; sometimes the characters will be superbly drawn, sometimes they will be only well drawn, and very often they will be badly or very badly drawn.

Full mastery of his technique will enable the reader to present a play many hundreds of times with a very high standard of excellence, and each time will seem to be the first time, with all the freshness of original spontaniety upon it.

Rhythm in Play-Reading

The rhythm of a play must be the rhythm of daily conversation. It may be speech of extraordinary and unusual beauty and melody, it may be sublime or magnificent, it may be colored by any mood that man is capable of feeling, or prompted by any type of thought he is capable of thinking, nevertheless, it should be the speech of conversation as it would be under such conditions. Hamlet, in his noblest or most melancholy moments, is the representation of a real human being *talking* to other human beings or to himself. Brutus *talks* to Cassius in indignation or in love, Iago *talks* to others in derision or in scorn, Nora *talks* to Thorval in disappointment or in sorrow, and if the reader presents characters truly he must make them *talk* as they would if they lived and moved and had their being there upon the stage.

In reading plays that are written in *prose* one should apply the combined principles of reading prose and of reading plays; in reading plays written in *verse* one should apply the combined principles of reading verse and of reading plays.

Scenes From Plays May Be Used as Readings

Individual scenes from plays may be used as short readings or several related scenes may be combined to advantage when it would not be expedient to read an entire play.

Almost all plays will have to be abridged, greatly, before they can be used by one person for purposes of entertainment. Such an evening's entertainment should not last longer than an hour and forty minutes under any circumstances; an hour and twenty minutes is usually sufficient time.

SCENES FROM *The Taming of the Shrew.* SHAKESPEARE

These scenes may be used as a reading. If the reader wishes to give a general idea of the play as a whole there is not much given here that may be dispensed with, but other scenes may be added if desired.

This arrangement of scenes is *based upon* the *Edwin Booth Prompt Book of Katharine and Petruchio,* edited by William Winter, and published by *The Penn Publishing Company* of Philadelphia.

CHARACTERS

Baptista, a rich gentleman of Padua.
Katharine, the shrew, his eldest daughter.
Petruchio, a young gentleman of Verona.
Hortensio, friend to Petruchio.
Grumio, servant to Petruchio.
Servants, attendants, etc.

Scene I. Padua. Before Hortensio's house.
        Hortensio (To Petruchio who has just arrived)
Petruchio, my friend! What happy gale
Blows you to Padua here from old Verona?

Petruchio

Such wind as scatters young men through the world
To seek their fortunes farther than at home.
Signior Hortensio, thus it stands with me:
Antonio, my father, is deceased:
And I have thrust myself into the world,
Haply to wive and thrive as best I may:
Therefore, if thou know
One rich enough to be Petruchio's wife,
Be she as old as Sibyl, and as curst and shrewd
As Socrates' Xantippe, she moves me not.

Hort.

I can, Petruchio, help thee to a wife,
With wealth enough, and young and beauteous,
Brought up as best becomes a gentlewoman;
Her only fault, and that is fault enough,

Is that she's intolerably curst
And shrewd and froward, beyond all measure,
And renowned in Padua for her scolding tongue.
I would not wed her for a mine of gold.

Pet.

Hortensio, peace! thou know'st not gold's effect.
Tell me her father's name and 'tis enough.

Hort.

Her father is Baptista Minola.
An affable and courteous gentleman:
Her name is Katharine.

Pet.

I know Baptista, though I know not her;
And he knew my father well.
I will not sleep, Hortensio, till I see her.

Scene II. Baptista's garden. (Katharine has just left her father after one of her frequent outbursts of bad temper).

Bap.

What a devilish spirit!
Was ever gentleman thus grieved as I?
But who comes here?   [*Petruchio enters*
Good morrow, sir.

Pet.

Good morrow, Signior Baptista.

Bap.

God save you, sir!

Pet.

And you, good sir! Pray, have you not a daughter,
Called Katharine, fair and virtuous?

Bap.

I have a daughter, sir, called Katharine.

Pet.

I am a gentleman of Verona,
That hearing of her beauty and her wit,
Her wondrous qualities and mild behavior,—
Am bold to show myself within your house.
Petruchio, is my name; Antonio's son,
A man well known throughout all Italy.

Bap.

I knew him well: You are welcome for his sake.
But for my daughter, Katharine, this I know
She's not for your turn, the more my grief.

Pet.

Signior Baptista, my business asketh haste
And every day I cannot come to woo.
Let specialties be therefore drawn between us,
That covenants may be kept on either hand.

Bap.

Yes, when the special thing is well obtained,—
My daughter's love; for that is all in all.

Pet.

Why, that is nothing; for I tell you, father,
I am as peremptory as she proud-minded;
And where two raging fires meet together
They do consume the thing that feeds their fury.
Though little fire grows great with little wind,
Yet extreme gusts will blow out fire and all;
So I to her, and so she yields to me;
For I am rough, and woo not like a babe.

Bap.

And will you woo her, sir?

Pet.

Why came I hither, but to that intent?
Think you a little din can daunt my ears?
Have I not in my time heard lions roar?
Have I not heard great ordnance in the field,
And heaven's artillery thunder in the skies?
Have I not, in a pitched battle, heard
Loud 'larums, neighing steeds, and trumpets' clang?
And do you tell me of a woman's tongue—
That gives not half so great a blow to hear
As will a chestnut in a farmer's fire?—
Tush, tush! fear boys with bugs.

Bap.

Then thou 'rt the man,
The man for Katharine, and her father too;
That shall she know, and know my mind at once
I'll portion her above her gentle sister,
New-married to Hortensio.

Pet.

Say'st thou me so?
Then, as your daughter, signior,
Is rich enough to be Petruchio's wife,
Were she as rough
As are the swelling Adriatic seas,
She moves me not a whit.
I come to wive it wealthily in Padua.
If wealthily, then happily, in Padua.

Bap.

Well may'st thou woo, and happy be thy speed!
But be thou armed for some unhappy words.`

Pet.

Ay, to the proof; as mountains are for winds.
O, how I long to have a grapple with her!

Bap.

O, by all means, sir.—Will you go with me,
Or shall I send my daughter Kate to you?

Pet.

I pray you send her: I'll await her here.

[*Exit Baptista, into house.*

I'll woo her with some spirit, when she comes:—
Say that she rail; why then, I'll tell her plain
She sings as sweetly as a nightingale:
Say that she frown; I'll say she looks as clear
As morning roses, newly washed with dew:
If she do bid me pack, I'll give her thanks,
As though she bade me stay by her a week:
If she deny to wed, I'll crave the day
When I shall ask the banns, and when be married.
But, here she comes: and now, Petruchio, speak.

[*Enter Katharine in a flaming rage.*

Kath.

Sent to be wooed, like bear unto the stake?
Trim wooing like to be!—and he the bear;
For I shall bait him. Yet, the man's a man.

Pet.

Good-morrow, Kate; for that's your name I hear.

Kath.

Well have you heard, but impudently said:
They call me Katharine, that do talk of me.

Pet.

You lie, in faith; for you are called plain Kate,
And bonny Kate, and sometimes Kate the curst.
But, Kate, the prettiest Kate in Christendom.
Take this of me, Kate of my consolation;
Hearing thy mildness praised in every town,
Thy virtue spoke of, and thy beauty sounded,
Thy affability, and bashful modesty
[Yet not so deeply as to thee belongs],
Myself am moved to woo thee for my wife.

Kath.

Moved in good time!
Let them that moved you hither,
Remove you hence: I knew you at the first,
You were a moveable.

Pet.

A moveable! Why, what's that?

Kath.

A joint-stool.

Pet.

Thou hast hit it: come sit on me.   [*Bends on one knee.*

Kath.

Asses are made to bear, and so are you.

Pet.

Women are made to bear, and so are you—
Alas, good Kate, I will not burden thee;
For, knowing thee to be but young and light—

Kath.

Too light, for such a swain as you to catch.   [*Crosses to* R.

Pet.

Come, come, you wasp; i' faith, you are too angry.

Kath.

If I be waspish, best beware my sting.

Pet.

My remedy then is, to pluck it out.

Kath.

Ay, if the fool could find it where it lies.

Pet.

The fool knows where the honey lies, sweet Kate.

Kath.

'T is not for drones to taste.

Pet.

That will I try.—   [*Offers to kiss her.—She strikes him.*
I swear I'll cuff you, if you strike again.—
Nay, come Kate, come: you must not look so sour.

Kath.

How can I help it, when I see that face?
But I'll be shocked no longer with the sight.
                                [*Crosses to* L., *going.*

Pet.

Nay, Kate; in sooth, you 'scape not so.

Kath.

I chafe you, if I tarry; let me go.

Pet.

No, not a whit; I find you passing gentle:
'T was told me you were rough, and coy, and sullen;
But now I find report a very liar.
For thou art pleasant, passing courteous.
Thou canst not frown, thou canst not look askance,
Nor bite the lip as angry wenches will,
Nor hast thou pleasure to be cross in talk:
But thou with mildness entertain'st thy wooers,

Kath.

This is beyond all patience;—   [*Walks majestically to and fro.*
Don't provoke me!

Pet.

Why doth the world report that Kate doth limp?
O, slanderous world! Kate, like the hazel-twig,
Is straight and slender, and as brown in hue
As hazel-nuts, and sweeter than the kernels.—
Thou dost not limp.—So, let me see thee walk:—
Walk, walk, walk, walk.   [*Katharine stops, suddenly,* R.

Kath.

Go, fool, and whom thou keep'st command.

Pet.

Did ever Dian so become a grove,
As Kate this garden with her princely gait?
O, be thou Dian, and let her be Kate,
And then let Kate be chaste, and Dian sportful!

Kath.

Where did you study all this goodly speech?

Pet.

Study!—
It is extempore, from my mother-wit.
Am I not wise?

Kath.

Yes, in your own conceit;
Keep yourself warm with that, or else you'll freeze.

Pet.

Or rather, warm me in thy arms, my Kate!
And therefore setting all this chat aside,
Thus in plain terms:—your father hath consented
That you shall be my wife; your dowry 'greed on;
And will you, nill you, I will marry you.

Kath.

Whether I will or no?—

Pet.

Nay, Kate, I am a husband for your turn;
For, by this light, whereby I see thy beauty,—
Thy beauty that doth make me love thee well,—
Thou must be married to no man but me;
For I am he that's born to tame you, Kate.

Kath.

That will admit dispute, my saucy groom.

Pet.

Here comes your father: never make denial;
I must and will have Katharine to my wife.

[*Enter Baptista, from house.*

Bap.

Now, signior, now,—
How speed you with my daughter?

Pet.

How should I speed, but well, sir?
How, but well?
It were impossible I should speed amiss.

Bap.

Why, how now, daughter Katharine! in your dumps?

Kath.

Call you me daughter? Now, I promise you,—
You have showed a tender fatherly regard,
To wish me wed to one half lunatic:
A mad-cap ruffian, and a swearing jack,
That thinks with oaths to face the matter out.

Bap.

Better this jack than starve;
And that's your portion—

Pet.

Father, 't is thus: yourself, and all the world
That talked of her, have talked of her amiss;
If she be curst, it is for policy;
For she's not froward, but modest as the dove;
She is not hot, but temperate as the morn;
And, to conclude, we have 'greed so well together,
We've fixed to-morrow for the wedding day.

Kath.

Tomorrow!
I'll see thee hanged to-morrow, first!—
To-morrow!

Bap.

Petruchio, hark—
She says, she'll see thee hanged first.

Pet.

What's that to you?
If she and I be pleased, what's that to you?
'T is bargained 'twixt us twain, being alone,
That she shall still be curst in company.

Kath.   [*Aside*

A plague upon his impudence!
I'll marry him, but I will tame him.

Pet.

I tell you, 't is incredible to believe
How much she loves me.
She hung about my neck,
And kiss on kiss
She vied so fast, protesting oath on oath,
That in a twink she won me to her love.
Give me thy hand, Kate.
I will now away,
To buy apparel for my gentle bride.
Father, provide the feast, and bid the guests.

Bap.

(Aside) Was ever match clapped up so suddenly?
What dost thou say, my Katharine?
Give thy hand.

Kath.

Never to man shall Katharine give her hand!
Here 't is,—and let him take it, an' he dare.

Pet.

Were it the fore-foot of an angry bear,
I'd shake it off;   [*Seizing her hand.*
But, as it's Kate's I kiss it.

Kath.

You'll kiss it closer, ere our moon be waned.

Pet.

Father, and wife, adieu! I must away,
Unto my country-house, and stir my grooms,
Scour off their country rust, and make 'em fine,
For the reception of my Katharine.
We will have rings, and things, and fine array;
To-morrow, Kate, shall be our wedding-day. [*Exit Petruchio* c.

Bap.

Well, daughter, though the man be somewhat wild,
And thereto frantic, yet his means are great:
Thou hast done well to seize the first kind offer;
For, by thy mother's soul, 't will be the last.

[*Exit Baptista, into house.*

Kath.

Why, yes; sister Bianca now shall see,
The poor abandoned Katharine, as she calls me,

Can make her husband stoop unto her lure,
And hold her head as high, and be as proud
As she, or e'er a wife in Padua.
As double as my portion be my scorn!
Look to your seat, Petruchio, or I throw you:
Katharine shall tame this haggard; or, if she fails,
Shall tie her tongue up, and pare down her nails.

CURTAIN.

Scene III. In Baptista's House.

*The wedding day has arrived,
the feast is prepared,
and the guests have assembled in Baptista's house.
All is in readiness,
The appointed hour is at hand,
But the bridegroom hasn't come.
Baptista, much too agitated to bear company,
has left the guests
and betaken himself to the quiet of the hall,
where he is pacing restlessly, up and down,
anxiously awaiting the tardy bridegroom.
Presently, a servant enters, calling*:

Master, master, news; and such news as you never heard of.

Bap.

Is Petruchio come?

Serv.

Why, sir.
He is coming: But how? Why, in a new hat and an old
jerkin; a pair of old breeches, thrice turned; a pair of boots that
have been candle-cases, one buckled, another laced; an old
rusty sword, with a broken hilt; his horse hipped with an old
mothy saddle, and stirrups of no kindred; besides, possessed
with the glanders, stark spoiled with the staggers, begnawn with
the bots, swayed in the back, and shoulder-shotten.

Bap.

I am glad he is come, howsoe'er he comes.

[*Enter Petruchio fantastically dressed.*

Pet.

Hoa!—
Where be these gallants? Who's at home?

Bap.

You're welcome, sir,
But not so well apparelled as I wish you were.

Pet.

But where is Kate? Where is my lovely bride?—
Wherefore gaze you thus—
As if you saw some wondrous monument,
Some comet, or unusual prodigy?

Bap.

Why, sir, this is your wedding-day.
First we were sad, fearing you would not come?
Now sadder, that you come so unprovided.
Fye! doff this habit, shame to your estate,
See not your bride in these unreverent robes,
Go to my chamber, put on clothes of mine.

Pet.

Not I, believe me; thus I'll visit her.
Therefore have done with words:
To me she's married, not unto my clothes:
But what a fool am I, to chat with you,
When I should bid good-morrow to my bride,
And seal the title with a loving kiss!
What ho! my Kate! my Kate!

[*Exit Petruchio,* R., *cracking his whip.*

Bap.

He hath some meaning in this mad attire:
I'll after him and see the event of this.

Scene IV. In Baptista's House.

*The bridegroom having arrived
the wedding party goes to the church
where the wedding ceremony is performed.
The occasion is brightened
by many high lights and unusual features
due to Petruchio's unconventional dress,
and his most extraordinary behavior.
The party has now returned to Baptista's house
in high good humor.*

Pet.

Gentlemen and friends, I thank you for your pains;
I know you think to dine with me to-day,

And have prepared great store of wedding-cheer,
But, so it is, my haste doth call me hence;
And, therefore, here I mean to take my leave.

Bap.

Is't possible, you will away to-night?

Pet.

I must away to-day, before night come.
Make it no wonder; if you knew my business,
You would entreat me rather go than stay.
Honest company, I thank you all,
That have beheld me give away myself
To this most patient, sweet, and virtuous wife;
Dine with my father, drink a health to me,
For I must hence, and farewell to you all.

Kath.

Sir, let me entreat you, stay till after dinner.

Pet.

It may not be.

Kath.

Let me *entreat* you.

Pet.

I am content.

Kath.

Are you content to stay?

Pet.

I am content you shall entreat my stay;
But yet not stay, entreat me how you can.

Kath.

Now, if you love me, stay.

Pet.

It may not be. What, ho, my horses there! My horses!

Kath.

Nay, then,
Do what thou canst, I will not go to-day;
No, nor to-morrow! nor till I please myself.
The door is open, sir: there lies your way:
You may be jogging, while your boots are green;
For me, I'll not go, till I please myself.—
'T is like you 'll prove a jolly surly groom,
To take it on you at the first so roughly.

Gentlemen, forward to the bridal dinner.—
He shall stay my leisure.
I see a woman may be made a fool,
If she had not a spirit to resist.

Pet.

They shall go forward, Kate, at thy command:
Obey the bride, you that attend on her:
Go to the feast, revel, and domineer;
Be mad and merry,—or go hang yourselves;
But, for my bonny Kate, she must with me.
Nay, look not big, nor stamp, nor stare, nor fret;
I will be master of what is mine own;
She is my goods, my chattels;
My horse, my ox, my field, my anything:
And here she stands, touch her whoever dare.
I'll bring my action on the proudest he
That stops my way in Padua.
Grumio,
Draw forth thy weapon, thou 'rt beset with thieves;

[Petruchio draws sword.

Rescue thy mistress, if thou be a man.—
Fear not, sweet wench;
They shall not touch thee,
I'll buckler thee against a million, Kate.

*Petruchio picks Katharine up in his arms and carries her out
regardless of her screams and protestations, much to the amazement and amusement of her father and the guests.*

Scene V. Petruchio's country home, the same evening.

*Petruchio and Katharine have just arrived, attended by Grumio.
There is no sign of the servants as they enter.*

Pet.

Hello, hello!
Where are these knaves?
What, no man at the door,
To hold my stirrup, nor to take my horse?
Where is Nathaniel, Gregory, Adam?

All the Servants.

Here, sir; here, sir; here, sir.

Pet.

Here, sir; here, sir; here, sir; here, sir!
You loggerheaded and unpolished grooms!
What, no attendance, no regard, no duty?
Go, rascals, go, fetch my supper in.

Pet. tenderly to Kath.

Sit down, Kate, and welcome.—
Nay, good, sweet Kate, be merry.—

to Grumio.

Grumio, pull off my boots!
Out, out, you rogue! You pluck my foot awry:
Take that, and mind the plucking of the other. [*Beats Grumio.*
You careless villain!

Kath.

Patience, I pray you; 't was a fault unwilling.

Pet.

Be merry Kate.
He's a blundering, beetle-headed, flap-eared knave.—
What, ho! my supper.— [*Enter servants,* R., *with the supper.*
Supper, supper!

Pet.

Come, Kate, sit down: I know you have a stomach.

Kath.

Indeed I have:
And never was repast so welcome to me. [*They sit.*

Pet.

What is this?
Mutton?
'T is burnt; and so is all the meat.
How durst you, villains,
Serve it thus to me that love it not?
There, take it to you, trenchers, cups, and all.
[*Throwing about the meats and dishes.*
The servants all run away, L.

Kath.

I pray you, husband, be not so disquiet;
The meat was well, and well I could have eat,
If you were so disposed; I'm sick with fasting.

Pet.

I tell thee, Kate, 't was burnt and dryed away,
And I expressly am forbid to touch it;
For it engenders choler, planteth anger;
And better 't were that both of us did fast,
Than feed us with such over-roasted flesh.
Be patient Kate to-morrow it shall be mended:
For this night, we'll fast for company.

Kath.

Fast?—Go to bed without my supper?

Pet.

'T is the wholesomest thing i' the world, sweet Kate.
Come, I will show thee to thy bridal chamber.

Scene VI. In Petruchio's house the following morning.

*Katharine has had no food since the wedding,
and she has passed the night without a moment's sleep.
Petruchio has thrown the furniture and furnishings about,
and has complained and grumbled all night long,
on the pretext that nothing was good enough for her.
Wan and haggard, and weakened in spirit,
she enters the cold, cheerless great-hall.*

Kath.

Did he marry me to famish me?
The more my wrong, the more his spite appears!
But that which plagues me more than all these wants,
He does it under name of perfect love.

[*Grumio enters.*

Oh, Grumio,
I pr'ythee, go and get me some repast
I care not what, so it be wholesome food.

[*Petruchio enters.*

Pet.

Hollo!—How fares my Kate?

Kath.

Faith, as cold as can be.

Pet.

Pluck up thy spirits; look cheerfully upon me:
For now, my honey-love, we are refreshed—

Kath.

Refreshed? With what?

Pet.

We will return unto thy father's house,
And revel it as bravely as the best.
Come, my Katharine: we will now away,
To feast and sport us at thy father's house.—
Grumio, go, call my men, and bring our horses out.

[*Exit Grumio* L.

Kath.

O, happy hearing! Let us straight be gone;
I cannot tarry here another day.

Pet.

Cannot, my Kate? O, yes, you can.

Kath.

Indeed I cannot.

Pet.

O, yes, you could, my Katharine, if I wished it.

Kath.

I tell you I'll not stay another moment.

Pet.

Grumio, put up the horses—On second thoughts, 't is now too
     late;   [*Grumio re-enters*
For, look, how bright and goodly shines the moon.

Kath.

The moon? the sun:—it is not moon-light now.

Pet.

I say, it is the moon that shines so bright.

Kath.

I say, it is the sun that shines so bright.

Pet.

Now, by my mother's son, and that's myself,
It shall be moon, or star, or what I list,
Or ere I journey to your father's house.—

Gru.   [*Aside to Katharine.*

Say as he says; or we shall never go.

Kath.

I see, 't is vain to struggle with my bonds.—
Sir, be it moon, or sun, or what you please;
And if you please to call it a rush-candle,
Henceforth, I vow, it shall be so for me.

Pet.

I say, it is the moon that shines so bright.

Kath.

I know, it is the moon.

Pet.

Nay then, you lie; it is the blessèd sun.

Kath.

Just as you please: it is the blessèd sun.
But sun it is not, when you say 'tis not;
And the moon changes, even as your mind:
What you will have it named, even that it is,
And so it shall be for your Katharine.

Pet. [*exultantly*]

Grumio,
Get out the horses.
But soft, some company is coming here,
And stops our journey.
    [*Baptista and Attendants enter and are warmly greeted. Baptista
    instantly senses that Katharine is not as she was.*

Bap.

How now, my child.
How lik'st thou wedlock? Art not altered, Kate?

Kath.

Indeed I am: almost transformed to stone.

Pet.

Changed for the better much; art not my Kate?

Kath.

So good a master cannot choose but mend me.

Bap.

Here is a wonder, if you talk of wonders.
I wonder what it bodes.

Pet.

Marry, peace it bodes, and love, and quiet life,
And lawful rule, and right supremacy.

Bap.

Now fair befall thee, son Petruchio,
I will add twenty thousand crowns;
Another dowry to another daughter,
For she is changed as she had never been.

Pet.

My fortune is sufficient—
Here's my wealth,
My Kate; and, since thou art become
So prudent, kind, and dutiful a wife,
Petruchio here shall doff the lordly husband;
An honest mask, which I throw off with pleasure.
Come, kiss me Kate.

Kath.

Nay, I'm all unworthy of thy love,
And look with blushes on my former self.—
A woman moved is like a fountain troubled,
Muddy, ill-seeming and bereft of beauty;
And while 'tis so none will touch a drop of it.
How shameful 't is, when women are so simple,
To offer war, where they should kneel for peace;
Or seek for rule, supremacy, and sway,
Where bound to love, to honour, and obey!
Such duty as a subject owes a prince,
A woman oweth to her husband.
My husband is my lord, my life, my soverign!

Pet.

Is not this well?
Come, my sweet Kate.

                                        [*Katharine goes to him*

Kiss me, Kate.

GENERAL INDEX

A

Action:
  arouse others to, 149, 315
  dramatic—in ode, 247
    extract which depicts, 145
    has little if any, 163
    imitated, 313
    of a monologue, 315, 318
    of characters in ballads, 191
    wish to depict, 119
Address: (see orations).
Affricates:
  formation of, 34, 35, 37
  on consonant chart, 38
  specimen words containing, 36
Alphabet:
  International Phonetic, 35
  Roman, 35
Art:
  chooses, 21
  greatest—is to conceal, 22
  imitation, not, 21
  of oral interpreter, 13
  of pronunciation, 32
  of reading well, 19
  oral reader's, 15
Articulation:
  careful of the, 191, 192
  phonetics applied to, 18
  pronunciation and, 71
Articulator, 31
Arts:
  basis of, 9
  fine, 9
  in all other, 13, 22
  practical, 13
Audience, audiences:
  attention of, 68, 72, 88
  before an, 114, 140, 332

Audience, Audiences: (*continued*)
  being aware of, 154
  contact with, 151, 152
  deadly for, 73
  definition of term, 113
  delivered to an, 152
  embarrassing for an, 73
  imagination of the, 333, 334
  interest an, 115
  lead the, 166
  lost to the, 151
  not embarrassed, 73
  not interested, 88
  offend an, 227
  people in an, 87
  presence of an, 332
  presenting it to an, 151
  reader or the, 68
  recognized by the, 335
  speaks to the, 5, 136, 150, 164,
    191, 205, 237, 246, 254, 305,
    322, 335
Author, Author's Authors:
  and audience, 182
  descriptions, 254, 336
  go to the, 124
  has made, 272
  heart of the, 205
  instead of the, 320
  lines, 113
  meaning, 12, 17, 69, 114, 115,
    153
  named by the, 317
  play fair with, 27
  refinement in, 80
  speak for the, 237
  speaks for himself, 180, 313
  speaks for the, 136, 164, 254, 305
  spokesman for the, 12

357

Story: (*continued*)
  oral interpretation of, 136
  purpose of the, 135
  rhythm of the, 137
  speaker and listener in the, 136
Stress:
  and intonation, 90-96, incl.
  and meaning, 58
  and rhythm, 85, 86
  degrees of, 62
  secondary, 63
  stress mark, 53
  strong, 63
  very strong, 63
  weak, 65
Stress group or groups:
  correct use of, 55
  explanation of, 55
  importance of, 56
  rhythmic value of, 56
  thought value of, 55
Suggestions:
  by following these, 2
  for delivery of an oration, 150
  for preparing a selection, 114
  for the study of this book, 2
Syllable:
  and stress, 58-62, incl.
  definition of, 53
  in intonation markings, 90-106, incl.
  stressed, 53
  unstressed, 80-86, incl.
Syllables:
  and metre, 85
  and rhythm, 181
  arrangement of, 70
  combinations of, 53
  crowding together, 80
  formation of, 53
  groups of, 24, 53, 192
  number of, 56
  stress on some, 80

Syllables: (*continued*)
  to form, 24
  unimportant, 80
  what—should be stressed, 59

T

Technical:
  knowledge, 18
  laws, 3
  means, 183
  study, 132
  suggestions, 132
  terminology, 118
  use, 12
Technique:
  by means of, 15
  highly developed, 334
  is the means, 132
  must be submerged, 3
  of:
    any art, 88
    expression, 2, 13, 15, 16
    his trade, 132
    reader, 20
    the writer, 20
    reader's, 3
    seems to be no, 3
Teeth, 30, 31, 38
Terminology, 113
Tone:
  color, 10, 46
  descending, 90
  fullness of, 24
  resonant, 50
  rising, 90
Tongue:
  organ of speech, 30
  position of the, 40
  tip of the, 38, 39, 40
Tongues, 13
Tragedy, 314

INDEX OF WRITINGS FROM WHICH LINES AND EXTRACTS HAVE BEEN TAKEN

369

INDEX OF COMPLETE SELECTIONS WITH AUTHORS

INDEX OF AUTHORS, TRANSLATORS AND
TITLES OF QUOTED MATERIAL